Ford Cortina Mk1 Corsair 1500 Owners Workshop Manual

by J H Haynes
Associate Member of the Guild of Motoring Writers
and P G Strasman
MISTC

Models covered

Cortina Saloon, 1200 and 1500
Cortina Estate, 1200 and 1500
Cortina GT, 1500
Corsair Saloon, 1500
Corsair GT, 1500
Corsair GT Estate, 1500

ISBN 0 85696 214 7

© J H Haynes and Company Limited 1974

2310/214

Printed in England

HAYNES PUBLISHING GROUP
SPARKFORD YEOVIL SOMERSET ENGLAND
distributed in the USA by
HAYNES PUBLICATIONS INC
861 LAWRENCE DRIVE
NEWBURY PARK
CALIFORNIA, 91320
USA

About this manual

This is a manual for do-it-yourself minded Cortina owners. It shows how to maintain these cars and how to carry out repairs when components become worn, or break. Regular and careful maintenance is essential if maximum reliability and minimum wear are to be achieved.

The step-by-step photographs and figures show how to deal with the major components and in conjunction with the text and exploded illustrations should make all the work quite clear - even to the novice who has never previously attempted the more complex job.

Although Cortinas are hardwearing and robust it is inevitable that their reliability and performance will decrease as they become older. Repairs and general reconditioning will become necessary if the car is to remain roadworthy. Early models requiring attention are frequently bought by the sort of motorist who can least afford the repair prices charged in garages, even though these prices are usually quite fair bearing in mind overheads and the high cost of capital equipment and skilled labour.

It is in these circumstances that this manual will prove to be of maximum assistance, as it is written from practical experience specially to help Cortina owners.

Manufacturers' official manuals are usually splendid publications which contain a wealth of technical information. However, as they are issued primarily to help the manufacturers' authorised dealers and distributors they tend to be written in very technical language, and tend to skip details of certain jobs which are common knowledge to garage mechanics. Owner's workshop manuals are different as they are intended primarily to help the owner. They therefore go into many of the jobs in great detail with extensive photographic support to ensure everything is properly understood so that the repair is done correctly.

Owners who intend to do their own maintenance and repairs should have a reasonably comprehensive tool kit. Some jobs require special service tools, but in many instances it is possible to get round their use with a little care and ingenuity.

Throughout this manual ingenious ways of avoiding the use of special equipment and tools are shown. In some cases the proper tool must be used. Where this is the case a description of the tool and its correct use is included.

When a component malfunctions, repairs are becoming more and more a case of replacing the defective item with an exchange rebuilt unit. This is excellent practice when a component is thoroughly worn out, but it is a waste of good money when overall the component is only half worn, and requires the replacement of but a single small item to effect a complete repair. As an example, a non-functioning dynamo can frequently be repaired quite satisfactorily just by fitting new brushes.

A further function of this manual is to show the owner how to examine malfunctioning parts; determine what is wrong, and then how to make the repair.

Given the time, mechanical do-it-yourself aptitude, and a reasonable collection of tools, this manual will show the ordinary private owner how to maintain and repair his car really economically.

Its arrangement

The manual is divided into twelve chapters, each covering a logical sub-division of the vehicle. The chapters are each divided into sections, numbered with single figures, eg 5; and the sections into paragraphs (or sub-sections), with decimal numbers following on from the section they are in; eg 5.1, 5.2, 5.3 etc.

The manual is freely illustrated, especially in those parts where there is a detailed sequence of operations to be carried out. There are two forms of illustration: figures and photographs. The figures are numbered in sequence with decimal numbers, according to their position in the chapter; eg Fig 6.4 is the 4th drawing/illustration in Chapter 6. Photographs are numbered either individually or in related groups the same as the section or sub-section of the text where the operation they show is described.

There is an alphabetical index at the back of the manual as well as a contents list at the front.

References to the 'left' or 'right' of the vehicle are in the sense of a person in a seat facing forwards towards the engine.

Every care has been taken to ensure the accuracy of this manual but no liability can be accepted by the authors and publishers for any loss, damage or injury caused by any errors in or omissions from the information given.

Contents

Model history and identification

The Cortina Mk I was introduced in September 1962 in standard or De luxe form to replace the Consul range. There was a choice of either two or four door saloons known at first as the Consul Cortina (Consul was soon dropped from the title). It transpired to be a conventional saloon car utilising many well proven components from previous Ford models.

Initially all models were fitted with a 1200 (1198 cc three bearing crankshaft) engine similar to the one used in the Anglia but in January 1963 a 1500 (1498 cc five bearing crankshaft) engine could be purchased as a factory optional extra. A four speed gearbox with a centrally mounted gear lever and rigid rear axle was used.

This 1500 engine was fitted as standard to the Cortina Super which was announced in January 1963 also. From the outside this car is easily recognisable by its twin chrome side flashes running the length of the body. Shortly afterwards in March 1963 two versions of an Estate car were announced; namely the De luxe version with the 1200 engine and the Super with the 1500. The Super is recognisable by its mock wood panelling on the sides and tailgate. The De luxe was available, however, with the 1500 engine as an optional extra.

Almost simultaneously a GT designated saloon was announced. This model used a modified 1500 engine fitted with a twin choke Weber carburettor, disc brakes on the front wheels, remote control gearchange and modified suspension as standard. It proved to have extra power and handling, often better then many sports cars.

In July 1963 all suspension and steering grease nipples were dispensed with by ball joints redesigned with greaseless seatings. This cut the service time considerably. In September of the same year childproof locks were fitted on the rear doors of all models. Similarly on all models except the GT a front bench seat with column gearchange was made available as an optional alternative to the normal layout of bucket seats and central gearchange.

Various modifications to the facia panel and instrument layout took place during the production run.

In December 1963 an automatic gearbox (Borg-Warner) became available as an optional extra on all 1500 models except the GT.

In October 1964 it was announced that all future models of the Cortina Mk I were to have disc brakes on the front wheels as standard equipment. At the same time the front grille was redesigned. The interior ventilation was greatly improved by fitting the new 'Aeroflow' system ensuring that a constant controllable flow of fresh air entered the car and was then expelled.

The GT models were given even larger front wheel disc brakes and self-adjusting rear brakes in October 1965.

The Cortina Mk I ceased production in September 1965. The Corsair which was essentially a variant of the Cortina Mk I was introduced in October 1963 in standard and GT form. The car was powered by the 1500 cc five bearing crankshaft engine. In December 1963 automatic transmission was available as an option but not on GT models. Production of the straight-four Corsair ceased in September 1965.

Cutaway drawing of the Corsair 1500

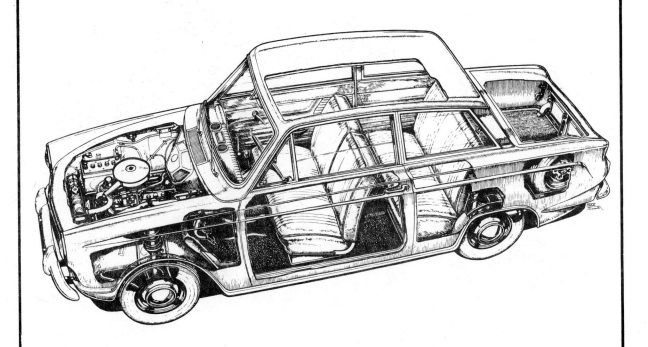

Cutaway drawing of the Cortina Mk 1 Saloon

Corsair 1500 Saloon

Interior view of the Cortina Mk 1 Saloon

Cortina Mk 1 Super Saloon

Cortina Mk 1 Estate with wood panelling

Ordering spare parts

Spare parts are available from many sources, for example: Ford garages, other garages and accessory shops, and motor factors. Our advice regarding spare part sources is as follows:

Officially appointed Ford garages - This is the best source of parts which are peculiar to your car and are otherwise not generally available (eg complete cylinder heads, internal gearbox components, badges, interior trim etc). It is also the only place at which you should buy parts if your car is still under warranty - non-Ford components may invalidate the warranty. To be sure of obtaining the correct parts it will always be necessary to give the storeman your car's engine and chassis number, and if possible, to take the 'old' part along for positive identification. Remember that many parts are available on a factory exchange scheme - any parts returned should always be clean! It obviously makes good sense to go straight to the specialists on your car for this type of part for they are best equipped to supply you.

Other garages and accessory shops - These are often very good places to buy materials and components needed for the maintenance of your car (e.g. oil filters, spark plugs, bulbs, fan belts, oils and greases, touch-up paint, filler paste etc). They also sell general accessories, usually have convenient opening hours, charge lower prices and can often be found not far from home.

Motor factors - Good factors will stock all of the more important components which wear out relatively quickly (e.g. clutch components, pistons, valves, exhaust systems, brake cylinders/pipes/seals/shoes and pads etc). Motor factors will often provide new or reconditioned components on a part exchange basis - this can save a considerable amount of money.

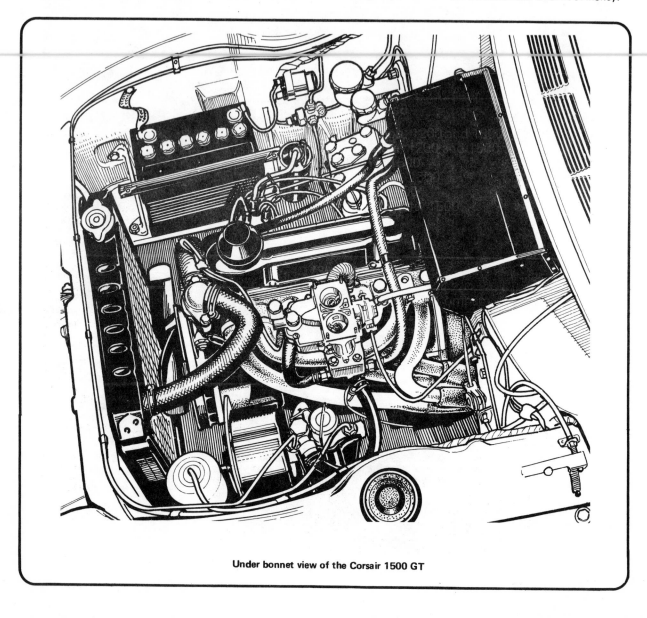

Under bonnet view of the Corsair 1500 GT

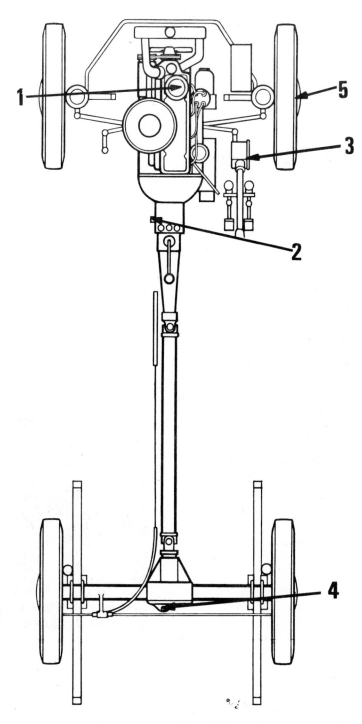

Lubrication chart

1 Engine - Castrol GTX
2 Gearbox - Castrol Hypoy Light
3 Steering box - Castrol Hypoy

4 Rear axle - Castrol Hypoy
5 Front hubs - Castrol LM Grease

Routine maintenance

The maintenance instructions listed below are basically those recommended by the manufacturer. They are supplemented by additional maintenance tasks which, through practical experience, the author recommends should be carried out at the intervals suggested.

The additional tasks are primarily of a preventative nature in that they will assist in eliminating the unexpected failure of a component due to fair wear and tear.

The levels of the engine oil, radiator cooling water, windscreen washer water and battery electrolyte, also the tyre pressures, should be checked weekly or more frequently if experience dictates this to be necessary. Similarly it is wise to check the level of the fluids in the clutch and brake master cylinder reservoirs at monthly intervals. If not checked at home it is advantageous to use regularly the same garage for this work as they will get to know your preferences for particular oils and the pressures at which you like to run your tyres.

Weekly or every 250 miles (400 km)

1 Check the oil level in the sump. Remove the dipstick; wipe it clean; re-insert it and then withdraw it again; check the oil level and top up as required.

2 Remove the radiator cap and check the coolant level which should be approximately 1 inch (25.4 mm) below the bottom of the filler neck. If the filler cap is removed immediately after a run, cover it with a cloth to prevent scalding when the pressure in the cooling system is released. Frequent topping up of the coolant may indicate a leak or a weak spring in the pressure cap. When a considerable loss of coolant has occurred through a leak, anti-freeze mixture should be added to the water used for topping up in order to maintain the strength of the anti-freeze.

3 Check the level of the electrolyte in the battery. Add only distilled water if necessary to bring the level of the electrolyte to just above the plate separators.

4 Check the tyre pressures (including the spare) and inflate if necessary to the pressures recommended (Specifications: Chapter 11). Check that the tyre wear pattern is uniform. If not, check the front wheel alignment.

5 Check the fluid level in the clutch and brake fluid reservoirs and top up if necessary.

6 Check and top up, if necessary, the level in the windscreen washer bottle.

7 Check all front and rear lamps for correct operation and renew any 'blown' bulbs.

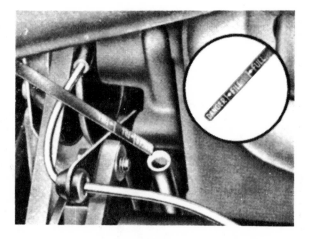

RM.1. Checking engine oil level

Every 5000 miles (8000 km) *

1 With the engine at normal operating temperature, drain the engine oil and renew the oil filter element. Fill with the correct grade and quantity of engine oil.

2 With the gearbox warm after a run, drain and refill with the correct grade and quantity of oil. It is recommended that further gearbox oil changes should be limited to 20,000 mile (32,000 km) intervals.

3 Check the fluid level in the automatic transmission unit (where fitted). Run the car for a minimum distance of 6 miles (9.6 km), place the speed selector lever in 'P' and allow the engine to idle for two minutes. Withdraw the dipstick, wipe clean and re-insert. Withdraw again and read off the fluid level. Top up if necessary with the correct grade and quantity of

fluid - **do not overfill.**

4 Wipe dirt from around the rear axle combined filler/level plug. Top up if necessary with the correct grade of oil.

5 On early models, grease steering and universal joint nipples and on all models check for play in ball joints.

6 Check the clutch pedal free movement and adjust the slave cylinder pushrod as described in Chapter 5.

7 Check the oil level in the steering box by removing the rubber plug and topping up if necessary with the correct grade of oil.

8 Check the tightness of the rear road spring 'U' bolts, clean the rear road springs and spray with penetrating oil.

9 Squirt two or three drops of engine oil into the dynamo rear bearing.

10 Lubricate the handbrake linkage.

11 Check and adjust the distributor contact breaker points and lubricate the distributor by applying two drops of engine oil to the cam centre screw (rotor arm removed) and a few drops through the baseplate to lubricate the mechanical advance components. Apply a smear of petroleum jelly to the high points of the cam.

12 Check and adjust the valve clearances.

13 Clean the interior of the fuel pump and its filter.

14 Check and adjust the fan belt.

15 Remove, clean and adjust the spark plugs.

16 Clean the engine oil filler cap gauze by washing it in paraffin.

17 Clean the air cleaner gauze element by washing it in paraffin, allowing it to drain and then applying a little engine oil. If a paper element type filter is fitted, refer to paragraph 33.

18 Check the wear of brake linings or disc pads.

19 Adjust the brakes if required and check the tyre tread depth.

RM.2. Checking coolant level

Every 15,000 miles (24,000 km)

These operations are additional to those already described for the repetitive 5000 mile (8000 km) service.

20 Change the wheels round to include the spare in order to make tyre wear even.

21 Check the torque wrench setting of the front suspension crossmember bolts.

22 Clean out, repack with grease and adjust the front hub bearings.

23 Examine the ball joint rubber gaiters for splits or deterioration and renew if necessary.

24 Check wheel alignment (toe-in).

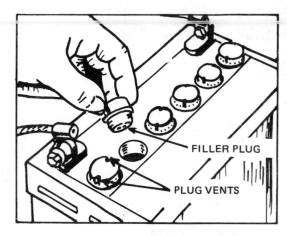

FILLER PLUG

PLUG VENTS

RM.3. Checking battery electrolyte level

Every 45,000 miles (72,000 km) or every 3 years

25 Renew all rubber seals in the brake and clutch master and slave cylinders. Bleed old hydraulic fluid from the system and refill with fluid which has been stored in an airtight container and has remained unshaken for 24 hours.

26 Check for wear in rear road spring shackle bushes and renew if necessary.

27 Check for resistance in shock absorbers and suspension legs and renew if weak.

Annually

28 Drain anti-freeze solution and refill with new mixture of the recommended concentration.

29 Examine seat belt anchorages and belts for wear or strain and renew as appropriate.

30 Examine brake pipes for rusting (rigid lines) or chafing or perishing (flexible hoses) and renew if evident.

31 Check for underbody rust particularly at rear road spring anchorages and front suspension leg upper mountings. De-rust and reinforce if necessary.

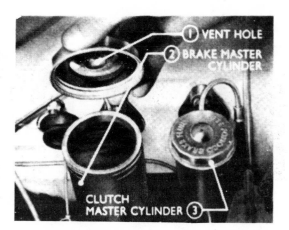

① VENT HOLE
② BRAKE MASTER CYLINDER

CLUTCH MASTER CYLINDER ③

RM.4. Checking hydraulic fluid reservoir level

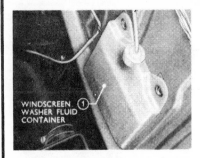

RM.5. Location of windscreen washer reservoir (Corsair)

RM.6. Changing engine oil filter

RM.7. Gearbox filler and drain plugs

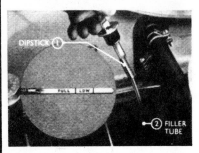

RM.8. Checking automatic transmission fluid level

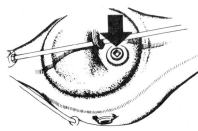

RM.9. Rear axle filler/level plug

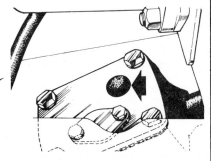

RM.10. Steering box filler/level plug

RM.11. Dynamo rear bearing lubrication hole

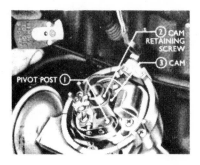

RM.12. Distributor lubrication points

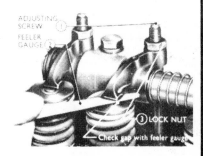

RM.13. Checking a valve clearance

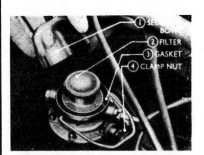

RM.14. Cleaning fuel pump

RM.15. Checking fan belt tension

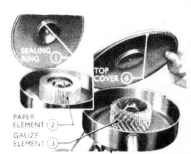

RM.16. Servicing air cleaner

* Estate car only
32 At 5000 mile (8000 km) intervals, remove the plug from the rear shock absorbers and check and top up the fluid level.

* GT models only
33 The air cleaner element is of paper type. It should be removed

at 5000 mile (8000 km) intervals and tapped on a block of wood to remove dust particles - do not attempt to clean it in any other way. At 15,000 mile (24,000 km) intervals renew the paper element. In very dusty operating conditions, the element should be renewed more frequently.

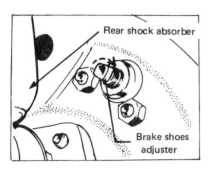

RM.17. Rear brake adjuster

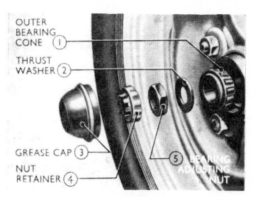

RM.18. Front hub bearing components

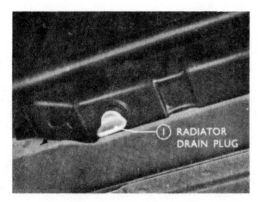

RM.19. Radiator drain tap

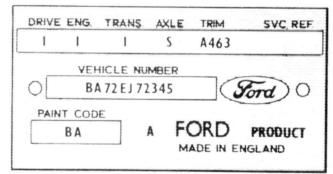

RM.20. Vehicle identification plate (after January 1965)

Chapter 1 Engine

Contents

Specifications

General

Type	4 cylinder, in-line, ohv		
	1200 cc	**1500 cc**	**1500 cc (GT)**
Bore	3.1875 in (80.96 mm)	3.1878 in (80.970 mm)	3.1878 in (80.970 mm)
Stroke	2.29 in (58.17 mm)	2.864 in (72.746 mm)	2.864 in (72.746 mm)
Cubic capacity	73.09 cu in (1197.8 cc)	91.43 cu in (1498 cc)	91.43 cu in (1498 cc)
Compression ratio:			
High	8.7 : 1	8.3 : 1	9.0 : 1
Low	7.3 : 1	7.0 : 1	—
Maximum Bhp (net):			
HC	48.5 @ 4800 rev/min	59.5 @ 4600 rev/min	78.0 @ 5200 rev/min
LC	46 @ 4800 rev/min	56.0 @ 4600 rev/min	—
Maximum torque (net):			
HC	63 lb ft (8.70 kg m) @ 2700 rev/min	81.5 lb ft (11.26 kg m) @ 2300 rev/min	91 lb ft (12.58 kg m) @ 3600 rev/min
LC	60 lb ft (8.30 kg m) @ 2700 rev/min	77.5 lb ft (10.72 kg m) @ 2700 rev/min	—
Firing order	1 2 4 3		

	1200 cc	1500 cc	1500 cc (GT)
Camshaft			
Journal diameter	1.5600 - 1.5605 in (39.624 - 39.637 mm)		
Bearing (inside diameter)	1.5615 - 1.5620 in (39.662 - 39.675 mm)		
Bearing length:			
Front and rear	0.75 in (19.0 mm)	0.79 in (20.07 mm)	0.79 in (20.07 mm)
Centre	0.64 in (16.3 mm)	0.68 in (17.27 mm)	0.68 in (17.27 mm)
Bearing running clearance	0.001 - 0.002 in (0.025 - 0.051 mm)		
End float	0.002 - 0.007 in (0.051 - 0.178 mm)		
Thrust plate thickness	0.176 - 0.178 in (4.470 - 4.521 mm)		
Maximum cam lift:			
Inlet	0.2108 in (5.350 mm)	0.2108 in (5.350 mm)	0.2309 in (5.865 mm)
Exhaust	0.2176 in (5.523 mm)	0.2176 in (5.523 mm)	0.2321 in (5.905 mm)
Connecting rods			
Length between centres	4.419 - 4.421 in (112.2 - 112.3 mm)	4.799 - 4.801 in (121.899 - 121.945 mm)	4.799 - 4.801 in (121.899 - 121.945 mm)
Big end bearing inside diameter	1.938 - 1.9392 in (4.9223 - 4.9254 mm)	2.0825 - 2.0830 in (52.896 - 52.908 mm)	2.0825 - 2.0830 in (52.896 - 52.908 mm)
Crankpin to bearing running clearance	0.0005 - 0.0022 in (0.0127 - 0.056 mm)		
Crankpin end float	0.004 - 0.010 in (0.102 - 0.254 mm)		
Small end bush inside diameter	0.8122 - 0.8125 in (20.630 - 20.638 mm)		
Crankshaft and main bearings			
Crankpin journal diameter	1.937 - 1.9375 in (49.200 - 49.213 mm)		
Main bearing journal diameter	2.1255 - 2.1260 in (52.988 - 54.000 mm)		
Undersize main bearing availability	0.010 in (0.254 mm); 0.020 in (0.508 mm); 0.030 in (0.762 mm)		
Main bearing running clearance	0.0005 - 0.0022 in (0.0127 - 0.056 mm)		
Crankshaft end float	0.003 - 0.011 in (0.076 - 0.279 mm)		
End float thrust washer thickness	0.091 - 0.093 in (2.31 - 2.36 mm)		
Cylinder block			
Type	Cast iron integral with crankcase		
Cylinder head			
Type	Cast iron		
Valve guide inside diameter	0.3113 - 0.3125 in (7.907 - 7.938 mm)		
Valve seat angle	44° 30' to 45°		
Valve seat width:			
Inlet	1/16 in (1.59 mm)		
Exhaust	5/64 in (1.98 mm)		
Flywheel and starter ring gear			
Type	Shrunk on ring gear; 110 teeth		
Clutch spigot bearing	Sintered bronze		
Lubrication system			
Oil pressure	35 - 40 lb in^2 (2.46 - 2.81 kg cm^2)		
Oil capacity (less filter):			
1200 cc (early)	4½ pints (2.56 litres)		
1200 cc (late)	5½ pints (3.12 litres)		
1500 cc (early)	5½ pints (3.12 litres)		
1500 cc (late)	7 pints (3.98 litres)		
Oil filter capacity	½ pint (0.285 litres)		
Oil pump (Eccentric bi-rotor type):			
Inner and outer rotor clearance	0.006 in (0.152 mm) maximum		
Outer rotor to housing clearance	0.010 in (0.254 mm) maximum		
Rotor end float	0.005 in (0.127 mm) maximum		
Oil pump (vane type):			
Vane to rotor clearance	0.005 in (0.127 mm) maximum		
Rotor and vane end float	0.005 in (0.127 mm) maximum		
Pistons			
Type	Aluminium; solid skirt		
Rings	2 compression; 1 oil control		
Ring groove width:			
Compression	0.0796 - 0.0806 in (2.022 - 2.047 mm)		
Oil control	0.1578 - 0.1588 in (4.008 - 4.034 mm)		
	1200 cc	**1500 cc**	**1500 cc (GT)**
Piston diameters:			
Grade 1	3.1858 - 3.1861 in	3.1858 - 3.1861 in	3.1855 - 3.1858 in

		(80.919 - 80.927 mm)	(90.919 - 80.927 mm)	(80.912 - 89.919 mm)

	Column 1	Column 2	Column 3
Grade 2	3.1861 - 3.1864 in (80.927 - 80.935 mm)	3.1861 - 3.1864 in (80.927 - 80.935 mm)	3.1858 - 3.1861 in (80.919 - 80.927 mm)
Grade 3	3.1864 - 3.1867 in (80.935 - 80.942 mm)	3.1864 - 3.1867 in (80.935 - 80.942 mm)	3.1861 - 3.1864 in (80.927 - 80.935 mm)
Grade 4	3.1867 - 3.1870 in (80.942 - 80.950 mm)	3.1867 - 3.1870 in (80.942 - 80.950 mm)	3.1864 - 3.1867 in (80.935 - 80.942 mm)
Grade 5 *	3.1870 - 3.1873 in (80.950 - 80.958 mm)	3.1870 - 3.1873 in (80.950 - 80.958 mm)	3.1867 - 3.1870 in (80.942 - 80.950 mm)
Grade 6 *	3.1873 - 3.1876 in (80.958 - 80.965 mm)	3.1873 - 3.1876 in (80.958 - 80.965 mm)	3.1870 - 3.1873 in (80.950 - 80.958 mm)

* Grades 5 and 6 only are supplied for replacement purposes

Oversize pistons available	0.0025 in (0.0635 mm); 0.005 in (0.127 mm); 0.015 in (0.381 mm) 0.030 in (0.762 mm)
Clearance between piston crown and cylinder block top face at tdc	0.022 - 0.038 in (0.559 and 0.965 mm)
Piston to cylinder bore clearance (1198 and 1498 cc)	0.0008 - 0.0014 in (0.0203 - 0.0356 mm)
Pull required to extract 0.0015 in (0.038 mm) feeler blade ½ in (12.7 mm) wide	3 to 7 lb (1.36 - 3.18 kg)
Piston to cylinder bore clearance (1498 cc GT)	0.0011 - 0.0017 in (0.0279 - 0.0432 mm)
Pull required to extract 0.002 in (0.051 mm) feeler blade ½ in (12.7 mm) wide	4 to 8 lb (1.81 - 3.63 kg)

Gudgeon pins:
Type	Fully floating, tubular
Outside diameter	0.8120 - 0.8123 in (20.625 - 20.632 mm)
Clearance in piston	0 - 0.0002 in (0 - 0.0051 mm)
Clearance in small end bush	0.0001 - 0.0003 in (0.0025 - 0.0076 mm)

Piston rings:
Top compression ring:
Type	Cast iron chrome plated
Radial thickness	0.122 - 0.130 in (3.099 - 3.302 mm)
Width	0.077 - 0.078 in (1.956 - 1.981 mm)
Ring to groove clearance	0.0016 - 0.0036 in (0.0406 - 0.0914 mm)
Ring gap	0.009 - 0.014 in (0.229 - 0.356 mm)

Lower compression ring:
Type	Cast iron (stepped on lower face)
Radial thickness	0.146 - 0.156 in (3.712 - 3.962 mm)
Width	0.077 - 0.078 in (1.956 - 1.981 mm)
Ring to groove clearance	0.0016 - 0.0036 in (0.0406 - 0.0914 mm)
Ring gap	0.009 - 0.014 in (0.229 - 0.356 mm)

Oil control ring:
Type	Cast iron slotted
Radial thickness	0.122 - 0.130 in (3.099 - 3.302 mm)
Width	0.155 - 0.156 in (3.937 - 3.962 mm)
Ring to groove clearance	0.0018 - 0.0038 in (0.0457 - 0.0965 mm)
Ring gap	0.009 - 0.014 in (0.229 - 0.356 mm)
Oversize rings available	0.0025 in (0.0635 mm); 0.005 in (0.127 mm); 0.015 in (0.381 mm); 0.030 in (0.762 mm)

Pushrods and tappets (cam followers)
Pushrod diameter	0.250 - 0.254 in (6.350 - 6.452 mm)
Pushrod length	7.40 - 7.43 in (178.82 - 178.89 mm)
Tappet length	1.85 in (46.99 mm)
Tappet stem diameter	0.436 - 0.4365 in (11.072 - 11.085 mm)
Tappet clearance in block	0.0005 - 0.002 in (0.0127 - 0.051 mm)

Timing chain
Type	Single roller
Pitch	0.375 in (9.525 mm)
Number of links	46
Roller width	0.225 in (5.615 mm)
Roller diameter	0.25 in (6.350 mm)

Valves
Valve stem diameter:
Inlet	0.3095 - 0.3105 in (7.861 - 7.887 mm)
Exhaust	0.3086 - 0.3096 in (7.838 - 7.864 mm)

Stem to guide clearance:

Inlet	0.0008 - 0.003 in (0.020 - 0.076 mm)		
Exhaust	0.0017 - 0.0039 in (0.043 - 0.099 mm)		
Oversize valve stems available	0.003 in (0.076 mm); 0.015 in (0.381 mm)		

	1200 cc	1498 cc	1498 cc (GT)
Valve head diameter:			
Inlet	1.262 - 1.272 in (32.050 - 32.310 mm)	1.497 to 1.507 in (38.02 to 38.28 mm)	1.405 - 1.415 in (35.687 - 35.941 mm)
Exhaust	1.183 - 1.193 in (30.040 - 30.030 mm)	1.240 to 1.250 in (31.50 to 31.75 mm)	1.240 - 1.250 in (31.496 - 31.750 mm)

Valve seat angle	45º 0' to 45º 15'	
Valve springs:		
Free length	1.48 in (37.59 mm)	
Internal diameter	0.802 - 0.814 in (20.371 - 20.672 mm)	

	1200 cc and 1500 cc	1500 cc GT
Valve timing:		
Inlet opens	17º BTDC	27º
Inlet closes	51º ABDC	65º
Exhaust opens	51º BBDC	65º
Exhaust closes	17º ATDC	27º
Valve lift:		
Inlet	0.315 in (8.001 mm)	0.3436 in (8.727 mm)
Exhaust	0.319 in (8.103 mm)	0.3354 in (8.519 mm)
Valve clearances (cold):		
Inlet	0.008 in (0.203 mm)	0.010 in (0.254 mm)
Exhaust	0.018 in (0.457 mm)	0.023 in (0.584 mm)
Valve clearances (hot):		
Inlet	0.010 in (0.254 mm)	0.012 in (0.305 mm)
Exhaust	0.017 in (0.432 mm)	0.022 in (0.559 mm)

Torque wrench settings	lb ft	kg m
Cylinder head bolts	65 - 70	8.983 - 9.674
Main bearings	55 - 60	7.601 - 8.292
Big ends	20 - 25	2.764 - 3.455
Flywheel	45 - 50	6.219 - 6.910
Manifolds	15 - 18	2.073 - 2.487
Rocker shaft pillars	17 - 22	2.349 - 3.040
Bellhousing to engine	40	5.53
Torque converter housing to engine	30	4.147

1 General description

The engine fitted to all models covered by this manual is of four cylinder, in-line, overhead valve type. The smaller 1198 cc version has three crankshaft main bearings and the larger 1498 cc has five main bearings. Alternative high and low compression ratios were available on Cortina and Corsair standard models but the GT versions of these cars were produced in high compression form only.

The cylinder block and head are of cast iron construction with fully machined combustion chambers. Vertically positioned in-line valves are located in guides which may be either directly machined in the cylinder head or pressed-in type.

The camshaft is located on the right hand side of the cylinder block and is driven by a single roller chain from a crankshaft sprocket. An automatic chain tensioner is fitted. The camshaft runs in three steel backed white metal bearings, endfloat being controlled by a thrust plate fitted at the front end. Machined onto the camshaft are the drive gears for the distributor and the oil pump and an eccentric cam operates the fuel pump arm.

The cast iron crankshaft runs in three (1198 cc) or five (1498 cc) shell bearings, endfloat being controlled by semi-circular thrust washers located one each side of the centre main bearing. GT engines have copper/lead or lead/bronze type main bearings, whereas, standard engines have white metal type.

The connecting rods are forged 'H' section having either copper/lead, lead/bronze or aluminium/tin shell type bearings according to application. The small end bushes are of bronze type.

Aluminium alloy pistons are used having two compression rings and one scraper (oil control) ring located above the gudgeon pin. The gudgeon pins are of fully floating type with circlips to secure them.

Pistons used in GT engines have concave, reinforced crowns.

The oil pump may be one of two types, either eccentric bi-rotor or sliding vane. Both pumps have an associated preset pressure relief valve.

2 Major operations possible with the engine in place

1 Removal of the valve rocker gear and cylinder head.
2 Removal of the carburettor and manifolds.
3 Removal of the sump, oil pump, connecting rod/piston assemblies.
4 Removal of the water pump.
5 Removal of the starter motor and dynamo.

3 Engine removal without gearbox

1 Mark the position of the bonnet hinges and then unscrew and remove the hinge bolts and with the help of an assistant lift the bonnet away (photo).
2 Disconnect the leads from the battery terminals.
3 Disconnect the battery case clamp and remove the battery (photo).

4 Drain the engine oil (photo).
5 Drain the coolant, retaining it for further use if it is a fresh anti-freeze mixture.
6 Remove the air cleaner from the carburettor by unscrewing the cover screw and the clamp screw at the carburettor throat.
7 Disconnect the top and bottom radiator hoses at the engine end, also the heater hoses (photos).
8 Unscrew and remove the four radiator securing bolts and lift the radiator from the engine compartment (photo).
9 Disconnect the fuel inlet pipe from the fuel pump and plug the pipe to prevent loss of fuel (photo).
10 Remove the engine breather after first unscrewing the engine to clutch bellhousing bolt which retains it.
11 Disconnect the lead from the starter motor terminal and then remove the two starter motor securing bolts and withdraw the starter motor.
12 Disconnect the HT and LT leads which run between the coil, distributor and spark plugs.
13 Unscrew and remove the coil from the battery platform.
14 Disconnect the leads from the oil pressure and water temperature transmitter units (photo).
15 Disconnect the leads from the rear of the dynamo.
16 Disconnect the manifold to exhaust downpipe clamp and support the exhaust pipe on a jack or block (photo).
17 Disconnect the choke cable and accelerator linkage at the carburettor (photo).
18 Detach the engine splash shield (four self-tapping screws).
19 Place suitable slings or chains under the engine and using a hoist, just take the weight of the engine.
20 Unscrew and remove the engine to clutch bellhousing (torque convertor housing - automatic transmission) securing bolts. The engine to bodyframe earthing strap is located under the top left hand bolt (photo).
21 Place a jack beneath the gearbox or automatic transmission unit to support its weight during engine removal.
22 Unscrew the bolts which secure the engine rear plate to the clutch bellhousing.
23 Unscrew and remove the bolts which secure the engine mountings to the crossmember (photo).
24 Pull the engine forward and then incline it upwards at an angle and hoist it from the engine compartment. Do not allow the weight of the engine to hang upon the gearbox input shaft, even momentarily, while the shaft is still engaged with the clutch driven plate, otherwise damage to the clutch and gearbox components will occur.

4 Engine removal without automatic transmission unit

1 The procedure is similar to that described in the preceding Section for removal leaving the manual gearbox in the car but the following additional operations are required.
2 Disconnect the downshift cable at the carburettor.
3 Disconnect the combined filler/breather tube bracket from the cylinder block.
4 Unscrew and remove the drive plate to torque converter securing bolts after first having marked the relative position of the drive plate to the torque converter for exact refitting. The bolts are accessible one at a time through the aperture in the engine rear cover plate and the engine will have to be turned slowly by means of the crankshaft pulley retaining bolt until each bolt comes into view.

5 Engine removal together with gearbox or automatic transmission unit

This is not recommended for the following reasons:
1 The car will have to be jacked up exceptionally high to provide sufficient clearance to drop the end of the transmission unit in order to attain the required lifting angle of the combined unit.
2 The combined weight of engine and transmission would be excessive.

3 The front crossmember and other steering components would have to be removed before withdrawal of the combined assembly could be achieved.

6 Engine dismantling - general

1 It is best to mount the engine on a dismantling stand, but if this is not available, stand the engine on a strong bench at a comfortable working height. Failing this, it can be stripped down on the floor.
2 During the dismantling process, the greatest care should be taken to keep the exposed parts free from dirt. As an aid to achieving this, thoroughly clean down the outside of the engine, first removing all traces of oil and congealed dirt.
3 A good grease solvent such as Gunk will make the job much easier, for, after the solvent has been applied and allowed to stand for a time, a vigorous jet of water will wash off the solvent and grease with it. If the dirt is thick and deeply embedded, work the solvent into it with a strong stiff brush.
4 Finally wipe down the exterior of the engine with a rag and only then, when it is quite clean, should the dismantling process begin. As the engine is stripped, clean each part in a bath of paraffin or petrol.
5 Never immerse parts with oilways in paraffin, eg crankshaft. To clean these parts, wipe down carefully with a petrol dampened rag. Oilways can be cleaned out with copper wire. If an air line is available, all parts can be blown dry and the oilways blown through as an added precaution.
6 Re-use of old gaskets is false economy. To avoid the possibility of trouble after the engine has been reassembled **always** use new gaskets throughout.
7 Do not throw away the old gaskets, for sometimes it happens that an immediate replacement cannot be found and the old gasket is then very useful as a template. Hang up the gaskets as they are removed.
8 To strip the engine, it is best to work from the top down. The crankcase provides a firm base on which the engine can be supported in an upright position. When the stage is reached where the crankshaft must be removed, the engine can be turned on its side and all other work carried out with it in this position.
9 Wherever possible, replace nuts, bolts and washers finger tight from wherever they were removed. This helps to avoid loss and muddle.

7 Engine dismantling - ancillary components

Before engine dismantling begins, it is necessary to strip it of ancillary components.

   a) Fuel system components
      Carburettor and manifold assembly
      Exhaust manifold
      Fuel pump
   b) Ignition system components
      Distributor
   c) Electrical system components
      Dynamo
   d) Cooling system components
      Fan and hub
      Water pump
      Thermostat housing and thermostat
      Water temperature indicator sender unit
   e) Engine
      Oil filter
      Oil pressure sender unit
      Oil level dipstick
      Oil filler cap and rocker cover
      Engine mountings
      Crankcase ventilation valve (where fitted)
   f) Clutch
      Clutch pressure plate assembly

3.1 Removing the bonnet lid

3.2 Removing the battery

3.4 Sump drain plug

3.7a Disconnecting heater hoses

3.7b Disconnecting heater hoses

3.8 Removing radiator

3.9 Disconnecting fuel pump inlet

3.14 Disconnecting water temperature transmitter lead

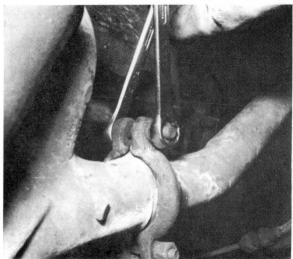

3.16 Disconnecting exhaust downpipe

3.17 Disconnecting the throttle linkage

3.20 Removing clutch bellhousing bolt and earth strap

3.23. Removing an engine mounting bolt

Fig. 1.1. Cut-away view of the 1198 cc engine (3 main bearings) and gearbox

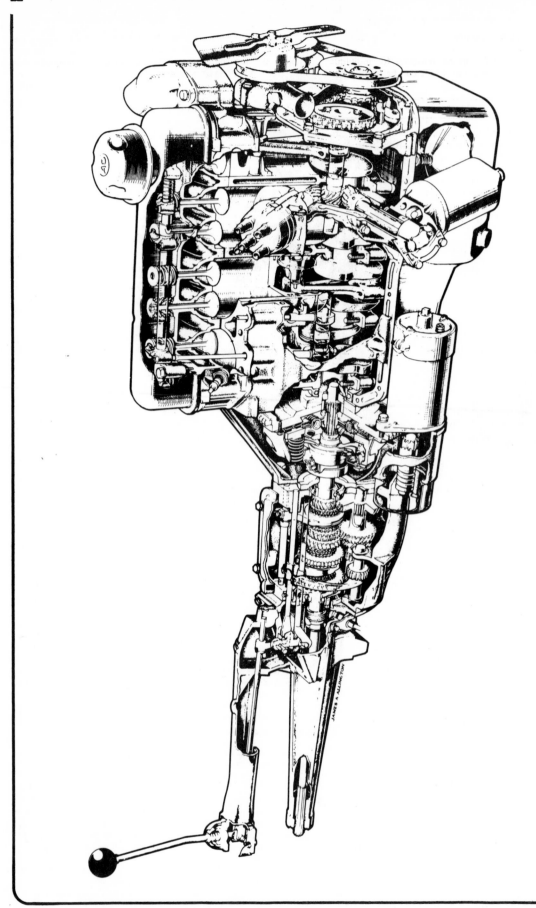

Fig. 1.2. Cut-away view of the 1498 cc engine (5 main bearings) and gearbox

Clutch friction plate assembly

Some of these items have to be removed for individual servicing or renewal periodically and details can be found under the appropriate Chapter.

8 Cylinder head - removal

1 Before removing the cylinder head, prepare to store the various components in numerical sequence (1 to 8) with No 1 nearest the radiator. A piece of wood with holes drilled in it or a long box with divisions would be suitable.
2 Unscrew and remove the rocker cover securing screws and lift the rocker cover from the cylinder head. If it is stuck tight, try and release the cork joint gasket from the cylinder head, using a sharp knife, but in any event it is wise to have a new gasket available for use on reassembly (photo).

8.2 Unscrewing a rocker box cover screw

3 Slacken each of the rocker pillar bolts a turn at a time (starting in the centre and working outwards) in order to prevent any undue strain on one section of the shaft which might be caused by the pressure of the valve springs on those valves which are open. Remove the bolts and lift away the rocker shaft as an assembly.
4 Withdraw each of the pushrods and store them in order in the rack previously prepared.
5 Unscrew the cylinder head bolts a turn at a time; starting with the corner ones, then the centre two and finally the remaining four in diagonal sequence.
6 Lift the cylinder head from the cylinder block. If it is stuck, do not attempt to prise it with a screwdriver inserted between the joint faces but tap the head on its sides using a hammer and a block of wood. Alternatively, refit the spark plugs and turn the engine over to allow compression to do the job.

9 Rocker assembly - dismantling

1 Withdraw the split pin from one end of the shaft and remove the flat washer, the spring cup washer and the second flat washer all of which bear against the rocker arm.
2 Withdraw the pillars, arms and springs from the shaft, keeping them in their correct sequence for exact refitment.

10 Valves - removal

1 The valves can be removed from the cylinder head by the following method: Compress each spring in turn with a valve spring compressor until the two halves of the collets can be removed. Release the compressor and remove the spring and spring retainer.

2 If, when the valve spring compressor is screwed down, the valve spring retaining cap refuses to free to expose the split collet, do not continue to screw down on the compressor as there is a likelihood of damaging it.
3 Gently tap the top of the tool directly over the cap with a light hammer. This will free the cap. To avoid the compressor jumping off the valve spring retaining cap when it is tapped, hold the compressor firmly in position with one hand.
4 Slide the rubber oil control seal off the top of each inlet valve stem and then drop out each valve through the combustion chamber.
5 Keep the valves, springs, seats and collets in correct sequence for refitment into their original positions.

11 Timing chain and gear - dismantling

1 With the water pump, fan and drive belt removed as described in the appropriate Chapter, unscrew and remove the crankchaft pulley bolt. This may be achieved by using a ring spanner and giving the spanner two or three clouts with a club hammer. If this method does not loosen the bolt then select a forward gear and pull the handbrake fully on. It should now be possible to unscrew the bolt using normal leverage on the spanner. On vehicles fitted with automatic transmission, remove the starter motor and jam the ring gear or the drive plate to torque converter bolts with a large screwdriver. This will prevent the engine rotating when the spanner is levered in an anticlockwise direction. When the pulley bolt is withdrawn, retain the spring locking washer and the large plain washer.
2 The crankshaft pulley wheel may pull off quite easily. If not, place two large screwdrivers behind the wheel at 180° to each other, and carefully lever the wheel off. It is preferable to use a proper pulley extractor if this is available, but large screwdrivers or tyre levers are quite suitable, providing care is taken not to damage the pulley.
3 Undo the bolts which hold the timing cover in place, noting that four sump bolts must also be removed before the cover can be taken off.
4 Check the chain for wear by measuring how much it can be depressed with the tensioner removed. More than ½ inch (12.7 mm) means a new chain must be fitted on reassembly.
5 With the timing cover off, take off the oil thrower. The concave side faces outwards.
6 With a drift or screwdriver tap back the tabs on the lockwasher under the two camshaft gearwheel retaining bolts and undo the bolts.
7 To remove the camshaft and crankshaft timing wheels complete with chain, ease each wheel forward a little at a time levering behind each gear wheel in turn with two large screwdrivers at 180° to each other. If the gearwheels are locked solid then it will be necessary to use a proper gearwheel and pulley extractor, and if one is available this should be used anyway in preference to screwdrivers. With both gearwheels safely off, remove the Woodruff key from the crankshaft with a pair of pliers.
8 Unscrew and remove the two bolts and their washers which secure the timing chain tensioner in position. Withdraw the tensioner and then pull the tensioner arm from its pivot pin.

12 Sump - removal

1 If the sump is to be removed with the engine in the car then it will be necessary to remove the splash shield and the starter motor and to disconnect the engine front mounting so that the engine can be jacked up (under the clutch bellhousing) sufficiently high to gain access to the sump bolts. Do not raise the engine so much that the water hoses, leads and control wires are strained.
2 If this operation is being carried out with the engine in the car, remember to drain the engine oil first!
3 Unscrew and remove the sump securing bolts working in a

diagonal sequence and unscrewing each bolt a turn at a time. If necessary turn the engine so that the crankshaft webs clear the inside of the sump.

4 Clean the old joint gasket from the mating faces of the crankcase and sump, also pick out the cork sealing strip from the recess at the front end of the crankshaft.

13 Oil pump - removal

1 The oil pump/filter assembly is mounted externally on the right hand side of the engine.

2 It will be easier if the filter is first detached by withdrawing the long centre securing bolt.

3 Remove the oil pump after unscrewing the three securing bolts.

14 Camshaft - removal

1 The camshaft cannot be removed with the engine in place in the car primarily because of the restriction imposed by the inverted umbrella shaped tappets which can only be removed downwards, ie towards the camshaft.

2 With the engine inverted and sump, rocker gear, pushrods, timing cover, oil pump, distributor, gearwheels, and timing chain removed, take off the chain tensioner and arm.

3 Bend back the locking tabs from the two bolts which hold the horseshoe shaped thrust plate in position behind the camshaft flange. Slide out the thrust plate.

4 Rotate the camshaft so that the tappets are fully home and then withdraw the camshaft from the block. Take great care that the cam lobe peaks do not damage the camshaft bearings as the shaft is pulled forward.

15 Tappets (cam followers) - removal

With the engine inverted and the camshaft withdrawn as described in the preceding Section, remove each tappet and keep it in correct sequence for exact refitment.

16 Piston, connecting rod and big end bearing - removal

1 The pistons and connecting rods can be removed with the engine still in the car or with the engine on the bench.

2 With the cylinder head and sump removed undo the big end retaining bolts.

3 The connecting rods and pistons are lifted out from the top of the cylinder block, after the carbon or wear ring at the top of the bore has been scraped away.

4 Remove the big end caps one at a time, taking care to keep them in the right order and the correct way round. Also ensure that the shell bearings are kept with their correct connecting rods and caps unless they are to be renewed. Normally, the numbers 1 to 4 are stamped on adjacent sides of the big end caps and connecting rods, indicating which cap fits on which rod and which way round the cap fits. Where no sequence numbers are to be found, mark each big end bearing cap and corresponding connecting rod with its number using quick drying paint. This will ensure there is no confusion later as it is most important that the caps go back in the correct position on the connecting rods from which they were removed.

5 If the big end caps are difficult to remove they may be gently tapped with a soft hammer.

6 To remove the shell bearings, press the bearing opposite the groove in both the connecting rod, and the connecting rod caps and the bearings will slide out easily.

7 Withdraw the pistons and connecting rods upwards and ensure they are kept in the correct order for replacement in the same bore. Refit the connecting rod, caps and bearings to the rods if the bearings do not require renewal, to minimise the risk of

16.3 Removing wear ring from cylinder bore using a scraper

getting the caps and rods muddled.

17 Gudgeon pin - removal

1 To remove the gudgeon pin to free the piston from the connecting rod, remove one of the circlips at either end of the pin with a pair of circlip pliers.

2 Press out the pin from the rod and piston with your finger.

3 If the pin shows reluctance to move, then on no account force it out, as this could damage the piston. Immerse the piston in a pan of boiling water for three minutes. On removal the expansion of the aluminium should allow the gudgeon pin to slide out easily.

4 Always use new circlips on reassembly.

18 Piston rings - removal

1 To remove the piston rings, slide them carefully over the top of the piston, taking care not to scratch the aluminium alloy; never slide them off the bottom of the piston skirt. It is very easy to break the cast iron piston rings if they are pulled off roughly, so this operation should be done with extreme care.

2 The use of three feeler blades or narrow strips of tin will facilitate their removal. Carefully lift one end of the piston ring and slide the feeler gauges under it. Turn them slowly round the piston so that they cause the ring to emerge from its groove. If the feeler blades are positioned at equidistant points round the periphery of the piston then the ring can be slid upwards, off the piston without dropping into an empty groove.

19 Flywheel - removal

1 Having removed the clutch assembly as described in Chapter 5, bend back the tabs on the lockplate and unscrew and remove the four securing bolts.

2 Gently tap the flywheel from the crankshaft flange using a hammer and block of wood or a plastic faced mallet.

3 There is no need to mark the position of the flywheel in relation to the crankshaft as it can only be located one way due to its positioning dowel.

20 Main bearings and crankshaft - removal

1 With the engine removed from the car and the timing gears, flywheel, connecting rods and pistons and sump removed as described in the previous Sections, remove the oil pump intake

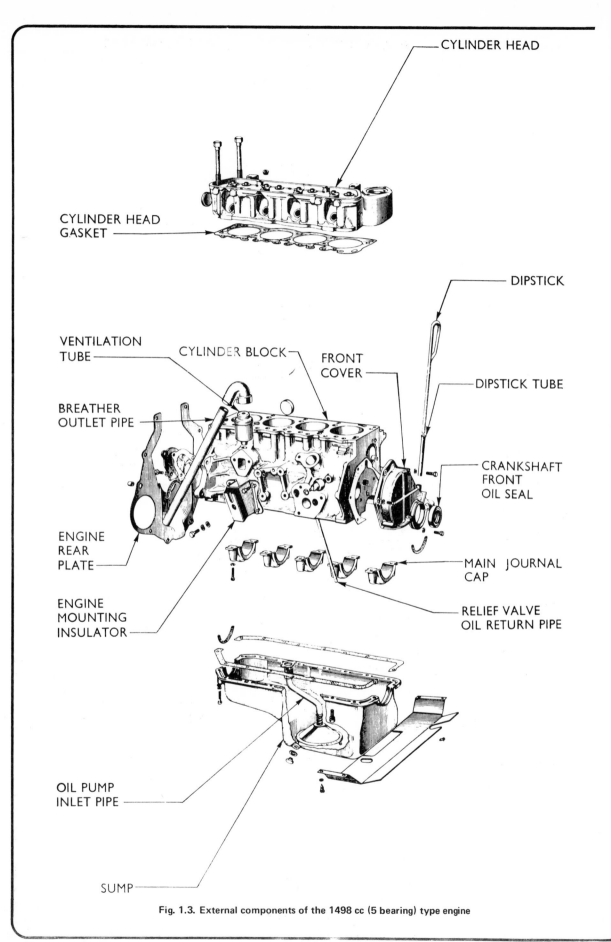

Fig. 1.3. External components of the 1498 cc (5 bearing) type engine

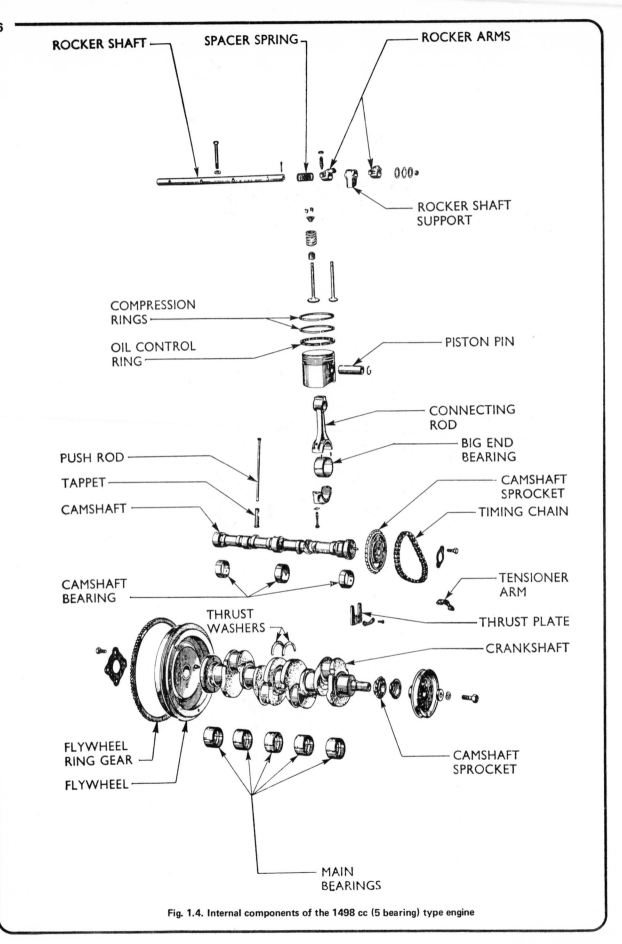

ROCKER SHAFT

SPACER SPRING

ROCKER ARMS

ROCKER SHAFT SUPPORT

COMPRESSION RINGS

OIL CONTROL RING

PISTON PIN

CONNECTING ROD

BIG END BEARING

PUSH ROD

TAPPET

CAMSHAFT

CAMSHAFT SPROCKET

TIMING CHAIN

CAMSHAFT BEARING

TENSIONER ARM

THRUST WASHERS

THRUST PLATE

CRANKSHAFT

CAMSHAFT SPROCKET

FLYWHEEL RING GEAR

FLYWHEEL

MAIN BEARINGS

Fig. 1.4. Internal components of the 1498 cc (5 bearing) type engine

pipe. To do this, first bend back the tab washer and then unscrew the union nut.

2 The pressure relief oil return pipe is a press fit in the cylinder block and if it is necessary to remove it, it should be drifted from its location.

3 Check that each of the three (1198 cc) or five (1498 cc) main bearing caps is marked with its position in relation to the crankcase. If not, mark them with quick drying paint.

4 Unscrew the bolts evenly from each main bearing cap and remove the caps complete with shell bearings.

5. Lift the crankshaft from the crankcase and withdraw the semi-circular thrust washers which are fitted one each side of the centre main bearing journal.

6 The half shell bearings located in the crankcase may now be removed. If they are not to be renewed then they must be kept in the correct order for refitment.

22.1 Unscrewing oil filter centre bolt

21 Lubrication system - description

1 The engine lubrication system is of forced feed type, the oil being circulated by the externally mounted oil pump. The pump may be of eccentric bi-rotor or sliding vane type driven by a gear on the camshaft.

2 Oil is drawn from the sump into the pump through a filter screen. Excess pressure is controlled by an integral relief valve and oil is returned through a pipe to the sump. Oil, under pressure from the pump, passes through a full-flow type filter which is attached to the pump and then through a gallery into which is screwed the oil pressure transmitter unit.

3 The oil then passes through a series of drillings and passages to lubricate all the bearings and moving parts of the engine.

22 Oil filter - removal and refitting

1 The full flow oil filter is attached to the oil pump on the right hand side of the engine toward the front. The element is removed by unscrewing the long centre bolt and carefully lifting away the filter bowl. This will be full of oil so have a large bowl located below it (photo).

2 Throw the old filter element away and thoroughly clean down the filter bowl and associated parts with paraffin and when perfectly clean, wipe dry with a non-fluffy rag.

3 A rubber sealing ring is located in a groove round the head of the oil filter and forms an effective leakproof joint between the filter head and the filter bowl. A new rubber sealing ring is supplied with each new filter element.

4 Carefully prise out the old sealing ring from the locating groove. If the ring has become hard and is difficult to move, take great care not to damage the sides of the sealing ring groove.

Fig. 1.5. Timing chain tensioner

Fig. 1.6. Camshaft thrust plate

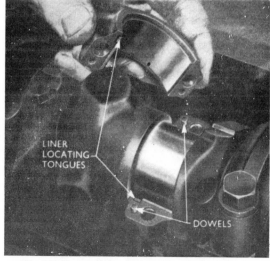

Fig. 1.7. Connecting rod big-end bearing and cap

5 With the old ring removed, fit the new ring in the groove at four equidistant points and press it home a segment at a time. Do not insert the ring at just one point and work round the groove pressing it home as, using this method, it is easy to stretch the ring and be left with a small loop of rubber which will not fit into the locating groove. Grease the exposed surface of the seal.

6 Offer up the bowl to the rubber sealing ring and check that the lip of the filter bowl is resting squarely on the rubber sealing ring.

7 Tighten the centre bolt sufficiently to create a good seal but do not overtighten it.

8 Run the engine and check for oil leaks.

23 Oil pump (eccentric bi-rotor type) - servicing

1 If the oil pump is worn it is best to purchase an exchange reconditioned unit as a good oil pump is at the very heart of long engine life. Generally speaking an exchange or overhauled pump should be fitted at a major engine reconditioning. If it is wished to overhaul the oil pump, detach the pump and filter unit from the cylinder block, and remove the filter body and element.

2 Remove the bolts and lockwashers securing the end plate and remove the plate. Lift away the 'O' ring from the sealing groove in the body.

3 Check the clearance between the lobes of the inner and outer rotors. The clearance must not exceed 0.006 inch (0.152 mm) when checked at two different points.

4 Check the clearance between the outer rotor and the housing, this should not exceed 0.0075 inch (0.19 mm). Replacement rotors are supplied only as a matched pair so that, if the clearance is excessive, a new rotor assembly must be fitted.

5 Lay a straight edge across the face of the pump in order to check the clearance between the faces of the rotors and the bottom of the straight edge. This clearance should not exceed 0.005 inch (0.13 mm). If the clearance is excessive the face of the pump body can be carefully lapped on a flat surface.

6 When it is necessary to renew the rotors, drive out the pin securing the skew gear and pull the gear from the shaft. Remove the inner rotor and drive shaft and withdraw the outer rotor. Install the outer rotor with the chamfered end towards the pump body.

7 Fit the inner rotor and drive shaft assembly, position the skew gear and install the pin. Tap over each end of the pin to prevent it loosening in service. Position a new 'O' ring in the groove in the pump body, fit the end plate in position and secure with the four bolts and lockwashers, tightening to a torque of 5 - 7 lb ft (0.690 - 0.966 kg m).

8 Refit the oil pump assembly together with a new gasket and secure in place with the bolts and lockwashers, tightening to a torque of 13 - 15 lb ft (1.794 - 2.070 kg m).

24 Oil pump (vane type) - servicing

1 Carry out the operations detailed in paragraphs 1, 2 and 5 of the preceding Section.

2 When reassembling, use a new 'O' ring seal.

25 Oil pump relief valve

This rarely requires attention but if essential, the valve and spring can be removed after withdrawing the spring seat which is a press fit in the oil pump body.

26 Oil filter relief valve

This valve is also a press fit in the filter body and does not normally require attention.

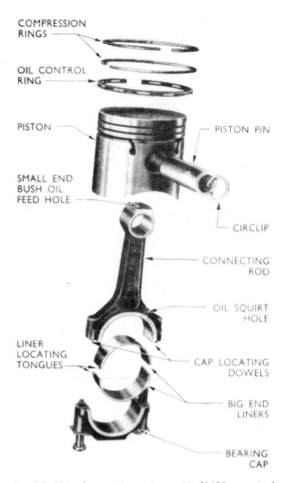

COMPRESSION RINGS

OIL CONTROL RING

PISTON

SMALL END BUSH OIL FEED HOLE

LINER LOCATING TONGUES

PISTON PIN

CIRCLIP

CONNECTING ROD

OIL SQUIRT HOLE

CAP LOCATING DOWELS

BIG END LINERS

BEARING CAP

Fig. 1.8. Piston/connecting rod assembly (1498 cc engine)

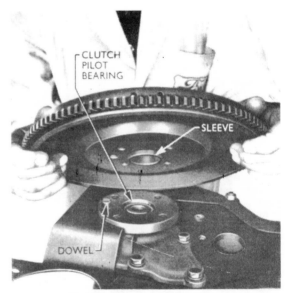

CLUTCH PILOT BEARING

SLEEVE

DOWEL

Fig. 1.9. Removing the flywheel

27 Crankcase ventilation systems - description and servicing

1 Air enters the crankcase through the gauze mesh incorporated in the oil filler cap.
2 Air and fumes are extracted from the crankcase by means of a breather on the right hand side of the engine. This breather incorporates a screen which prevents the emission of oil droplets.
3 Servicing is restricted to removing the oil filler cap every 5000 miles (8000 km) and washing it in fuel and shaking it dry.
4 If an oil bath type oil filler cap is encountered the oil should be discarded every 5000 miles (8000 km), the gauze washed in fuel and fresh engine oil applied.
5 Some later models are equipped with a semi-closed fume emission control system. Check the security of the connecting rubber hoses and renew any that have deteriorated.
6 Every 5000 miles (8000 km) remove the spring retainers from the valve cap which is mounted on the rocker box cover. Clean the assembly in paraffin and reassemble.

28 Engine mountings - removal and refitting

1 The rubber insulators which support the engine are fitted between mounting brackets (one on each side of the crankcase) and the front bodyframe crossmember.
2 If the insulators become distorted, compressed or detached from their bonded reinforcement plates then they should be renewed.
3 Lockplates are used with the engine mounting bolts and their tabs should first be bent back.
4 Renewal of engine mountings can be carried out with the engine in position in the car provided that the engine is first jacked up an inch or two using a block of wood under the sump to protect it.

29 Examination and renovation - general

With the engine stripped down and all parts thoroughly cleaned, it is now time to examine everything for wear. The following items should be checked and where necessary renewed or renovated as described in the following Sections.

30 Crankshaft - examination and renovation

1 Examine the crankpin and main journal surfaces for signs of scoring and scratches. Check the ovality of the crankpins at different positions with a micrometer. If more than 0.001 inch (0.0254 mm) out of round, the crankpin will have to be reground. It will also have to be reground if there are any scores or scratches present. Also check the journals in the same fashion.
2 If it is necessary to regrind the crankshaft and fit new bearings your local Ford garage or engineering works will be able to decide how much metal to grind off and the size of new bearing shells.
3 Remove the crankshaft rear oil seal retainer and renew the semi-circular oil seal. The new seal should stand proud by 1/32 inch (0.79 mm) at the ends.

31 Big end and main bearings - examination and renovation

1 Big end bearing failure is accompanied by a noisy knocking from the crankcase, and a slight drop in oil pressure. Main bearing failure is accompanied by vibration which can be quite severe as the engine speed rises and falls, and a drop in oil pressure.
2 Bearings which have not broken up, but are badly worn, will give rise to low oil pressure and some vibration. Inspect the big ends, main bearings, and thrust washers for signs of general wear, scoring, pitting and scratches. The bearings should be matt grey

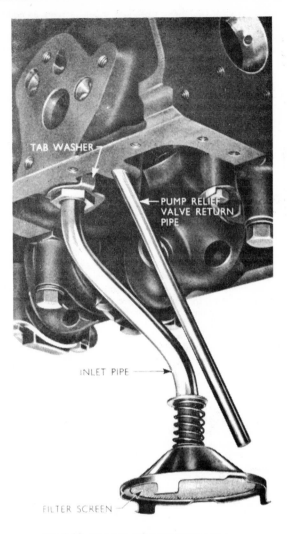

Fig. 1.10. Oil pump inlet and return pipes

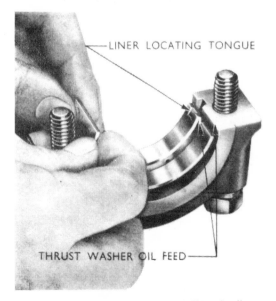

Fig. 1.11. Main bearing cap and shell bearing liner

in colour. With lead-indium bearings should a trace of copper colour be noticed the bearings are badly worn as the lead bearing material has worn away to expose the indium underlay. Renew the bearings if they are in this condition or if there is any sign of scoring or pitting.

3   The undersizes available are designed to correspond with the regrind sizes, ie 0.010 inch (0.25 mm) bearings are correct for a crankshaft reground 0.010 inch (0.25 mm) undersize. The bearings are in fact slightly more than the stated undersize as running clearances have been allowed for during their manufacture. Crankshafts normally have to be reground because of scoring due to bearing failure. Refer to the Specifications for full information regarding regrinding tolerances.

32 Cylinder bores - examination and renovation

1   The cylinder bores must be examined for taper, ovality, scoring and scratches. Start by carefully examining the top of the cylinder bores. If they are at all worn a very slight ridge will be found on the thrust side. This marks the top of the piston ring travel. The owner will have a good indication of the bore wear prior to dismantling the engine or removing the cylinder head. Excessive oil consumption accompanied by blue smoke from the exhaust is a sure sign of worn cylinder bores and piston rings.

2   Measure the bore diameter just under the ridge with a micrometer and compare it with the diameter at the bottom of the bore, which is not subject to wear. If the difference between the two measurements is more than 0.006 inch (0.1524 mm) then it will be necessary to fit special pistons and rings or to have the cylinders rebored and fit oversize pistons. If no micrometer is available remove the rings from a piston and place the piston in each bore in turn about ¾ inch (19.05 mm) below the top of the bore. If an 0.010 inch (0.25 mm) feeler gauge can be slid between the piston and the cylinder wall on the thrust side of the bore then remedial action must be taken. Oversize pistons are available as listed in the Specifications.

3   These are accurately machined to just below the indicated measurements so as to provide correct running clearances in bores bored out to the exact oversize dimensions.

4   If the bores are slightly worn but not so badly worn as to justify reboring them, then special oil control rings and pistons can be fitted which will restore compression and stop the engine burning oil. Several different types are available and the manufacturer's instructions concerning their fitting must be followed closely.

5   If new pistons are being fitted and the bores have not been reground, it is essential to slightly roughen the hard glaze on the sides of the bores with fine glass paper so the new piston rings will have a chance to bed in properly.

33 Pistons and piston rings - examination and renovation

1   If the old pistons are to be refitted, carefully remove the piston rings and then thoroughly clean them. Take particular care to clean out the piston ring grooves. At the same time do not scratch the aluminium in any way. If new rings are to be fitted to the old pistons then the top ring should be stepped so as to clear the ridge left in the cylinder bore, above the previous top ring. If a normal but oversize new ring is fitted, it will hit the ridge and break because the new ring will not have worn in the same way as the old, which will have worn in unison with the ridge.

2   Before fitting the rings on the pistons each should be inserted approximately 2 inches (50.8 mm) down the cylinder bore and the gap measured with a feeler gauge. This should be between 0.009 inch and 0.014 inch (0.23 mm and 0.36 mm). It is essential that the gap should be measured at the bottom of the ring travel, as if it is measured at the top of a worn bore and gives a perfect fit, it could easily seize at the bottom. If the ring gap is too

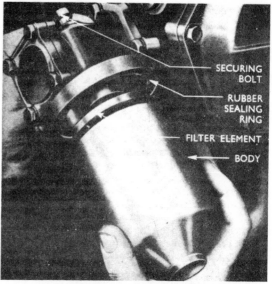

Fig. 1.12. Removing the engine oil filter

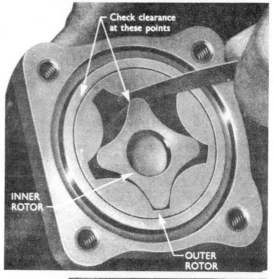

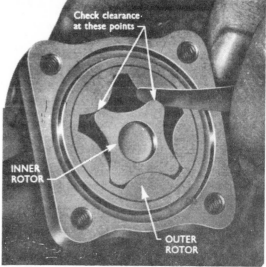

Fig. 1.13. Checking eccentric bi-rotor type oil pump for wear

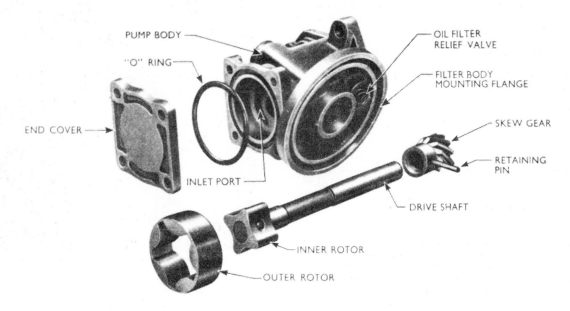

PUMP BODY

"O" RING

END COVER

OIL FILTER
RELIEF VALVE

FILTER BODY
MOUNTING FLANGE

SKEW GEAR

RETAINING
PIN

DRIVE SHAFT

INLET PORT

INNER ROTOR

OUTER ROTOR

Fig. 1.14. Exploded view of eccentric bi-rotor type oil pump

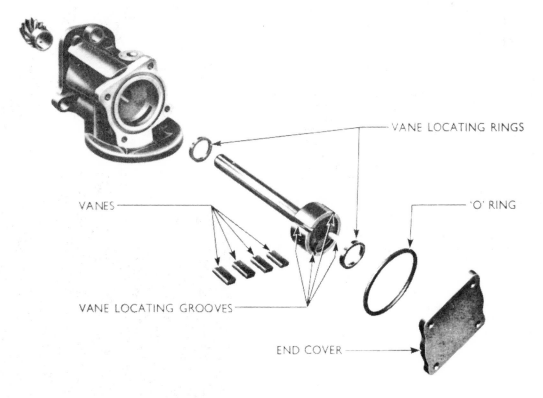

VANE LOCATING RINGS

VANES

'O' RING

VANE LOCATING GROOVES

END COVER

Fig. 1.15. Exploded view of vane type oil pump

small rub down the ends of the ring with a very fine file until
the gap, when fitted, is correct. To keep the rings square in the
bore for measurement, line each up in turn by inserting an old
piston in the bore upside down and use the piston to push the
ring down about 2 inches (50.8 mm). Remove the piston and
measure the piston ring gap.

3   The correct piston ring to groove clearances are as follows:

Top compression	0.0016 - 0.0036 inch
Second compression	(0.0406 - 0.0194 mm)
Oil control (scraper)	0.0018 - 0.0038 inch
	(0.0457 - 0.0965 mm)

When new pistons are being installed these clearances will
automatically be correct but if proprietary rings are being
fitted then the grooves may have to be widened on a lathe.

34 Camshaft and camshaft bearings - examination and renovation

1   Carefully examine the camshaft bearings for wear. If the
bearings are obviously worn or pitted then they must be
renewed. This is an operation for your local Ford dealer or local
engineering works as it demands the use of specialised equipment. The bearings are removed with a special drift after which
new bearings are pressed in, care being taken to ensure the oil
holes in the bearings line up with those in the block.
2   The camshaft itself should show no signs of wear, but if very
slight scoring on the cams is noticed, the score marks can be
removed by very gentle rubbing down with a very fine emery
cloth. The greatest care should be taken to keep the cam profiles
smooth.
3   Examine the skew gear for wear, chipped teeth or other
damage.
4   Carefully examine the camshaft thrust plate. Excessive wear
will be visually self-evident and will require the fitting of a new
plate.

35 Valves and valve seats - examination and renovation

1   Examine the heads of the valves for pitting and burning,
especially the heads of the exhaust valves. The valve seatings
should be examined at the same time. If the pitting on valve and
seat is very slight the marks can be removed by grinding the
exhaust seats and valve together with coarse, and then fine,
valve grinding paste. The inlet valves should not be ground in as
they are specially coated to resist corrosion. If necessary grind
an inlet valve seat using a spare valve. If the inlet valve is badly
pitted it should be renewed.
2   Where bad pitting has occurred to the valve seats it will be
necessary to recut them and fit new valves. If the valve seats
are so worn that they cannot be recut then it will be necessary
to fit new valve seat inserts. These latter two jobs should be
entrusted to the local Ford agent or engineering works. In
practice it is very seldom that the seats are so badly worn that
they require renewal.
3   Valve grinding is carried out as follows: Smear a trace of
coarse carborundum paste on the seat face and apply a suction
grinder tool to the valve head. With a semi-rotary motion, grind
the valve head to its seat, lifting the valve occasionally to
redistribute the grinding paste. When a dull matt even surface
finish is produced on both the valve seat and the valve, wipe off
the paste and repeat the process with fine carborundum paste,
lifting and turning the valve to redistribute the paste as before.
A light spring placed under the valve head will greatly ease this
operation. When a smooth unbroken ring of light grey matt
finish is produced, on both valve and valve seat faces, the grinding
operation is completed.
4   Scrape away all carbon from the valve head and the valve
stem. Carefully clean away every trace of grinding compound,
taking great care to leave none in the ports or in the valve

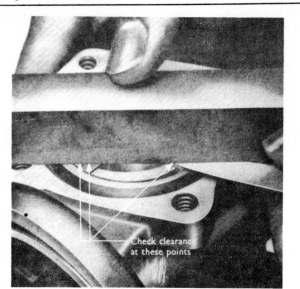

Fig. 1.16. Checking end clearance of oil pump rotor and vane

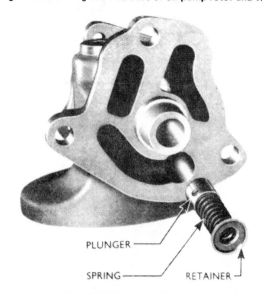

PLUNGER

SPRING   RETAINER

Fig. 1.17. Oil pump relief valve

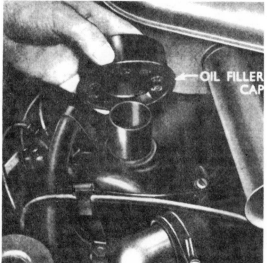

OIL FILLER
CAP

Fig. 1.18. Oil filler cap mesh

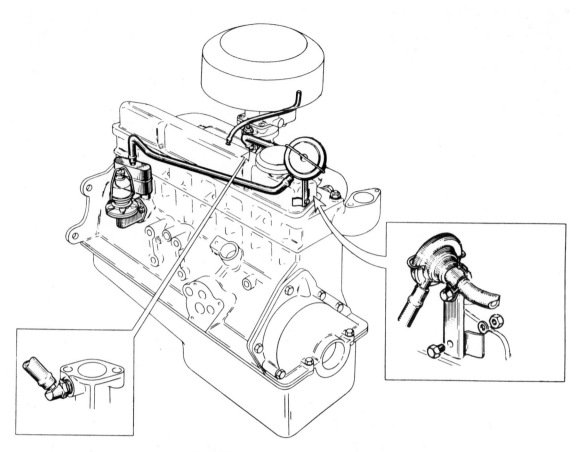

Fig. 1.19. Crankcase emission control system

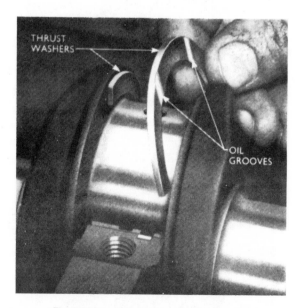

Fig. 1.20. Crankshaft thrust washer location

Fig. 1.21. Timing mark location

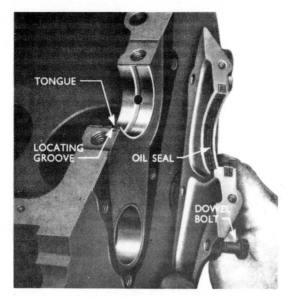

Fig. 1.22. Installing crankshaft rear oil seal retainer

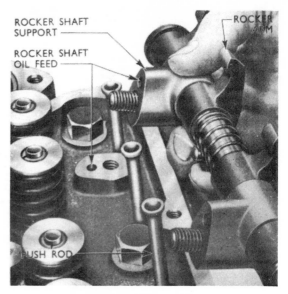

Fig. 1.24. Re-fitting rocker shaft assembly

Fig. 1.23. Cylinder head bolt tightening sequence

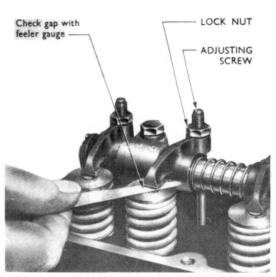

Fig. 1.25. Adjusting a valve clearance

Fig. 1.26. Location of ignition timing marks

guides. Clean the valves and valve seats with a paraffin soaked rag then with a clean rag, and finally, if an air line is available, blow the valves, valve guides and valve ports clean.

36 Valve guides - examination and renovation

1 Test each valve in its guide for wear. After a considerable mileage, the valve guide bore may wear elliptically and can be tested by rocking the valve.
2 The remedy for wear is to ream the valve guide bores by the minimum amount to accommodate the smallest oversize valves as listed in the Specifications.
3 It is preferable to leave this operation to a Ford dealer but where the home mechanic is competent then the reaming should be carried out from the valve seat end using paraffin as a cutting lubricant.

37 Timing chain and gear - examination and renovation

1 Examine the teeth on both the crankshaft gearwheel and the camshaft gearwheel for wear. Each tooth forms an inverted 'V' with the gearwheel periphery and if worn the side of each tooth under tension will be slightly concave in shape when compared with the other side of the tooth, ie one side of the inverted 'V' will be concave when compared with the other. If any sign of wear is present the gearwheels must be renewed.
2 Examine the links of the chain for side slackness and renew the chain if any slackness is noticeable when compared with a new chain. It is a sensible precaution to renew the chain at about 30,000 miles (48,000 km) and at a lesser mileage if the engine is stripped down for a major overhaul. The actual rollers on a very badly worn chain may be slightly grooved.

38 Rockers and rocker shaft - examination and renovation

1 Thoroughly clean the rocker shaft and then check the shaft for straightness. The surface of the shaft should be free from any worn ridges caused by the rocker arms. If any wear is present, renew the shaft.
2 Check the rocker arms for wear of the rocker bushes, for wear at the rocker arm face which bears on the valve stem, and for wear of the adjusting ball ended screws. Wear in the rocker arm bush can be checked by gripping the rocker arm tip and holding the rocker arm in place on the shaft, noting if there is any lateral rocker arm shake. If shake is present, and the arm is very loose on the shaft, a new bush or rocker arm must be fitted.
3 Check the tip of the rocker arm where it bears on the valve head for cracking or serious wear on the case hardening. If none is present re-use the rocker arm. Check the lower half of the ball on the end of the rocker arm adjusting screw. Check the pushrods for straightness. Renew any that are bent.

39 Tappets - examination and renovation

Examine the bearing surface of the mushroom tappets which lie on the camshaft. Any indentation in this surface or any cracks indicate serious wear and the tappets should be renewed. Thoroughly clean them out, removing all traces of sludge. It is most unlikely that the sides of the tappets will prove worn, but if they are a very loose fit in their bores and can readily be rocked, they should be renewed.

40 Connecting rods - examination and renovation

1 Examine the mating faces of the big end caps to see if they have ever been filed in a mistaken attempt to take up wear. If so the offending rods must be renewed.
2 Insert the gudgeon pin into the little end of the connecting

rod. It should go in fairly easily, but if any slackness is present then take the rod to your local Ford dealer or engineering works and exchange it for a rod of identical weight.

41 Starter ring gear - examination and renovation

1 If the teeth on the flywheel or driveplate (automatic transmission) starter ring are badly worn or if some are missing, then it will be necessary to exchange the assembly for a new or reconditioned unit.
2 For those who feel competent, the ring gear attached to the flywheel or driveplate (automatic transmission) can be removed and a new gear fitted.
3 Split the ring with a cold chisel after making a cut with a hacksaw blade between two teeth. Take great care not to damage the flywheel during this process.
4 Heat the new ring in an electric oven to about 400°F (204°C) or immerse in a pan of boiling oil.
5 Hold the ring at this temperature for five minutes and then quickly fit it to the flywheel so the chamfered portion of the teeth faces the gearbox side of the flywheel.
6 The ring should be tapped gently down onto its register and left to cool naturally when the contraction of the metal on cooling will ensure that it is a secure and permanent fit. Great care must be taken not to overheat the ring, indicated by it turning light metallic blue, as if this happens the temper of the ring will be lost.

42 Cylinder head - decarbonising

1 This can be carried out with the engine either in or out of the car. With the cylinder head off carefully remove with a wire brush mounted in an electric drill and blunt scraper, all traces of carbon deposits from the combustion spaces and the ports. The valve head stems and valve guides should also be freed from any carbon deposits. Wash the combustion spaces and ports down with petrol and scrape the cylinder head surface free of any foreign matter with the side of a steel rule or a similar article.
2 Clean the pistons and top of the cylinder bores. If the pistons are still in the block then it is essential that great care is taken to ensure that no carbon gets into the cylinder bores as this could scratch the cylinder walls or cause damage to the piston and rings. To ensure this does not happen, first turn the crankshaft so that two of the pistons are at the top of their bores. Stuff rag into the other two bores or seal them off with paper and masking tape. The waterways should also be covered with small pieces of masking tape to prevent particles of carbon entering the cooling system and damaging the water pump.
3 There are two schools of thought as to how much carbon should be removed from the piston crown. One recommendation is that a ring of carbon should be left round the edge of the piston and on the cylinder bore wall as an aid to low oil consumption. Although this is probably true for early engines with worn bores, on later engines for effective decarbonisation all traces of carbon should be removed.
4 If all traces of carbon are to be removed, press a little grease into the gap between the cylinder walls and the two pistons which are to be worked on. With a blunt scraper carefully scrape away the carbon from the piston crown, taking great care not to scratch the aluminium. Also scrape away the carbon from the surrounding lip of the cylinder wall. When all carbon has been removed, scrape away the grease which will now be contaminated with carbon particles, taking care not to press any into the bores. To assist prevention of carbon build-up, the piston crown can be polished with a metal polish. Remove the rags or masking tape from the other two cylinders and turn the crankshaft so that the two pistons which were at the bottom are now at the top. Place rag or masking tape in the cylinders which have been decarbonised and proceed as just described.
5 If a ring of carbon is going to be left round the piston, then this can be helped by inserting an old piston ring into the top of

the bore to rest on the piston and ensure that the carbon is not accidentally removed. Check that there are no particles of carbon in the cylinder bores. Decarbonising is now complete.

43 Engine reassembly - general

1 To ensure maximum life with minimum trouble from a rebuilt engine, not only must everything be correctly assembled, but everything must be spotlessly clean, all the oilways must be clear, locking washers and spring washers must always be fitted where indicated and all bearing and other working surfaces must be thoroughly lubricated during assembly.

2 Before assembly begins renew any bolts or studs if the threads of which are in any way damaged, and whenever possible use new spring washers.

3 Apart from your normal tools, a supply of clean rag; an oil can filled with engine oil (an empty plastic detergent bottle thoroughly cleaned and washed out, will invariably do just as well); a new supply of assorted spring washers; a set of new gaskets; and a torque spanner, should be collected together.

44 Assembling the engine

1 Thoroughly clean the engine block and remove all traces of old gaskets and jointing compound.

2 Position the upper halves of the main shell bearings in their locations so that the tabs engage in the machined keyways.

3 Oil the main bearing shells after they have been fitted in position.

4 Thoroughly clean out the oilways in the crankshaft with the aid of a thin wire.

5 To check for the possibility of an error in the grinding of the crankshaft journal (presuming the crankshaft has been reground) smear engineer's blue evenly over each big end journal in turn with the crankshaft end flange held firmly in position in a vice.

6 With new shell bearings fitted to the connecting rods fit the correct rod to each journal in turn fully tightening down the securing bolts.

7 Spin the rod on the crankshaft a few times and then remove the big end cap. A fine unbroken layer of engineer's blue should cover the whole of the journal. If the blue is much darker on one side than the other or if the blue has disappeared from a certain area (ignore the very edge of the journal) then something is wrong and the journal will have to be checked with a micrometer.

8 The main journals should also be checked in similar fashion with the crankshaft in the crankcase. On completion of these tests, remove all traces of the engineer's blue.

9 The crankshaft can now be lowered carefully into place.

10 Fit new end float thrust washers. These locate in recesses on either side of the centre main bearing in the cylinder block and must be fitted with the oil grooves facing outwards. With the crankshaft in position, check for float which should be between 0.003 and 0.011 inch (0.076 to 0.279 mm). If the end float is incorrect remove the thrust washers and fit new ones to give the correct end float.

11 Place the lower halves of the main bearing shells in their caps making sure that the locking tabs fit into the machined grooves. Refit the main bearing caps ensuring that they are the correct way round and that the correct gap is on the correct journal. Tighten the cap bolts to a torque of 65 to 70 lb ft (8.280 to 9.660 kg m). Spin the crankshaft to make certain it is turning freely.

12 Check that the piston ring grooves and oilways are thoroughly clean and unblocked. Piston rings must always be fitted over the head of the piston and never from the bottom.

13 Fit the piston rings by reversing the method described for their removal (Section 18). The compression rings are marked 'TOP' and the upper one is chromium plated. The lower compression ring is stepped on its bottom face.

14 When all the rings have been fitted, stagger their gaps at equidistant points of a circle to prevent gas 'blow-by' which would occur if the gaps were in alignment.

15 If the original pistons are being refitted, mate them to their original connecting rods and gudgeon pins. If new pistons are being installed this requirement does not arise.

16 Check that the piston is fitted so that the arrow on its crown is facing the timing cover end of the engine; that the numbers or marks on the two halves of the big end bearing caps are together and on the camshaft side of the engine; that the word 'FRONT' is also cast into the side of the connecting rod and is facing in the same direction as the arrow on the piston crown.

17 Fit one new circlip into its recess in the gudgeon pin hole in the piston and from the other side push in the gudgeon pin. Use only finger pressure and immerse the piston in hot water if necessary to expand the gudgeon pin bore.

18 Fit the second circlip in position. Repeat this procedure for the remaining three pistons and connecting rods.

19 Fit the connecting rod in position and check that the oil hole in the upper half of each bearing shell aligns with the oil jet hole in the connecting rod.

20 Wipe the cylinder bores clean and oil them liberally with clean engine oil. The pistons complete with connecting rods are fitted to their bores from above. As each piston is inserted into its bore, ensure that it is the correct piston/connecting rod assembly for that particular bore and that the connecting rod is the right way round, and that the front of the piston is towards the front of the bore, ie towards the front of the engine.

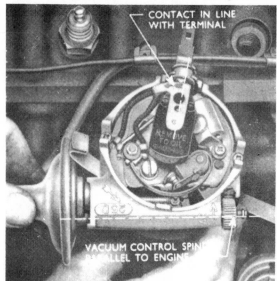

Fig. 1.27. Distributor ready to push into mesh with camshaft gear

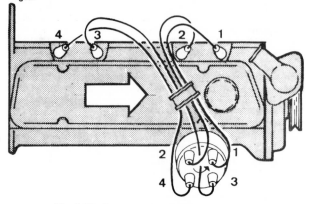

Fig. 1.28. Correct order of HT lead connection

44.9 Lowering crankshaft into position

44.11. Tightening a main bearing cap bolt

44.12 Fitting a piston ring

44.17 Fitting a gudgeon pin

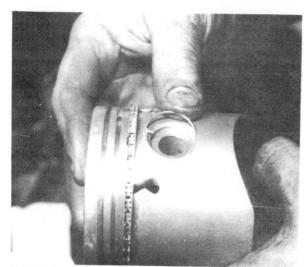

44.18 Fitting a gudgeon pin circlip

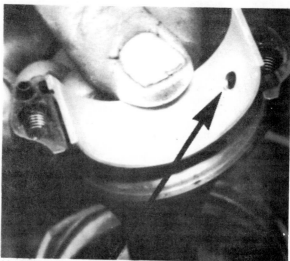

44.19 Big end shell bearing oil hole

21 The piston will only slide into the bore as far as the oil control ring. It is then necessary to compress the piston rings in a clamp.

22 Drive each piston/connecting rod assembly down into its cylinder bore using the wooden handle of a hammer for the purpose. Do not strike the piston crown with the hammer handle but rest it on the piston crown and then strike the head of the hammer with the palm of the hand. Provided the piston rings have been sufficiently clamped into their grooves and the space between clamp and ring has been very liberally lubricated, the piston assembly will pass into the cylinder bore with little resistance.

23 Fit the shell bearings to the big end caps so the tongue on the back of each bearing lies in the machined recess.

24 Generously oil the crankshaft connecting rod journals and then replace each big end cap on the same connecting rod from which it was removed. Fit the locking plates under the head of the big end bolts, tap the caps right home on the dowels and then tighten the bolts to a torque of 20 to 25 lb ft (2.760 to 3.450 kg m). Lock the bolts in position by knocking up the tabs on the locking washer.

25 The semi-rebuilt engine is ready for the cam followers (tappets) and camshaft to be fitted.

26 Fit the eight cam followers into the same hole in the block from which each was removed. The cam followers can only be fitted with the block upside down.

27 Fit the Woodruff key in its slot on the front of the crankshaft and then press the timing sprocket into place so the timing mark faces forward. Oil the camshaft shell bearings and insert the camshaft into the block (which should still be upside down).

28 Make sure the camshaft turns freely and then fit the thrust plate behind the camshaft flange as shown in the photo. Measure the end float with a feeler gauge - it should be between 0.0025 and 0.0075 inch (0.0635 and 0.2032 mm). If this is not so then renew the plate.

29 Fit the two camshaft flange bolts into their joint washer and screw down the bolts securely.

30 Turn up the tab under the head of each bolt to lock it in place.

31 When refitting the timing chain round the gearwheels and to the engine, the two timing lines must be adjacent to each other on an imaginary line passing through each gearwheel centre.

32 With the timing marks correctly aligned turn the camshaft until the protruding dowel locates in the hole in the camshaft sprocket wheel.

33 Tighten the two retaining bolts and bend up the tabs on the lockwasher.

34 Fit the oil slinger to the nose of the crankshaft, concave side facing outwards. The cut-out locates over the Woodruff key.

35 Then slide the timing chain tensioner arm over its hinge pin on the front of the block.

36 Turn the tensioner back from its free position so it will apply pressure to the tensioner arm and replace the tensioner on the block sump flange.

37 Bolt the tensioner to the block using spring washers under the heads of the two bolts.

38 Remove the front oil seal from the timing chain cover and with the aid of a vice, carefully press a new seal into position. Lightly lubricate the face of the seal which will bear against the crankshaft.

39 Use jointing compound and a new gasket on the mating faces of the timing cover and block, and locate the timing cover on the front face of the block.

40 Screw in and tighten the two dowel bolts first. These fit in the holes nearest the sump flange and serve to align the timing cover. Use new lockwashers and tighten the bolts evenly.

41 Refit the tube or oil breather device to its recess in the top of the petrol pump housing on the block, tapping it gently into place. Replace the oil pump suction pipe using a new tab washer and position the gauze head so it clears the crankshaft throw and the oil return pipe. Tighten the nut and bend back the tab of the lockwasher.

42 Locate the crankshaft rear oil seal retainer on the cylinder block. Coat both mating faces of a new gasket with jointing compound. The oil seal will already have been renewed as described in Section 29. Enter all four securing bolts but the two nearer the sump should be tightened first as they also function as alignment dowels. Finally tighten all four bolts equally.

43 Locate new cork sealing gaskets to each side of the crankcase flange. It is essential that the ends of these gaskets enter the cork strip recess at the front so that they will be held in position by the ends of the cork strip. At the rear of the engine, the ends of the side gaskets will abut the crankshaft so that they will be held in position by the semi-circular seal when the sump is bolted up.

44 Fit the sump which will have been fitted with a new semi-circular seal at its rear end. The longer two sump securing bolts are fitted at the rear.

45 Clean the mating faces of the flywheel flange and the flywheel and locate the flywheel on the flange so that the dowel engages correctly.

46 Screw in the flywheel retaining bolts to a torque of between 50 and 55 lb ft (6.9 and 7.590 kg m).

47 Bend up the tab washers under the flywheel bolts.

48 The engine can now be turned over so it is the right way up. Coat the oil pump flanges with jointing compound.

49 Fit a new gasket in place on the oil pump.

50 Position the oil pump against the block ensuring the skew gear teeth on the drive shaft mate with those on the camshaft.

51 Replace the three securing bolts and spring washers and tighten them down evenly.

52 Moving to the front of the engine, align the slot in the crankshaft pulley wheel with the key on the crankshaft and gently tap the pulley wheel home.

53 Secure the pulley wheel by fitting the large flat washer, the spring washer and then the bolt which should be tightened securely.

54 The next step is to thoroughly clean the faces of the block and cylinder head. Then fit a new cylinder head gasket.

55 With the cylinder head on its side, lubricate the valve stems and refit the valves to their correct guides. The valves should previously have been ground in.

56 Then fit new valve stem umbrella oil seals, open ends down.

57 Next slide the valve spring into place. Use new springs if the old ones have seen more than 20,000 miles (32,000 km) service.

58 Slide the valve spring retainer over the valve stem.

59 Compress the valve spring with a compressor.

60 Then refit the split collets. A trace of grease will help to hold them to the valve stem recess until the spring compressor is slackened off and the collets are wedged in place by the spring.

61 Carefully lower the cylinder head onto the block.

62 Replace the cylinder head bolts and screw them down finger tight.

63 With a torque wrench tighten the bolts to 65 to 70 lb ft (8.970 to 9.660 kg m), in the order shown.

64 Fit the pushrods into the same holes in the block from which they were removed. Make sure the pushrods seat properly in the cam followers (tappet blocks).

65 Reassemble the rocker gear onto the rocker shaft and fit the shaft to the cylinder head. Ensure that the oil holes are clear and that the cut-outs for the securing bolts lie facing the holes in the brackets.

66 Tighten down the four rocker bracket washers and bolts to a torque of 17 to 22 lb ft (2.346 to 3.036 kg m).

67 The valve adjustments should be made initially with the engine cold. The importance of correct rocker arm/valve stem clearances cannot be overstressed as they vitally affect the performance of the engine. If the clearances are set too open, the efficiency of the engine is reduced as the valves open late and close earlier than was intended. If, on the other hand, the clearances are set too close there is a danger that the stems will expand upon heating and not allow the valves to close properly which will cause burning of the valve head and seat and possible warping. If the engine is in the car, access to the rockers is by removing the two holding down studs from the rocker cover and then lifting the rocker cover and gasket away.

68 It is important that the clearance is set when the tappet of the valve being adjusted is on the heel of the cam (ie opposite the peak). This can be ensured by carrying out adjustments in the following order (which also avoids turning the crankshaft more than necessary):

Valves fully open	Check and adjust
1 and 6	3 inlet 8 exhaust
3 and 8	1 exhaust 6 inlet
2 and 4	5 exhaust 7 inlet
5 and 7	2 inlet 4 exhaust

69 The valves are counted from the front of the engine.

70 The valve clearances **cold** are inlet 0.008 inch (0.203 mm) and exhaust 0.018 inch (0.457 mm). When the engine has been fully assembled and run to normal operating temperature, the valve clearances should be checked and re-adjusted to inlet 0.010 inch (0.254 mm) and exhaust 0.017 inch (0.532 mm). GT valve clearances are **cold**: inlet 0.010 inch (0.254 mm) exhaust 0.023 inch (0.584 mm); **hot**: inlet 0.012 inch (0.305 mm) exhaust 0.022 inch (0.559 mm).

71 To adjust a valve clearance, slacken the adjuster screw locknut and insert a feeler blade between the rocker arm and the end of the valve stem. Turn the adjuster screw until the feeler blade is a stiff sliding fit and tighten the locknut. Re-check the gap.

72 Do not refit the rocker cover before replacing the distributor and setting the ignition timing. It is important to set the distributor drive correctly as otherwise the ignition timing will be totally incorrect. It is possible to set the distributor drive in apparently the right position, but, in fact, 180° out, by omitting to select the correct cylinder which must not only be at tdc but also must be on its firing stroke with both valves closed. The distributor drive should therefore not be fitted until the cylinder head is in position and the valves can be observed. Alternatively, if the timing cover has not been replaced, the distributor drive can be replaced when the lines on the timing wheels are adjacent to each other.

73 Rotate the crankshaft so that No 1 piston is at tdc and on its firing stroke (the lines in the timing gears will be adjacent to each other). When No 1 piston is at tdc both valves will be closed and both rocker arms will 'rock' slightly because of the stem to arm pad clearance.

74 The ignition timing marks comprise a notch in the crankshaft pulley and two marks moulded onto the timing cover. The mark nearer the engine is the 10° btdc index and the outer (lower) is the 6° btdc index. A point midway between the two marks is 8° btdc. All 1198 cc engines should be timed to the 6° mark, 1498 cc engines to the 8° mark and GT versions to the 10° mark.

75 Hold the distributor above its crankcase opening so that the vacuum unit is towards the rear of the engine and parallel to the cylinder block and then turn the rotor arm so that it points to the distributor LT terminal. Push the distributor into its recess and as the drive gears mesh, the rotor will turn to point at No 1 segment in the distributor cap.

76 Tighten the distributor clamp plate bolt to secure the unit.

77 Using the timing light method (as described in Chapter 4) check that the contact breaker points are just about to open, if not, slacken the clamp bolt and turn the distributor as necessary.

78 Using a new gasket, bolt the water pump to the front of the engine.

79 Note that the dynamo support strap fits under the head of the lower bolt on the water pump. The bolt should not be tightened at this stage.

80 Replace the fuel pump using a new gasket and tighten the two securing bolts.

81 Fit the thermostat, noting carefully its correct orientation. Use a new gasket and then fit the top housing water outlet.

82 Fit the rocker cover and if the old gasket has broken or deteriorated, use a new one, making sure to engage the lugs of the cork in the rocker cover recesses (photo).

83 Fit the dynamo to its mountings and after fitting the fan belt, adjust the belt tension to permit not more than ½ inch (12.5 mm) free movement between the water pump and generating unit pulleys. Tighten the strap bolts fully.

84 Refit the vacuum advance pipe between the distributor and the carburettor and refit the oil and water temperature sender units.

85 Replace the engine ancillary components such as the oil filter, oil breather separator, engine mountings and inlet and exhaust manifolds, using new gaskets for the latter.

86 Refit the carburettor but at this stage do not fit the spark plugs. The engine is now ready for refitting to the vehicle.

44.21 Fitting a piston ring clamp

44.22 Inserting a piston/connecting rod assembly into a cylinder bore

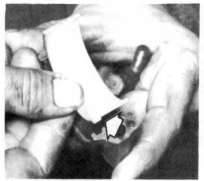
44.23 Big end shell bearing alignment tag

44.24a Tightening a big-end bolt

44.24b Bending up a big end bolt lock plate tab

44.27 Inserting the camshaft

44.28 Fitting camshaft thrust plate

44.29 Tightening camshaft thrust plate bolts

44.30 Camshaft thrust plate lock plate tab

44.32 Camshaft sprocket alignment dowel

44.33 Bending up a camshaft sprocket lock plate tab

44.34 Fitting crankshaft oil slinger

44.35 Locating timing chain slipper

44.36 Locating timing chain tensioner

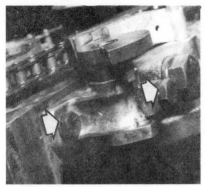
44.37 Timing chain tensioner securing bolts and spring washers

44.38 Pressing a new timing cover oil seal into position

44.39 Installing the timing cover

44.41 Tapping the oil breather into the crankcase

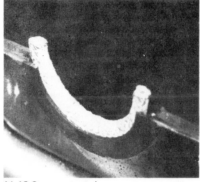
44.43 Sump rear seal

44.44 Inserting the two (longer) rear sump bolts

44.45 Locating flywheel to crankshaft rear flange

44.46 Tightening a flywheel bolt (note lever to prevent rotation)

44.47 Bending up a flywheel bolt lock plate tab

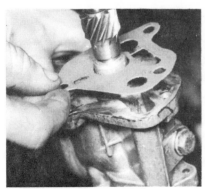
44.49 Fitting a new oil pump flange gasket

44.50 Engaging the oil pump drive

44.51 Tightening an oil pump securing bolt

44.52 Fitting the crankshaft pulley

44.53 Screwing in the crankshaft pulley retaining bolt

44.54 Placing a new cylinder head gasket on the block

44.61 Lowering the cylinder head into position

44.65 Fitting the rocker gear

44.66 Tightening a rocker pillar bolt

44.71 Adjusting a valve clearance

44.77 Distributor clamp plate pinch bolt

44.78 Fitting the water pump

44.79 Fitting the alternator adjustment strap bolt

44.82 Refitting the rocker box cover

45 Engine replacement - general

1 Although the engine can be replaced with one man and a suitable winch, it is easier if two are present, one to lower the engine into the engine compartment and the other to guide the engine into position and to ensure it does not foul anything.
2 At this stage one or two tips may come in useful. Ensure all the loose leads, cables, etc are tucked out of the way. If not, it is easy to trap one and so cause much additional work after the engine is replaced. Smear grease on the tip of the gearbox input shaft before fitting the gearbox.
3 Always fit a new fan belt and new cooling hoses and Jubilee clips as this will help eliminate the possibility of failure while on the road. An exchange rebuilt carburettor also helps!
4 Two pairs of hands are better than one when refitting the bonnet. Do not tighten the bonnet securing bolts fully until it is ascertained that the bonnet is on straight.

46 Engine - replacement (manual gearbox)

1 Position a sling around the engine and support its weight on suitable lifting tackle.
2 Lower the engine into the engine compartment ensuring that nothing is fouling. Line up the engine and gearbox raising the height of the gearbox if necessary with the jack until the splines on the gearbox input shaft mate with the splined grooves in the clutch disc centre. As the spark plugs have not yet been fitted, the crankshaft pulley may be easily turned by hand to facilitate engagement of the splined components. Do not allow the weight of the engine to hang upon the gearbox input shaft, even momentarily.
3 To line up the mounting bracket holes it may be necessary to move the engine about slightly and this will be found to be much easier if the lifting slings are still in position and taking most of the weight.
4 Replace the bolts and washers - one on each side - which hold the engine mountings to the bodyframe.
5 Do up those engine to clutch housing bolts which are accessible from above. The earth strap for the engine is secured by the top left hand bolt. Remove the slings from the engine, and jack up the front of the car securely so it can be worked on from underneath.
6 Working underneath the car, replace the lower clutch housing cover and all the lower clutch housing bolts. Do up the bolts holding the clutch housing to the rear of the engine.
7 Refit the starter motor, replace the retaining bolts, and the starter cable which is held in place with a nut and washer.
8 Reconnect the fuel lines to the pump.
9 Reconnect the HT lead to the coil centre terminal and the LT lead to the distributor.
10 Screw in the spark plugs, cleaned and set to the correct gap of 0.23 inch (0.58 mm) and connect the leads from the distributor cap.
11 Connect the exhaust downpipe and the throttle and choke controls; connect the temperature gauge lead.
12 Replace the radiator and reconnect the top and bottom hoses

and the heater hoses.
13 Replace the engine splash shield (where fitted); the air cleaner; the bonnet; and reconnect the two leads to the rear of the dynamo.
14 Reconnect the battery.

47 Engine - replacement (automatic transmission)

1 The procedure is similar to that described in the preceding Section but observe the following points:
2 If the torque converter has been drawn forward during the engine removal operation, it will be necessary to align the front drive tangs with the slots in the inner gear and then carefully slide the torque converter rearwards into position. Take great care not to damage the oil seal at the front of the transmission.
3 Align the driveplate to torque converter marks made prior to removal and then screw in and tighten the securing bolts. These are accessible one at a time through the starter motor aperture, the engine being turned slowly by applying a spanner to the crankshaft pulley bolt.
4 Reconnect the downshift cable at the carburettor and also the speed selector linkage.
5 Insert and tighten the securing bolt at the upper end of the filler/breather tube.

48 Engine - initial start up after major servicing

1 Make sure that the battery is fully charged and that all lubricants, coolant and fuel are replenished.
2 If the fuel system has been dismantled it will require several revolutions of the engine on the starter motor to pump the petrol up to the carburettor.
3 As soon as the engine fires and runs, keep it going at a fast tickover only (no faster) and bring it up to normal working temperature.
4 As the engine warms up there will be odd smells and some smoke from parts getting hot and burning off oil deposits. The signs to look for are leaks of water or oil which will be obvious, if serious. Check also the exhaust pipe and manifold connections as these do not always find their exact gas tight position until the warmth and vibration have acted on them and it is almost certain that they will need tightening further. This should be done, of course, with the engine stopped.
5 When normal running temperature has been reached, adjust the engine idle speed as described in Chapter 3.
6 Stop the engine and wait a few minutes to see if any lubricant or coolant is dripping out when the engine is stationary.
7 With the engine at normal operating temperature, check the torque settings of the cylinder head and sump bolts. Check and adjust if necessary the valve clearances.
8 Road test the car to check that the timing is correct and that the engine is giving the necessary smoothness and power. Do not race the engine - if new bearings and/or pistons have been fitted, it should be treated as a new engine and run in at a reduced speed for the first 1000 miles (2000 km).

49 Fault diagnosis - engine

Symptom	Reason/s	Remedy
Engine fails to turn over when starter button operated	Discharged or defective battery	Charge or replace battery, push-start car (Manual gearbox only).
	Dirty or loose battery leads	Clean and tighten both terminals and earth ends of earth lead.
	Defective starter solenoid or switch	Run a heavy duty wire direct from the battery to the starter motor or by-pass the solenoid.
	Engine earth strip disconnected	Check and retighten strap.
	Jammed starter motor drive pinion	Place car in gear and rock from side to side.

Symptom	Reason/s	Remedy
		Alternatively, free exposed square end of shaft with spanner.
	Defective starter motor	Remove and recondition.
Engine turns over but will not start	Ignition damp or wet	Wipe dry the distributor cap and ignition leads.
	Ignition leads to spark plugs loose	Check and tighten at both spark plug and distributor cap ends.
	Shorted or disconnected low tension leads	Check the wiring on the CB and SW terminals of the coil and to the distributor.
	Dirty, incorrectly set or pitted contact breaker points	Clean, file smooth and adjust.
	Faulty condenser	Check contact breaker points for arcing, remove and fit new condenser.
	Defective ignition switch	By-pass switch with wire.
	Ignition LT leads connected wrong way round	Remove and replace leads to coil in correct order.
	Faulty coil	Remove and fit new coil.
	Contact breaker point spring earthed or broken	Check spring is not touching metal part of distributor. Check insulator washers are correctly placed. Renew points if the spring is broken.
	No fuel in fuel tank	Refill tank!
	Vapour lock in fuel line (in hot conditions or at high altitude)	Blow into fuel tank, allow engine to cool, or apply a cold wet rag to the fuel line in engine compartment.
	Blocked float chamber needle valve	Remove, clean and replace.
	Fuel pump filter blocked	Remove, clean and replace.
	Choked or blocked carburettor jets	Dismantle and clean.
	Faulty fuel pump	Remove, overhaul and replace.
	Too much choke allowing too rich a mixture to wet plugs	Remove and dry spark plugs or with wide open throttle, push-start the car (manual gearbox only).
	Float damaged or leaking or needle not seating	Remove, examine, clean and replace float and needle valve as necessary.
	Float lever incorrectly adjusted	Remove and adjust correctly.
Engine stalls and will not start	Ignition failure - sudden	Check over low and high tension circuits for breaks in wiring.
	Ignition failure - misfiring precludes total stoppage	Check contact breaker points, clean and adjust. Renew condenser if faulty.
	Ignition failure - in severe rain or after traversing water splash	Dry out ignition leads and distributor cap.
	No fuel in fuel tank	Refill tank.
	Fuel tank breather choked	Remove fuel cap and clean out breather hole or pipe.
	Sudden obstruction in carburettor	Check jets, filter, and needle valve in float chamber for blockage.
Engine misfires or idles unevenly	Water in fuel system	Drain tank and blow out fuel lines.
	Ignition leads loose	Check and tighten as necessary at spark plug and distributor cap ends.
	Battery leads loose on terminals	Check and tighten terminal leads.
	Battery earth strap loose on body attachment point	Check and tighten earth lead to body attachment point.
	Engine earth lead loose	Tighten lead.
	Low tension leads to SW and CB terminals on coil loose	Check and tighten leads if found loose.
	Low tension lead from CB terminal side to distributor loose	Check and tighten if found loose.
	Dirty or incorrectly gapped spark plugs	Remove, clean and regap.
	Dirty, incorrectly set or pitted contact breaker points	Clean, file smooth and adjust.
	Tracking across distributor cap	Remove and fit new cap.
	Ignition too retarded	Check and adjust ignition timing.
	Faulty coil	Remove and fit new coil.
	Mixture too weak	Check jets, float chamber needle valve and filters for obstruction. Clean as necessary. Carburettor incorrectly adjusted.
	Air leak in carburettor	Remove and overhaul carburettor.
	Air leak at inlet manifold to cylinder head,	Test by pouring oil along joints. Bubbles

Symptom	Reason/s	Remedy
	or inlet manifold to carburettor	indicate leak. Renew manifold gasket as appropriate.
	Incorrect valve clearances	Adjust rocker arm clearances.
Engine misfires or idles unevenly	Burnt out exhaust valves	Remove cylinder head and renew defective valves.
	Sticking or leaking valves	Remove cylinder head, clean, check and renew valves as necessary.
	Wear or broken valve springs	Check and renew as necessary.
	Worn valve guides or stems	Renew valves.
	Worn pistons and piston rings	Dismantle engine, renew pistons and rings.
Lack of power and poor compression	Burnt out exhaust valves	Remove cylinder head, renew defective valves.
	Sticking or leaking valves	Remove cylinder head, clean, check and renew valves as necessary.
	Worn valve guides and stems	Remove cylinder head and renew valves.
	Weak or broken valve springs	Remove cylinder head, renew defective springs.
	Blown cylinder head gasket (accompanied by increase in noise)	Remove cylinder head and fit new gasket.
	Worn pistons and piston rings	Dismantle engine, renew pistons and rings.
	Worn or scored cylinder bores	Dismantle engine, rebore, renew pistons and rings.
	Ignition timing wrongly set. Too advanced or retarded	Check and reset ignition timing.
	Contact breaker points incorrectly gapped	Check and reset contact breaker points.
	Incorrect valve clearances	Adjust rocker arm clearances.
	Incorrectly set spark plugs	Remove, clean and regap.
	Carburettor too rich or too weak	Tune carburettor for optimum performance.
	Dirty contact breaker points	Remove, clean and replace.
	Fuel filters blocked causing top end fuel starvation	Dismantle, inspect, clean, and replace all fuel filters.
	Distributor automatic balance weights or vacuum advance and retard mechanisms not functioning correctly	Overhaul distributor.
	Faulty fuel pump giving top end fuel starvation	Remove, overhaul, or fit exchange reconditioned fuel pump.
Excessive oil consumption	Badly worn, perished or missing valve stem oil seals	Remove, fit new oil seals to valve stems.
	Excessively worn valve stems and valve guides	Remove cylinder head and fit new valves.
	Worn piston rings	Fit oil control rings to existing pistons or purchase new pistons.
	Worn pistons and cylinder bores	Fit new pistons and rings, rebore cylinders.
	Excessive piston ring gap allowing blow-by	Fit new piston rings and set gap correctly.
Oil being lost due to leaks	Leaking oil filter gasket	Inspect and fit new gasket as necessary.
	Leaking rocker cover gasket	Inspect and fit new gasket as necessary.
	Leaking timing case gasket	Inspect and fit new gasket as necessary.
	Leaking sump gasket	Inspect and fit new gasket as necessary.
	Loose sump plug	Tighten, fit new gasket as necessary.
Unusual noises from engine	Worn valve gear (noisy tapping from rocker box)	Inspect and renew rocker shaft, rocker arms and ball pins as necessary.
	Worn big end bearing (regular heavy knocking)	Drop sump. If bearings broken up clean out oil pump and oilways, fit new bearings. If bearings not broken but worn fit bearing shells.
	Worn timing gears (rattling from front of engine)	Remove timing cover, fit new timing gears.
	Worn main bearings (rumbling and vibration)	Drop sump, remove crankshaft. If bearings worn but not broken up, renew. If broken up strip oil pump and clean out.
	Worn crankshaft (knocking, rumbling and vibration)	Regrind crankshaft, fit new main and big end bearings.

Chapter 2 Cooling system

Contents

Specifications

Capacity (1198 cc)
Without heater ... ...   9 pints (5.1 litres)
With heater ... ...   10½ pints (5.8 litres)

Capacity (1498 cc)
Without heater ... ...   10½ pints (5.98 litres)
With heater ... ...   12 pints (6.58 litres)

Radiator cap release pressure
1198 cc ... ...   7 lb in^2 (0.492 kg cm^2)
1498 cc ... ...   10 lb in^2 (0.703 kg cm^2)

Thermostat (1198 cc)
Starts to open ... ...   82 to 88°C (180 to 190°F)
Fully open ... ...   101°C (214°F)

Thermostat (1498 cc)
Starts to open ... ...   85 to 88.9°C (185 to 192°F)
Fully open ... ...   98.9 to 101.7°C (210 to 215°F)

Torque wrench settings

	lb ft	kg m
Fan blade	5 - 7	0.69 - 0.97
Water pump	5 - 7	0.69 - 0.97
Thermostat housing	12 - 15	1.66 - 2.07

1 General description

The engine cooling water is circulated by a thermo-syphon water pump assisted system, and the whole system is pressurised. This is both to prevent the loss of water down the overflow pipe with the radiator cap in position and to prevent premature boiling in adverse conditions. The radiator cap is pressurised to 7 lb sq in (0.492 kg sq cm) for 1198 cc engines and 10 lb sq in (0.703 kg sq cm) for 1498 cc engines. This has the effect of considerably increasing the boiling point of the coolant. If the water temperature goes above the increased boiling point the extra pressure in the system forces the internal part of the cap off its

seat, thus exposing the overflow pipe down which the steam from the boiling water escapes thereby relieving the pressure. It is, therefore, important to check that the radiator cap is in good condition and that the spring behind the sealing washer has not weakened. The cooling system comprises the radiator, top and bottom water hoses, heater hoses, the impeller water pump (mounted on the front of the engine, it carries the fan blades, and is driven by the fan belt), the thermostat and the two drain taps.

The system functions in the following fashion. Cold water in the bottom of the radiator circulates up the lower radiator hose to the water pump where it is pushed round the water passages in the cylinder block, helping to keep the cylinder bores and pistons cool.

The water then travels up into the cylinder head and circulates round the combustion spaces and valve seats absorbing more heat and then, when the engine is at its correct operating temperature, travels out of the cylinder head, past the open thermostat into the upper radiator hose and so into the radiator header tank.

The water travels down the radiator where it is rapidly cooled by the in-rush of cold air through the radiator core, which is created by both the fan and the forward motion of the car. The water, now much cooler, reaches the bottom of the radiator when the cycle is repeated.

When the engine is cold the thermostat (which is a valve which opens and closes according to the temperature of the water) arrests the circulation of the water in the engine.

Only when the correct minimum operating temperature has been reached, as shown in the Specifications, does the thermostat begin to open, allowing water to return to the radiator.

On GT models the inlet manifold is heated by the coolant.

2 Cooling system - draining

1 If the engine is cold, remove the filler cap from the radiator by turning the cap anticlockwise. If the engine is hot, then turn the filler cap very slightly until pressure in the system has had time to be released. Use a rag over the cap to protect your hand from escaping steam. If with the engine very hot the cap is released suddenly, the drop in pressure can result in the water boiling. With the pressure released the cap can be removed.
2 If anti-freeze is used in the cooling system, drain it into a bowl having a capacity of at least 12 pints (6.80 litres) for re-use.
3 Open the drain plug located on the rear of the radiator lower tank next to the bottom hose. Also remove the engine drain plug which is located at the rear right hand side of the cylinder block (photos).
4 When the water has finished running, probe the drain plug orifices with a short piece of wire to dislodge any particles of rust or sediment which may be causing a blockage.
5 It is important to note that the heater cannot be drained completely during the cold weather so an anti-freeze solution must be used. Always use an anti-freeze with an ethylene glycol base.

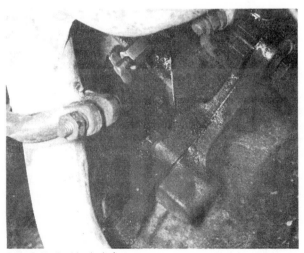

2.3b Cylinder block drain tap

2.3a Radiator drain tap

3 Cooling system - flushing

1 In time the cooling system will gradually lose its efficiency as the radiator becomes choked with rust, scale deposits from the water, and other sediment. To clean the system out, remove the radiator filler cap and drain plug and leave a hose running in the filler cap neck for ten to fifteen minutes.
2 In very bad cases the radiator should be reverse flushed. This can be done with the radiator in position. The cylinder block plug is removed and a hose with a suitable tapered adaptor placed in the drain plug hole. Water under pressure is then forced through the radiator and out of the header tank filler cap neck.
3 It is recommended that some polythene sheeting is placed over the engine to stop water finding its way into the electrical system.
4 The hose should now be removed and placed in the radiator cap filler neck and the radiator washed out in the usual manner.

4 Cooling system - filling

1 Tighten the cylinder block and radiator drain plugs.
2 Fill the system slowly to ensure that no air lock develops. If a heater is fitted, check that the valve in the heater is open (control at HOT), otherwise an air lock may form in the heater. The best type of water to use in the cooling system is rain water; use this whenever possible.
3 Do not fill the system higher than within ½ inch (12.5 mm) of the filler neck. Overfilling will merely result in wastage, which is especially to be avoided when anti-freeze is in use.
4 It is usually found that air locks develop in the heater radiator so the system should be vented during refilling by detaching the heater supply hose from the elbow connection on the water pump housing.
5 Pour coolant into the radiator filler neck whilst the end of the heater supply hose is held at the elbow connection height. When a constant stream of water flows from the supply hose quickly refit the hose. If venting is not carried out it is possible for the engine to overheat. Should the engine overheat for no apparent reason then the system should be vented before seeking other causes.
6 Only use anti-freeze mixture with ethylene glycol base.
7 Replace the filler cap and turn it firmly clockwise to lock it in position.

5 Radiator - removal, inspection, cleaning, refitting

1 Drain the cooling system as described in Section 2 of this Chapter.
2 Slacken the two clips which hold the top and bottom radiator

hoses on the radiator and carefully pull off the two hoses (photos).

3   Undo and remove the four bolts that secure the radiator to the front panel. The radiator may now be lifted upwards and away from the engine compartment. The fragile matrix must not be touched by the fan blades as it easily punctures (photo).

4   With the radiator away from the car any leaks can be soldered or repaired with a suitable substance such as Cataloy. Clean out the inside of the radiator by flushing as described earlier in this Chapter. When the radiator is out of the car it is advantageous to turn it upside down and reverse flush. Clean the exterior of the radiator by carefully using a compressed air jet or a strong jet of water to clear away any road dirt, flies etc.

5   Inspect the radiator hoses for cracks, internal or external perishing and damage by overtightening of the securing clips. Also inspect the overflow pipe. Renew the hoses if suspect. Examine the radiator hose clips and renew them if they are rusted or distorted.

6   The drain plug and washer should be renewed if leaking or with worn threads, but first ensure the leak is not caused by a faulty rubber washer.

7   Refitting is a reversal of removal. Refill the cooling system as described in Section 4.

6 Thermostat - removal, testing, refitting

1   Partially drain the cooling system *usually 4 pints (2.27 litres) is enough) as described in Section 2.

2   Slacken the top radiator hose to the thermostat housing and remove the hose.

3   Undo and remove the two bolts and spring washers that secure the thermostat housing to the cylinder head.

4   Carefully lift the thermostat housing away from the cylinder head. Recover the joint washer adhering to either the housing or cylinder head.

5   Lift the thermostat from its recess. Do not attempt to prise it if it is stuck but cut round the edge of its periphery until it is released, using a sharp knife.

6   Test the thermostat for correct functioning by suspending it on a string in a saucepan of cold water together with a thermometer. Heat the water and note the temperature at which the thermostat begins to open. This should be 82 - 88ºC (180 - 190ºF). It is advantageous in winter to fit a thermostat that does not open too early. Continue heating the water until the thermostat is fully open. Then let it cool down naturally.

7   If the thermostat does not fully open in boiling water, or does not close down as the water cools, then it must be discarded and a new one fitted. Should the thermostat be stuck open when cold this will usually be apparent when removing it from the housing.

8   Refitting the thermostat is the reverse sequence to removal. Always ensure that the thermostat housing and cylinder head mating faces are clean and flat. If the thermostat housing is badly corroded fit a new housing. Always use a new gasket. Tighten the two securing bolts to a torque wrench setting of 12 - 15 lb ft (1.66 - 2.07 kg m).

7 Water pump - removal and refitting

1   Drain the cooling system as previously described.

2   Detach the radiator and heater hoses from the water pump.

3   Slacken the dynamo mounting bolts and adjuster strap bolts, push the unit in towards the engine and remove the fan belt.

4   Unscrew and remove the four bolts which secure the fan blades to the water pump pulley hub and remove the fan blades.

5   Unscrew and remove the three bolts which secure the water pump to the front face of the engine block.

6   Withdraw the water pump and its gasket.

7   Refitting is a reversal of removal but use a new gasket, refill the cooling system and adjust the tension of the fan belt as

5.2a Removing lower radiator hose

5.2b Removing top radiator hose

5.3 Removing a radiator securing bolt

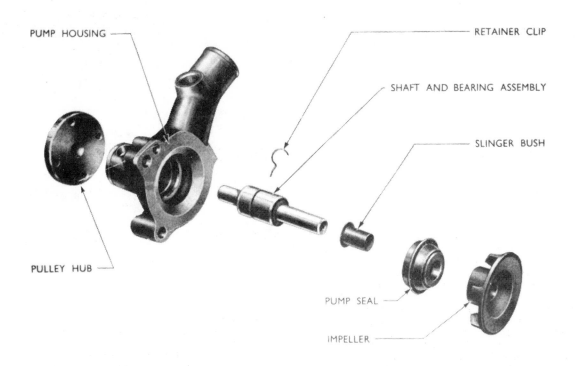

PUMP HOUSING

RETAINER CLIP

SHAFT AND BEARING ASSEMBLY

SLINGER BUSH

PULLEY HUB

PUMP SEAL

IMPELLER

Fig. 2.1. Exploded view of the water pump

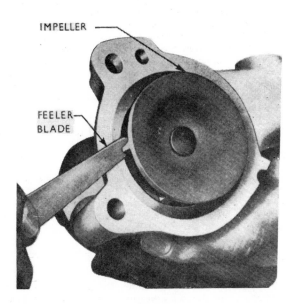

IMPELLER

FEELER BLADE

Fig. 2.2. Checking the impeller blades to water pump housing clearance

⅞ in. FREE MOVEMENT

ADJUSTMENT BOLTS

Fig. 2.3. Fan belt adjustment diagram

described in Section 9.

8 Water pump - dismantling and reassembly

1   Before undertaking the dismantling of a water pump to effect
a repair, check that all parts are available. It may be quicker and
more economical to replace the complete unit.
2   Pull out the bearing retainer clip from its slot in the water
pump housing.
3   Using a suitable puller, draw the hub from the shaft.
4   Using a soft faced hammer drive the shaft and bearing
assembly out towards the rear of the pump body.
5   The impeller vane is removed from the spindle by using a
universal three legged puller and suitable thrust block.
6   Remove the seal and the slinger by splitting the latter with
the aid of a sharp cold chisel.
7   Carefully inspect the condition of the shaft and bearing
assembly and if it shows signs of wear or corrosion, new parts
should be obtained. If it was found that coolant was leaking from
the pump, a new seal should be obtained. If it was evident that
the pulley hub or impeller were a loose fit they must be renewed.
The repair kit available comprises a new shaft and bearing
assembly, a slinger seal, bush, clip and gasket.
8   To reassemble the water pump first fit the shaft and bearing
assembly to the housing, larger end of the shaft to the front of
the housing, and press the assembly into the housing until the
front of the bearing is flush with the pump housing.
9   Refit the bearing locating clip.
10 Next press the pump pulley onto the front end of the shaft
until the end of the shaft is flush with the end of the hub.
11 Press the new slinger flanged end first onto the shaft until
the non-flanged end is approximately 0.5 inch (13 mm) from the
shaft end. To act as a rough guide the flanged end on the slinger
will be just in line with the impeller side of the window in the
water pump body.
12 Place the new seal over the shaft and into the counterbore
in the water pump housing (carbon face towards impeller) and
then press the impeller onto the shaft until a clearance of
0.030 inch (0.762 mm) is obtained between the impeller and the
housing face. Whilst this is being carried out the slinger will be
pushed onto its final position by the impeller.

9 Fan belt - adjustment

1   It is important to keep the fan belt correctly adjusted and it
is considered that this should be a regular maintenance task
every 6000 miles (10,000 km). If the belt is loose it will slip,
wear rapidly and cause the dynamo and water pump to
malfunction. If the belt is too tight the dynamo and water
pump bearings will wear rapidly causing premature failure of
these components.
2   The fan belt tension is correct when there is 0.5 inch (12.7 mm)
of lateral movement at the midpoint position of the belt run
between the dynamo pulley and the water pump.
3   To adjust the fan belt, slacken the dynamo securing bolts
and move the dynamo in or out until the correct tension is
obtained. It is easier if the dynamo bolts are only slackened a
little so it requires some effort to move the dynamo. In this
way the tension of the belt can be arrived at more quickly than
by making frequent adjustment (photo).
4   When the correct adjustment has been obtained fully tighten
the dynamo mounting bolts.

10 Fan belt - renewal

1   If the fan belt is worn or has stretched unduly, it should be
renewed. The most usual reason for replacement is that the belt
has broken in service. It is recommended that a spare belt be
always carried in the car.
2   Loosen the dynamo mounting bolts and push the unit in

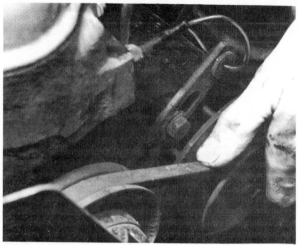

9.3 Testing fan belt adjustment

towards the engine.
3   Slip the old belt over the dynamo pulley and then detach it
from the crankshaft and water pump pulleys.
4   Install the new belt by fitting it first round the crankshaft
and water pump pulleys and then locating it over the rim of the
dynamo pulley.
5   Adjust the tension as described in the preceding Section.
When a new belt is fitted, it will require re-adjustment after the
first 250 miles (400 km) of use.

11 Temperature warning light - fault finding

1   On deluxe versions, a temperature warning light is fitted on
the speedometer dial. The light illuminates when the coolant
temperature passes its normal level.
2   To check the serviceability of the bulb, disconnect the
green/blue lead from the switch which is screwed into the
thermostat housing. Switch on the ignition and earth the
disconnected lead. The bulb should illuminate, if not, renew it.

12 Temperature gauge - fault finding

1   A temperature gauge is fitted to 1498 cc standard and GT
models.
2   If the temperature gauge fails to work, either the gauge, the
sender unit, the wiring or the connections are at fault.
3   It is not possible to repair the gauge or the sender unit and
they must be replaced by new units if at fault.
4   First check the wiring connections are sound. Check the
wiring for breaks using an ohmmeter. The sender unit and
gauge should be tested by substitution.

13 Anti-freeze mixture

1   Apart from the obvious reason for using a recommended
anti-freeze, its use also prevents corrosion and rusting of
internal surfaces of the cooling system.
2   It is recommended that the mixture is of the strength
indicated in the following table.
3   Each autumn, drain the old coolant and refill with new
anti-freeze mixture. The corrosion inhibitors in the anti-freeze
begin to lose their effectiveness after an operating life of about
twelve months.

4 The table below gives the amount of anti-freeze and degree of protection.

Anti-freeze %	Commences to freeze °C	°F	Frozen solid °C	°F	Amount of anti-freeze pints	litres
25	-13	9	-26	-15	2½	1.42
33¹/3	-19	-2	-36	-33	3	1.71
50	-36	-33	-48	-53	4½	2.56

Note: Never use anti-freeze in the windscreen washer reservoir as it will cause damage to the paintwork.

14 Fault diagnosis - cooling system

Symptom	Reason/s	Remedy
Overheating	Insufficient water in cooling system	Top up radiator
	Fan belt slipping (accompanied by a shrieking noise on rapid engine acceleration)	Tighten fan belt to recommended tension or replace if worn
	Radiator core blocked or radiator grille restricted	Reverse flush radiator, remove obstructions
	Bottom water hose collapsed, impeding flow	Remove and fit new hose
	Thermostat not opening properly	Remove and fit new thermostat
	Ignition advance and retard incorrectly set (accompanied by loss of power, and perhaps, misfiring)	Check and reset ignition timing
	Carburettor incorrectly adjusted (mixture too weak)	Tune carburettor
	Exhaust system partially blocked	Check exhaust pipe for constrictive dents and blockages
	Oil level in sump too low	Top up sump to full mark on dipstick
	Blown cylinder head gasket (water/steam being forced down the radiator overflow pipe under pressure)	Remove cylinder head, fit new gasket
	Engine not yet run-in	Run-in slowly and carefully
	Brakes binding	Check and adjust brakes if necessary
Cool running	Thermostat jammed open	Remove and renew thermostat
	Incorrect thermostat fitted, allowing premature opening of valve	Remove and replace with new thermostat which opens at a higher temperature
	Thermostat missing	Check and fit correct thermostat
Loss of cooling water	Loose clips on water hoses	Check and tighten clips if necessary
	Top, bottom, or by-pass water hoses perished and leaking	Check and replace any faulty hoses
	Radiator core leaking	Remove radiator and repair
	Thermostat gasket leaking	Inspect and renew gasket
	Radiator pressure cap spring worn or seal ineffective	Renew radiator pressure cap
	Blown cylinder head gasket (pressure in system forcing water/steam down overflow pipe	Remove cylinder head and fit new gasket
	Cylinder wall or head cracked	Dismantle engine, despatch to engineering works for repair

Chapter 3 Fuel system

Contents

Specifications

Fuel pump

Type	Mechanical, camshaft operated
Delivery pressure	1 to 2 lb in^2 (0.070 to 0.141 kg cm^2)

Carburettors

Type:

1198 cc and 1498 cc	Single venturi downdraught
1498 cc GT	Dual barrel, downdraught (two venturis each barrel)

Single venturi data

	1198 cc	1498 cc
Main jet	110	92
Compensating jet	—	112
Air correction jet	200	
Compensating jet air bleed	—	2.6 mm
Accelerator pump jet	40	50
Idling air bleed	60	70
Idling jet	50	55
Economy jet	65	—
Econostat air jet	130	—
Econostat fuel jet	80	—
Choke tube	23 mm	29 mm
Needle valve (fuel inlet)	1.6 mm	1.75 mm

Dual barrel data

	Primary	Secondary
Venturi diameter	26 mm	27 mm
Auxiliary venturi diameter	4.5 mm	4.5 mm
Main jet	140	155
Air correction jet	230	180
Emulsion tube type	F30	F30
Slow-running fuel jet	50	70
Slow-running air jet	200	70
Progression holes	2 x 120	1 x 120
Slow-running volume control port	1.5 mm	—

Air bleed in throttle plate	1 mm
Needle valve (fuel inlet)	1.75 mm
Starter fuel jet	190
Starter air correction jet	100
Starter air passage diameter	6 mm
Air bleed above starter reservoir diameter	1.25 mm
Starter progression hole diameter	2 x 2.5 mm
Air to starter progression hole diameter	3.5 mm
Accelerator pump jet	60
Accelerator pump inlet valve lateral bleed	50

Fuel tank

Capacity	8 gals (36.3 litres)

1 General description

The fuel system on all models is similar and includes a rear mounted tank, a camshaft operated mechanical fuel pump and a downdraught carburettor of differing type according to model type.

The necessary rigid and flexible fuel lines and a fuel gauge and transmitter unit are incorporated.

The air cleaner may be of oil-wetted gauze type or disposable paper element; according to vehicle operating application.

A non-vented fuel filler cap is fitted to all models. The exhaust system on all models except the GT is of single downpipe type. GT models have a four branch downpipe and the inlet manifold is water heated from a take off point at the base of the thermostat housing.

A manually operated choke is fitted and accelerator linkage is of the rod and ball joint type.

2 Air cleaner - removal, servicing, refitting

1 Both types of air cleaner are serviced as described in the Routine Maintenance Section at the front of this manual.

2 Removal and dismantling of the paper element and oil-wetted gauze types is similar.

3 Loosen the clamp which secures the air cleaner flexible collar to the carburettor.

4 Unscrew and remove the centre wing nut. Lift the cover (photo).

5 Prise the air cleaner from the carburettor. The rubber connector to the carburettor may need releasing by inserting a blunt screwdriver between it and the carburettor intake. The use of brute force can cause the carburettor cover to crack or break off.

6 Refitting is a reversal of removal.

7 If necessary, the air cleaner body can be removed simply by lifting it from its rocker cover platform but when refitting it ensure that the locating dowel engages correctly.

3 Fuel pump - description

1 The mechanically operated fuel pump is actuated through a spring loaded rocker arm. One arm of the rocker (8) (Fig 3.2) bears against an eccentric on the camshaft and the other arm operates a diaphragm pull rod.

2 As the engine camshaft rotates, the eccentric moves the pivoted rocker arm outwards which in turn pulls the diaphragm pull rod and the diaphragm (5) down against the pressure of the diaphragm spring.

3 This creates sufficient vacuum in the pump chamber to draw in fuel from the tank through the fuel filter gauze and non-return inlet valve (21).

4 The rocker arm is held in constant contact with the eccentric by an anti-rattle spring (6) and as the engine camshaft continues

to rotate the eccentric allows the rocker arm to move inwards. The diaphragm spring (20) is thus free to push the diaphragm (5) upwards forcing the fuel in the pump chamber out to the carburettor through the non-return outlet valve (21). On some models a metal dome cover is used instead of the transparent bowl (24) illustrated. The metal dome is held in place by a centre bolt, the layout of the fuel pump being otherwise identical.

5 When the float chamber in the carburettor is full, the float chamber needle valve will close so preventing further flow from the fuel pump.

6 The pressure in the delivery line will hold the diaphragm downwards against the pressure of the diaphragm spring, and it will remain in this position until the needle valve in the float chamber opens to admit more fuel.

4 Fuel pump - testing in position

1 Presuming that the fuel lines and unions are in good condition and that there are no leaks anywhere, check the performance of the fuel pump in the following manner.

2 Disconnect the fuel pump at the carburettor inlet union and the high tension lead to the coil, and with a jar or a large rag in position to catch the ejected fuel, turn the engine over on the starter motor solenoid.

3 A good spurt of fuel should emerge from the end of the pipe every second revolution.

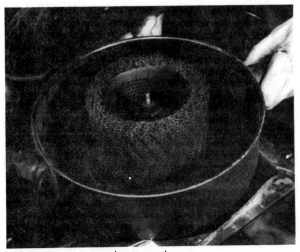

2.4 Air cleaner element (gauze type)

5 Fuel pump - removal and refitting

1   The fuel pump is mounted on the right hand side of the engine on a level with the camshaft.
2   Remove the fuel inlet and outlet pipes by unscrewing the union nuts.
3   Unscrew the two set bolts and spring washers which hold the pump to the crankcase.
4   Lift the pump together with the gasket away from the crankcase.
5   Replacement of the pump is a reversal of the above process. Remember to use a new crankcase to fuel pump gasket to ensure no oil leaks, ensure that both faces of the flange are perfectly clean, and check that the rocker arm lies on top of the camshaft eccentric and not underneath it.

6 Fuel pump - dismantling, servicing, reassembly

1   Unscrew the knurled pressure cap (glass bowl type) or the centre bolt (metal cover) and remove the cover and filter screen.
2   Make file marks across the edges of the upper and lower body mating flanges to assist in reassembly. Make the marks on each side of the projecting tag of the diaphragm.
3   Remove the screws and spring washers which secure the two halves of the pump body together and separate, taking care not to damage the diaphragm which is clamped between the two flanges.
4   The diaphragm can be removed by turning a quarter turn in either direction in order to free the centre rod from the operating lever. Remove the spring, oil seal retaining washer and rubber seal.
5   Inlet and outlet valves are retained by a spring steel plate, the two valve assemblies together with a special gasket can be lifted from the body. To dismantle the lower body, remove the circlip from one end of the pivot pin on which the rocker arm operates and press out the pin. The rocker arm, spring, link and two washers can then be removed.
6   To reassemble the pump after a new diaphragm has been obtained, assemble the spring oil seal washer and seal to the pull rod of the new diaphragm. Insert the end of the rod in the slotted end of the link engaging the grooves in the pull rod by turning it one quarter of a turn at the same time depressing it against the pressure of the spring.
7   Support the pump upper body so that the valve locations are uppermost and insert the figure '8' gasket. Fit the two valve assemblies and secure the retaining plate with two screws.
8   Locate the upper body over the diaphragm so that the mating marks are in alignment. Depress the rocker arm until the diaphragm is flush with the body flange. Hold the rocker arm in this position and insert the flange screws and spring washers, screwing them in finger tight at this stage.
9   Operate the rocker arm several times to centralise the diaphragm and with the rocker arm fully depressed, tighten the flange screws fully in diametrically opposite sequence.
10 Refit the filter screen and the metal cover or glass bowl, according to type. Always take the opportunity of installing a new cover sealing ring and cover bolt fibre washer.

7 Fuel tank - servicing

1   Due to the ingress of water into the fuel tank caused by condensation and water percolation into filling station fuel tanks it is recommended that annually the drain plug is removed from the base of the fuel tank and about a pint of fuel drained and discarded. As, of course, fuel always floats on water, any water present in the tank will be drawn off first.
2   In the event of a leak developing in a fuel tank, restrict any repair methods to the use of fibre glass or similar filler. **Never be tempted to solder or braze a fuel tank** even if it has remained empty for weeks.
3   Leave major fuel tank repairs to professionals or purchase a new tank which will probably be just as economical as having a faulty one repaired.

8 Fuel tank - removal and refitting

1   Unscrew and remove the drain plug and drain the fuel.
2   Remove the covering from the luggage boot floor.
3   Disconnect the leads from the fuel tank transmitter unit.
4   Disconnect the fuel outlet pipe from the tank.
5   Loosen the hose clips which secure the filler and vent pipes to the tank.
6   Unscrew and remove the self-tapping screws which secure the fuel tank flange to the floor pan.
7   Unscrew and remove the filler cap and ease the tank from its location.
8   If necessary and after testing in position as described in Section 9, the tank transmitter unit can be unscrewed and carefully removed to avoid damage to the float mechanism. A special spanner is required to unscrew the bayonet type fitting of the transmitter unit but a 'C' spanner or the careful use of a drift will provide a substitute (photo). Always use a new rubber sealing ring when refitting the transmitter unit.
9   Installation of the fuel tank is a reversal of removal.

9 Fuel contents gauge and transmitter unit - testing

1   The transmitter consists of a float hinged and provided with a wiper contact so that when the float rises and falls a rheostat controls the electrical current voltage which is reflected at the fuel tank gauge on the dashboard.
2   The float may be sluggish in operation, or may not work at all.
3   Examine the tank unit to ensure that the rheostat is not damaged and that the wiper contact is bearing against the coil. Check the float for any accumulation of dirt which will give it additional weight and the pivot of the arm for easy movement, without excessive side play.
4   Check the security of all leads and terminals at both the gauge and the transmitter.
5   If the fuel gauge still does not operate correctly, the fault must lie in either the gauge or the transmitter or the connecting wiring.
6   To check the transmitter, disconnect teh wire from the 'live' terminal on the unit. Switch on the ignition and the gauge should read 'FULL'.
7   Now connect this same lead to earth and the gauge should read 'EMPTY'. If both these tests are satisfactory then it is the transmitter which is faulty.

8.8 Fuel tank transmitter, lead and fuel outlet pipe

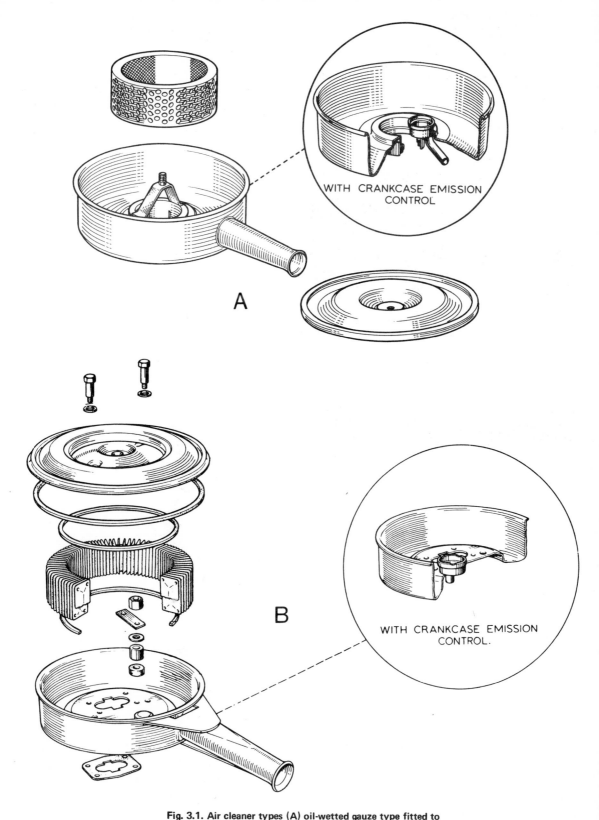

WITH CRANKCASE EMISSION CONTROL

A

WITH CRANKCASE EMISSION CONTROL.

B

Fig. 3.1. Air cleaner types (A) oil-wetted gauze type fitted to standard models (paper element in certain applications) (B) paper element type fitted to GT models

8   If during the preceding test the gauge does not read 'FULL' then disconnect the same wire from the gauge. If it registers 'FULL' then the connecting wire is faulty. If it still does not register 'FULL' then it is the gauge which is at fault.

9   With the connecting lead disconnected at the transmitter end and the wire earthed, if the gauge registers anything but 'EMPTY' then there is probably an insulation fault somewhere in the circuit wiring.

10 Carburettors - general description

1   The carburettor fitted to 1198 cc models is of single venturi downdraught type. It incorporates an accelerator pump, an economy device controlled by depression in the manifold and a hand operated choke valve (strangler). The latter is interconnected by a rod to the throttle butterfly valve to provide an automatically set fast idle.

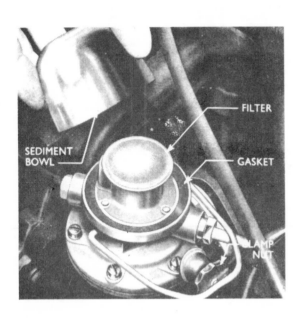

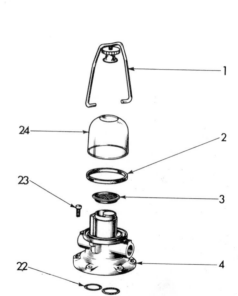

Fig. 3.2. Removing the sediment bowl from fuel pump

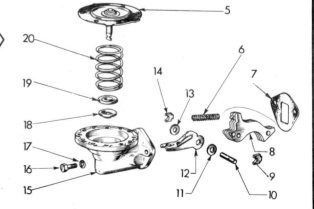

Fig. 3.3. Exploded view of the fuel pump

1	Clamp	13	Washer
2	Gasket	14	Rocker arm pin
3	Filter		retainer
4	Upper pump body	15	Lower pump body
5	Diaphragm	16	Bolt
6	Rocker arm spring	17	Spring washer
7	Gasket	18	Fuel pump oil seal
8	Rocker arm	19	Oil seal retainer
9	Rocker arm pin	20	Diaphragm spring
	retainer	21	Inlet and outlet valves
10	Rocker arm pin	22	Gasket
11	Washer	23	Screw
12	Rocker arm link	24	Sediment bowl

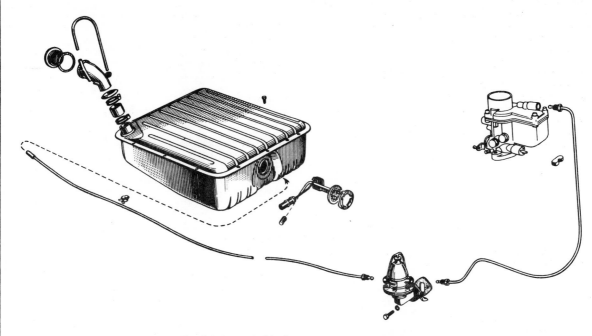

Fig. 3.4. Layout of fuel system on standard models

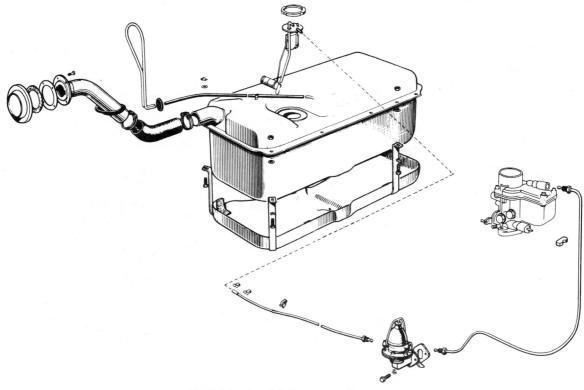

Fig. 3.5. Layout of fuel system on Estate cars

2 The carburettor fitted to 1498 cc Cortina and Corsair models is similar in construction and operation to that fitted in the smaller engined models but differs in detail and reference should be made to the Specifications for full details of jet sizes and other components.

3 The carburettor fitted to 1498 cc Cortina and Corsair GT models differs considerably from the models described above, largely because of the additional performance characteristics made possible by the small modifications to the engine. The type used is a vertical downdraught of double barrel or double choke type.

4 Small auxiliary venturi tubes are located at the top of each barrel and these discharge fuel into the narrowest parts of the larger venturis which are located further down the barrels.

5 The throttle plate in one barrel opens before that in the other barrel to ensure good performance at high revolutions as well as smooth progression when the throttle is operated at low engine speeds.

6 At about every 5000 miles (8000 km) this carburettor should be checked for slow running and at the same time the float level needs to be checked to ensure that the correct amount of fuel is being retained. At the same time the float bowl should be cleaned of any sediment which may have collected.

11 Carburettor adjustments (1198 cc engine)

a) Choke and fast idle

1 The choke cable must be adjusted so that with the facia panel control pushed fully home there is a free movement when the control is pulled out before the cable commences to operate. The correct amount of free movement is 1/8 inch (3.175 mm).

2 With the choke cable correctly set and pulled fully out (choke plate shut) a 1.1 mm (No 57) twist drill should slide between the edge of the throttle butterfly and the carburettor throat wall. Adjust the length of the choke to throttle connecting link if required to obtain the correct setting.

b) Slow-running adjustment

3 To obtain the best slow-running adjustment the engine should be tuned against a vacuum gauge connected to the inlet manifold. To enable this to be accomplished a blanking plug will be found in the carburettor flange, and it is first necessary to remove this plug and fit in a screwed adaptor. To this is connected a plastic tube which in turn is connected to the rear of a vacuum gauge. Before commencing any adjustments make sure that the air cleaner is clean and not blocked, since this will affect the amount of air in the fuel mixture.

4 No adjustments to the carburettor should be attempted until the engine has been run to bring it up to working temperature. To obtain correct mixture, screw in the throttle stop until a reasonable idling speed is attained, and then turn the volume control screw either one way or the other until the maximum vacuum reading, usually between 19º and 22º, is attained and the needle remains steady. Ease back the throttle screw and continue adjustment of the volume control screw, watching the vacuum gauge needle at each adjustment until the maximum reading is obtained with the engine at a reasonable slow running speed. To obtain the most satisfactory result it may be necessary to adjust the ignition setting described later. If a satisfactory reading cannot be obtained the reasons are set out in the Section dealing with the engine fault diagnosis.

c) Accelerator pump stroke adjustment

5 For normal operating conditions set the accelerator pump so that the pushrod passes through the outer elongated hole in the operating lever and the split pin through the outer hole in the pushrod (B) (Fig 3.10). For cold climatic conditions the setting requires that the pushrod passes through the inner elongated hole in the operating lever and the split pin through the inner hole in the pushrod (A).

12 Carburettor adjustments (1498 cc engine)

a) Choke and fast idle

1 The adjustment is similar to that described in the preceding Section except that a 0.914 mm (No 64) twist drill should be used for setting the fast idle position of the throttle plate.

b) Slow-running adjustment

2 The procedure is identical to that described in the preceding Section.

c) Accelerator pump stroke adjustment

3 The accelerator pump stroke can be varied between a long stroke and a short stroke according to climatic operating conditions. In temperate climates the shorter stroke should be used and the longer stroke in cold climates. To alter the setting, lift the spring loaded stop plate and rotate it through 180º.

13 Carburettor adjustment (1498 cc GT engine)

The slow running on this type of carburettor is carried out in a similar manner to that described in Section 11 using a vacuum gauge. The gauge should be connected to the inlet manifold, a socket type screw being provided for the purpose.

14 Carburettor - removal and refitting

1 The carburettor is removed by first unscrewing the bolts securing the air cleaner and then disconnecting the feed pipe union and the pipe to the ignition distributor. Continue by disconnecting the choke control cable at the operating cam and detach the clip which secures the outer cable in position, and then unscrew the two (four on GT carburettors) nuts and spring washers which hold the carburettor flange to the inlet manifold and lift away (photo).

2 A new gasket should be fitted when the carburettor is replaced.

3 Normally the carburettor should not be stripped unnecessarily, but rather attention should be given to periodic cleaning out. The use of a fuel filter system in the pump, described earlier, together with the efficient air cleaning through the filter will keep most of the foreign matter out of the carburettor.

4 For the most satisfactory operation the controls should be kept in good working order, and the carburettor in association with the ignition, should be kept in tune.

14.1 Throttle and choke connections at carburettor

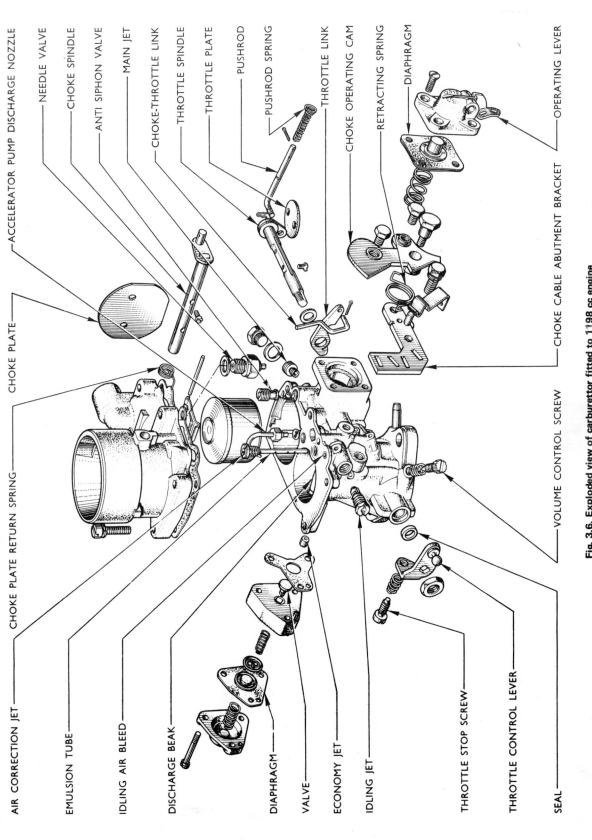

AIR CORRECTION JET

CHOKE PLATE RETURN SPRING

CHOKE PLATE

ACCELERATOR PUMP DISCHARGE NOZZLE

NEEDLE VALVE

CHOKE SPINDLE

ANTI SIPHON VALVE

MAIN JET

CHOKE-THROTTLE LINK

THROTTLE SPINDLE

THROTTLE PLATE

PUSHROD

PUSHROD SPRING

THROTTLE LINK

CHOKE OPERATING CAM

RETRACTING SPRING

DIAPHRAGM

OPERATING LEVER

CHOKE CABLE ABUTMENT BRACKET

EMULSION TUBE

IDLING AIR BLEED

DISCHARGE BEAK

DIAPHRAGM

VALVE

ECONOMY JET

IDLING JET

VOLUME CONTROL SCREW

THROTTLE STOP SCREW

THROTTLE CONTROL LEVER

SEAL

Fig. 3.6. Exploded view of carburettor fitted to 1198 cc engine

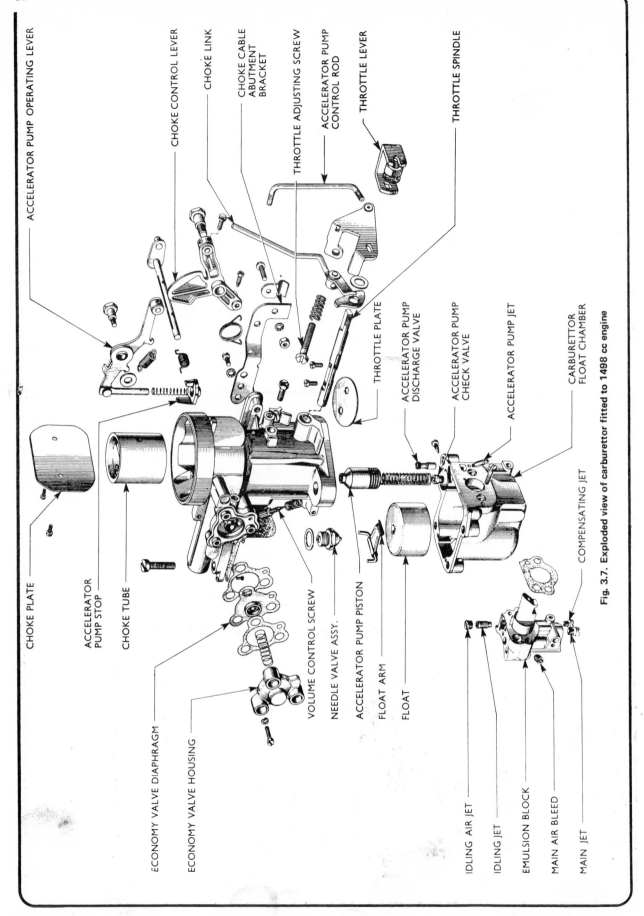

ACCELERATOR PUMP OPERATING LEVER

CHOKE CONTROL LEVER

CHOKE LINK

CHOKE CABLE ABUTMENT BRACKET

THROTTLE ADJUSTING SCREW

ACCELERATOR PUMP CONTROL ROD

THROTTLE LEVER

THROTTLE SPINDLE

THROTTLE PLATE

ACCELERATOR PUMP DISCHARGE VALVE

ACCELERATOR PUMP CHECK VALVE

ACCELERATOR PUMP JET

CARBURETTOR FLOAT CHAMBER

COMPENSATING JET

CHOKE PLATE

ACCELERATOR PUMP STOP

CHOKE TUBE

ECONOMY VALVE DIAPHRAGM

ECONOMY VALVE HOUSING

VOLUME CONTROL SCREW

NEEDLE VALVE ASSY.

ACCELERATOR PUMP PISTON

FLOAT ARM

FLOAT

IDLING AIR JET

IDLING JET

EMULSION BLOCK

MAIN AIR BLEED

MAIN JET

Fig. 3.7. Exploded view of carburettor fitted to 1498 cc engine

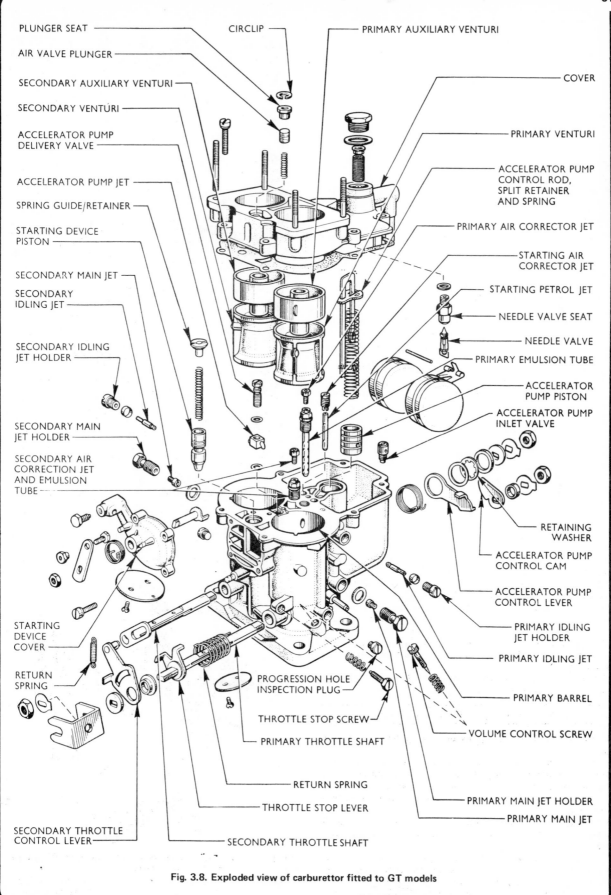

PLUNGER SEAT

AIR VALVE PLUNGER

SECONDARY AUXILIARY VENTURI

SECONDARY VENTURI

ACCELERATOR PUMP DELIVERY VALVE

ACCELERATOR PUMP JET

SPRING GUIDE/RETAINER

STARTING DEVICE PISTON

SECONDARY MAIN JET

SECONDARY IDLING JET

SECONDARY IDLING JET HOLDER

SECONDARY MAIN JET HOLDER

SECONDARY AIR CORRECTION JET AND EMULSION TUBE

STARTING DEVICE COVER

RETURN SPRING

SECONDARY THROTTLE CONTROL LEVER

CIRCLIP

PRIMARY AUXILIARY VENTURI

COVER

PRIMARY VENTURI

ACCELERATOR PUMP CONTROL ROD, SPLIT RETAINER AND SPRING

PRIMARY AIR CORRECTOR JET

STARTING AIR CORRECTOR JET

STARTING PETROL JET

NEEDLE VALVE SEAT

NEEDLE VALVE

PRIMARY EMULSION TUBE

ACCELERATOR PUMP PISTON

ACCELERATOR PUMP INLET VALVE

RETAINING WASHER

ACCELERATOR PUMP CONTROL CAM

ACCELERATOR PUMP CONTROL LEVER

PRIMARY IDLING JET HOLDER

PRIMARY IDLING JET

PRIMARY BARREL

VOLUME CONTROL SCREW

PRIMARY MAIN JET HOLDER

PRIMARY MAIN JET

PROGRESSION HOLE INSPECTION PLUG

THROTTLE STOP SCREW

PRIMARY THROTTLE SHAFT

RETURN SPRING

THROTTLE STOP LEVER

SECONDARY THROTTLE SHAFT

Fig. 3.8. Exploded view of carburettor fitted to GT models

15 Carburettor (1198 cc type) - dismantling and reassembly

1 To dismantle the carburettor first unscrew the five screws with spring washers securing the float chamber cover to the body and lift away the body together with the gasket. Lift out the float arm and hinge pin and remove the float (photo). Detach the split pin which retains the pushrod and spring, and then remove the four screws holding the accelerator pump in position, lifting away the pump body and operating arm together with diaphragm and return spring.

2 Lift the float arm and hinge pivot pin from the float chamber and extract the float.

3 Detach the outer clip which retains the choke throttle link and then loosen the screws which secure the link to the choke operating cam.

4 Remove the choke operating cam centre bolt.

5 Unscrew and remove the screw which secures the choke cable abutment bracket. Detach the bracket.

6 Remove the economy unit (three screws) and then unscrew the economy jet.

7 Unscrew the idling and air correction jets, also the emulsion tube assembly and lift off the accelerator pump discharge nozzle.

8 Unscrew the anti-syphon valve and extract the glass ball.

9 If necessary remove the discharge beak by unscrewing the tapered screw. When refitting, the tapered screw will have to be locked in position by dropping a lead shot into the drilling which is located above it.

10 Unscrew the plug and washer and unscrew the main jet.

11 Remove the throttle plate and spindle only if essential as the two retaining screws are an interference fit in the spindle tapped holes.

12 If there is wear between the spindle and carburettor body it is recommended that a reconditioned unit is obtained as the defect cannot be remedied and it will be impossible to obtain satisfactory slow-running with wear in these components.

13 Check the original jet calibrations with those listed in the Specifications in case a previous owner has substituted any of them.

14 Never attempt to clean out jets by probing with wire. Use air pressure from a tyre pump only.

15 Obtain a repair kit for the carburettor which will contain all the necessary components which should be renewed at major overhaul.

16 Reassembly is a reversal of dismantling but the following points must be observed: Refit the throttle plate so that when it is closed, the '8' stamped on it faces downwards and away from the accelerator pump. Peen the ends of the securing screws.

17 Ensure that the inner end of the choke retracting spring is located in the slot in the abutment bracket and the outer end against the 'V' in the cam.

18 Check that the float is installed with its attached cup washer uppermost and the float lever with its curved float contact area downwards.

19 Carry out the adjustments described in Section 11 once the carburettor has been refitted to the engine.

16 Carburettor (1498 cc type) - dismantling and reassembly

1 Remove the float chamber by unscrewing the four retaining bolts.

2 Remove the screw which secures the choke link to the choke control lever and then the bolt which retains the control lever to the carburettor body. Remove the lever and spring.

3 Remove the choke cable abutment bracket from the carburettor body.

4 Remove the nut and lockwasher which retain the throttle operating lever to the spindle and withdraw the lever, stop lever and choke link connection.

5 Remove the accelerator pump lever pivot bolt and withdraw the two halves of the lever together with the connecting spring. Note the washers fitted one each side of the operating lever.

6 Withdraw the accelerator pump adjustment stop from the top

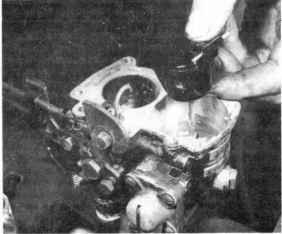

15.1 Removing the carburettor float

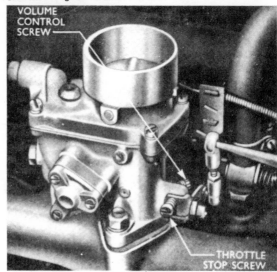

Fig. 3.9. Slow-running adjustment screws (1198 cc type carburettor)

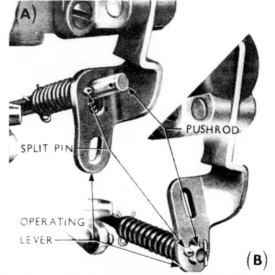

Fig. 3.10. Accelerator pump stroke adjustment (1198 cc type carburettor)

(A) Cold operating setting   (B)   Temperate or hot operating setting

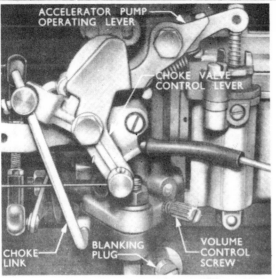

Fig. 3.11. Slow-running adjustment screws (1498 cc type carburettor)

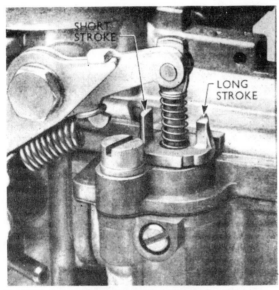

Fig. 3.12. Accelerator pump stroke adjustment (1498 cc type carburettor)

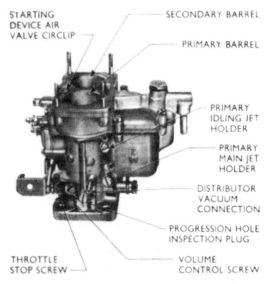

Fig. 3.13. Slow-running adjustment screws (1498 cc GT carburettor)

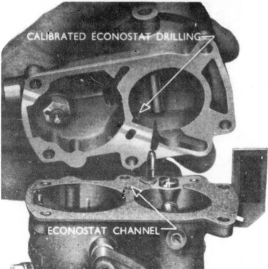

Fig. 3.14. Removing float chamber cover (1198 cc type carburettor)

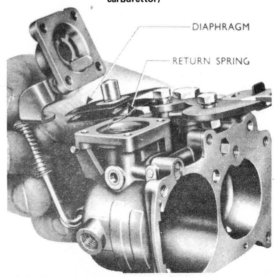

Fig. 3.15. Removing accelerator pump (1198 cc type carburettor)

of the float chamber together with seal and retainer.

7 Remove the economy valve housing (three screws) and withdraw the spring and diaphragm noting the gaskets fitted to both sides of the diaphragm.

8 Unscrew the float chamber fuel inlet needle valve assembly.

9 If necessary, remove the choke and throttle plates from their spindles.

10 Remove the choke tube after flattening the tab washer and removing the securing screw.

11 Remove the float pivot bracket and float from the float chamber.

12 Remove the emulsion block (two screws) and then unscrew all the jets for cleaning and checking of their calibration against those specified (see Specifications).

13 Remove the accelerator pump piston retaining screw and withdraw the piston and spring. Extract the pump non-return valve and the discharge valve.

14 If there is wear between the throttle spindle and the carburettor body the unit should be renewed on an exchange basis. It will be impossible to obtain satisfactory slow-running with wear in these components.

15 Never attempt to clean out jets by probing with wire. Use air pressure from a tyre pump only.

16 Obtain a repair kit for the carburettor which will contain all the necessary components which will require renewal at major overhaul. The gaskets which are located between the float chamber and carburettor body are retained by small drive pins. When renewing the gaskets remove the pins with pliers and tap them into position using a hammer of light weight.

17 Reassembly is a reversal of dismantling but the following should be observed. The throttle spindle should have its larger flat facing toward the volume control screw.

18 Fit the choke plate to its spindle so that the larger offset segment is towards the float chamber. Centre punch the butterfly plate screws to secure them.

19 Ensure that the two seating washers are refitted under the inlet needle valve body.

20 Carry out the adjustments described in Section 12 once the carburettor has been refitted to the engine.

17 Carburettor (1498 cc GT type) - dismantling and reassembly

1 Unscrew and remove the fuel filter assembly from the carburettor top cover.

2 Remove the carburettor cover after removing the six securing screws.

3 Remove the floats and needle valve from the cover.

4 Where necessary, the starting device air valve can be removed from the cover by relieving the staking which secures the retaining circlip.

5 Withdraw the accelerator pump assembly by pulling out the control rod, retainer, spring and piston. To dismantle the pump, compress the spring and rotate the piston slightly.

6 Unscrew the accelerator pump inlet valve from the bottom of the float chamber, also the delivery valve which is located between the carburettor barrels.

7 Unscrew the starting air correction jet and starting fuel jet assembly from the top face of the carburettor. Separate the two jets.

8 Unscrew the primary air correction jet and emulsion tube assembly then follow with the removal of the secondary air correction jet and emulsion tube assembly. Secure the hexagons of the emulsion tubes and unscrew the air correction jets from them.

9 Remove the circular idling jet holders from the side of the carburettor body. Withdraw the jets from their holders and check the condition of the sealing rings.

10 Unscrew the main jets from the outside of the carburettor noting the copper seating washers.

11 Unscrew and remove the starting device cover (four screws) and dismantle if necessary by removing the nut and spring washer. After prising out the starting device piston spring guide

retainer, turn the carburettor upside down to extract the piston.

12 Dismantle the throttle and accelerator pump linkage after reference to the relevant illustration.

13 If essential, remove the throttle plates from their shafts and then withdraw the auxiliary venturis followed by the primary and then the secondary ones.

14 Clean all jets by blowing them clear with air pressure from a tyre pump. Check their calibration marks with those listed in the Specifications Section.

15 Obtain a repair kit which will contain all the necessary gaskets and renewable components required at major overhaul.

16 If there is wear between the throttle spindles and the carburettor body, the unit should be renewed complete on an exchange basis, as satisfactory slow running will never be achieved with wear in these components.

17 Reassembly is a reversal of dismantling but the following must be observed: The secondary throttle spindle has a right-angled section at one end of it.

18 Ensure that the primary main jet (140) is screwed into the jet holder on the primary barrel side of the carburettor.

19 Ensure that the primary idling jet (50) is screwed into the jet holder on the primary barrel side of the carburettor.

20 Ensure that the primary air correction jet (230) is screwed into the emulsion tube which is towards the primary barrel.

21 Check that the balls in the accelerator pump delivery and inlet valves move freely.

22 Once the floats have been reassembled, check their setting. To do this, first hold the carburettor cover in a vertical position so that the floats hang down with the needle valve tab in light contact with the ball. The float to top cover (gasket removed) dimension should be 7/32 inch (5.5 mm). If necessary, bend the float arms (at the float ends) to correct the setting.

23 Now check the stroke (fully open position) which should be correct when the float to cover dimension is 9/16 inch (14.0 mm). Adjust if necessary by bending the tab which abuts the needle valve seat.

24 Clean the fuel filter gauze before refitting it.

25 If the throttle stop and volume control screws have been removed, replace them as follows to provide a starting point pending precise adjustment and tuning. Screw in the volume control screw until it just seats and then unscrew it two turns. Fit the throttle stop screw until it just contacts the throttle stop lever and then screw it in a further half a turn.

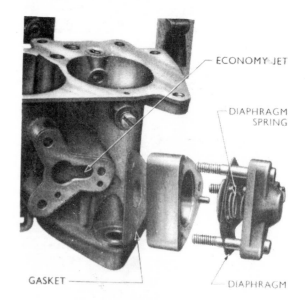

Fig. 3.16. Removing economy unit (1198 cc type carburettor)

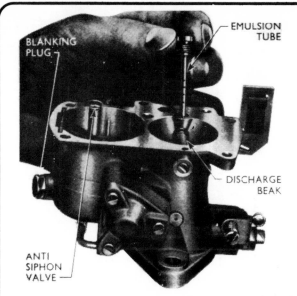

Fig. 3.17. Removing emulsion tube (1198 cc type carburettor)

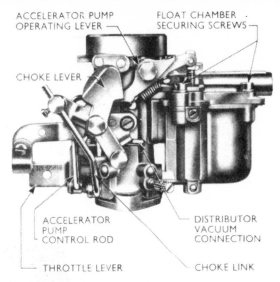

Fig. 3.18. Carburettor linkage (1498 cc type carburettor)

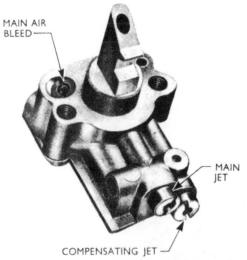

Fig. 3.19. Emulsion block (1498 cc type carburettor)

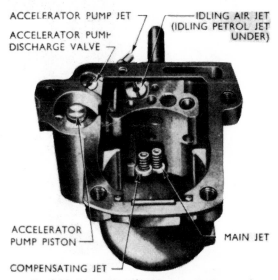

Fig. 3.20. Jet locations (1498 cc type carburettor)

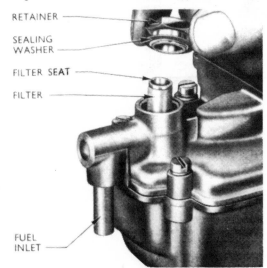

Fig. 3.21. Fuel filter (GT carburettor)

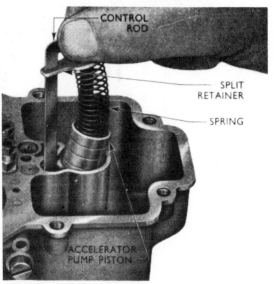

Fig. 3.22. Accelerator pump components (GT carburettor)

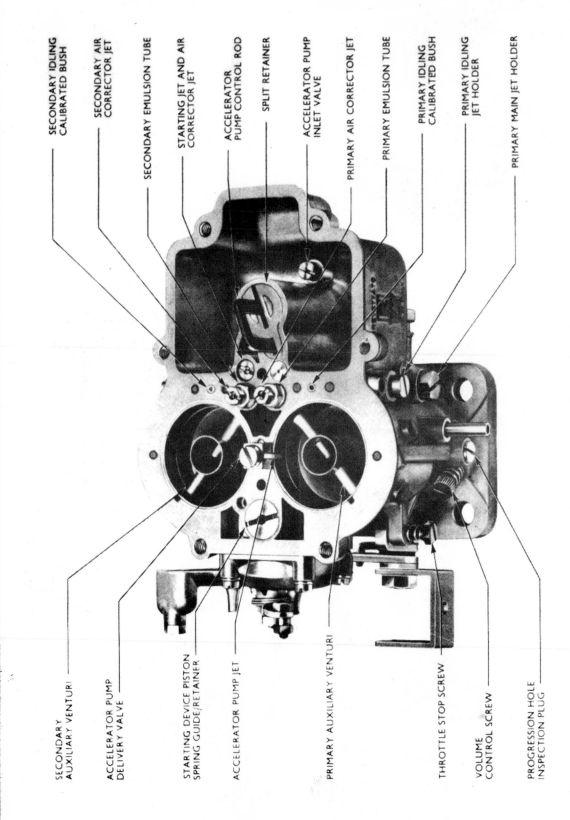

66

SECONDARY IDLING CALIBRATED BUSH

SECONDARY AIR CORRECTOR JET

SECONDARY EMULSION TUBE

STARTING JET AND AIR CORRECTOR JET

ACCELERATOR PUMP CONTROL ROD

SPLIT RETAINER

ACCELERATOR PUMP INLET VALVE

PRIMARY AIR CORRECTOR JET

PRIMARY EMULSION TUBE

PRIMARY IDLING CALIBRATED BUSH

PRIMARY IDLING JET HOLDER

PRIMARY MAIN JET HOLDER

SECONDARY AUXILIARY VENTURI

ACCELERATOR PUMP DELIVERY VALVE

STARTING DEVICE PISTON SPRING GUIDE/RETAINER

ACCELERATOR PUMP JET

PRIMARY AUXILIARY VENTURI

THROTTLE STOP SCREW

VOLUME CONTROL SCREW

PROGRESSION HOLE INSPECTION PLUG

Fig. 3.23. Jet locations (GT carburettor)

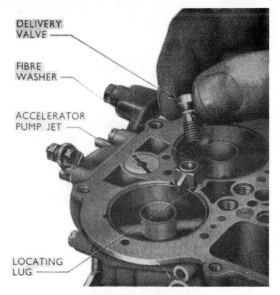

DELIVERY VALVE

FIBRE WASHER

ACCELERATOR PUMP JET

LOCATING LUG

Fig. 3.24. Accelerator pump jet and delivery valve (GT carburettor)

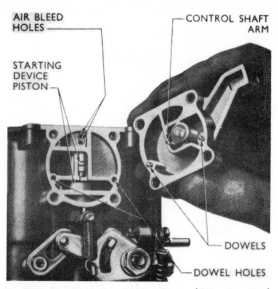

AIR BLEED HOLES

STARTING DEVICE PISTON

CONTROL SHAFT ARM

DOWELS

DOWEL HOLES

Fig. 3.25. Starting device piston and cover (GT carburettor)

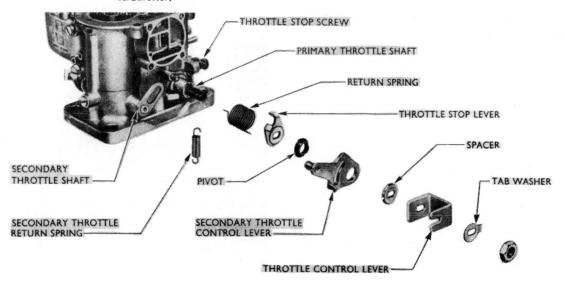

THROTTLE STOP SCREW

PRIMARY THROTTLE SHAFT

RETURN SPRING

THROTTLE STOP LEVER

SPACER

TAB WASHER

SECONDARY THROTTLE SHAFT

PIVOT

SECONDARY THROTTLE RETURN SPRING

SECONDARY THROTTLE CONTROL LEVER

THROTTLE CONTROL LEVER

Fig. 3.26. Throttle linkage components (GT carburettor)

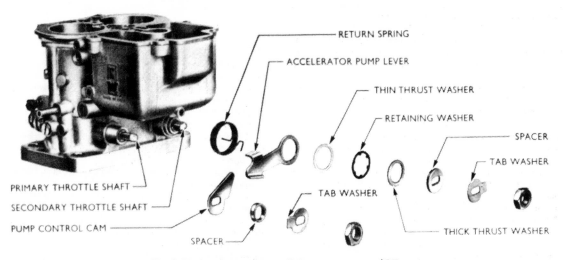

RETURN SPRING

ACCELERATOR PUMP LEVER

THIN THRUST WASHER

RETAINING WASHER

SPACER

TAB WASHER

PRIMARY THROTTLE SHAFT

SECONDARY THROTTLE SHAFT

PUMP CONTROL CAM

SPACER

TAB WASHER

THICK THRUST WASHER

Fig. 3.27. Accelerator pump linkage components (GT carburettor)

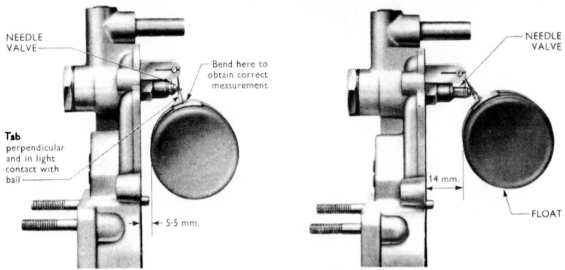

Fig. 3.28. Float adjustment diagrams (GT carburettor)

18 Accelerator pedal and linkage - adjustment

1   Set the slow-running as described earlier in this Chapter.
2   Disconnect the linkage at the carburettor.
3   Loosen the locknut on the pedal return stop and adjust the stop bolt so that the distance between the outside edge of the centre of the brake pedal pad and the outside edge of the centre of the accelerator pedal pad is for rhd vehicles 1¼ to 1½ inches (31.15 to 38.1 mm) or for lhd vehicles 1.88 to 2.12 inches (47.78 to 53.85 mm).
4   Tighten the stop bolt locknut, reconnect the linkage at the carburettor and then with the accelerator pedal fully depressed to its stop, check that the throttle butterfly valve plate is fully open. If this is not the case, do not re-adjust the return stop bolt but adjust the length of the ball jointed link which connects with the throttle control shaft.
5   There are detail differences between components used on the different vehicle models but the basic principle of adjustment applies. On vehicles fitted with automatic transmission, the 'kick-down' cable must be checked and adjusted after the accelerator linkage has been finally set. This is described in Chapter 6, part 2.

19 Exhaust systems - description and servicing

1   All models are fitted with a two section exhaust system. The front downpipe is connected to a socket at the front end of an expansion box while the rear silencer and tailpipe are a combined unit.
2   The system is suspended at the silencer by means of rubber rings and at the tailpipe by a flexible strap (photo).
3   Examination of the exhaust pipe and silencers at regular intervals is worthwhile as small defects may be repairable when, if left they will almost certainly require renewal of one of the sections of the system. Also, any leaks, apart from the noise factor, may cause poisonous exhaust gases to get inside the car which can be unpleasant, to say the least, even in mild concentrations. Prolonged inhalation could cause sickness and giddiness.
4   As the sleeve connections and clamps are usually very difficult to separate it is quicker and easier in the long run to remove the complete system from the car when renewing a section. It can be expensive if another section is damaged when trying to separate a bad section from it.
5   To remove the system first remove the bolts holding the tail pipe bracket to the body. Support the rear silencer on something

19.2 Exhaust suspension ring

to prevent cracking or kinking the pipes elsewhere.
6   Unhook the rubber rings supporting the front silencer.
7   Disconnect the manifold to downpipe connecting flange and then withdraw the complete exhaust system from below and out to the rear of the vehicle. If necessary, jack up the rear of the vehicle to provide more clearance.
8   When separating the damaged section to be renewed, cut away the damaged part from the adjoining good section rather than risk damaging the latter.
9   If small repairs are being carried out it is best, if possible, not to try and pull the sections apart.
10 Refitting should be carried out after connecting the two sections together. De-burr and grease the connecting socket and make sure that the clamp is in good condition and slipped over the front pipe but do not tighten it at this stage.
11 Connect the system to the manifold and connect the rear support strap. Now adjust the attitude of the silencer so that the tension on the two rubber support rings will be equalised when fitted.

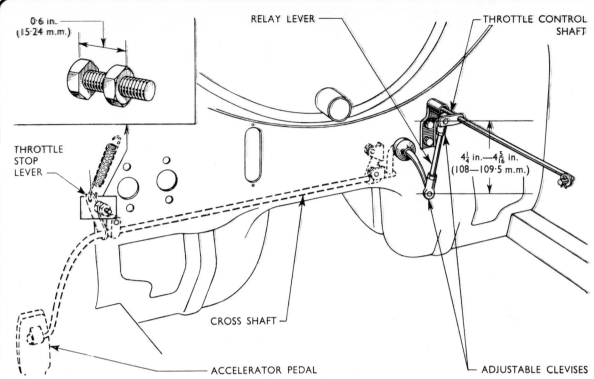

0·6 in.
(15·24 m.m.)

THROTTLE
STOP
LEVER

RELAY LEVER

THROTTLE CONTROL
SHAFT

$4\frac{1}{4}$ in.—$4\frac{5}{16}$ in.
(108—109·5 m.m.)

CROSS SHAFT

ACCELERATOR PEDAL

ADJUSTABLE CLEVISES

Fig. 3.29. Accelerator linkage adjustment. This is for initial setting, for precise adjustment procedure see text

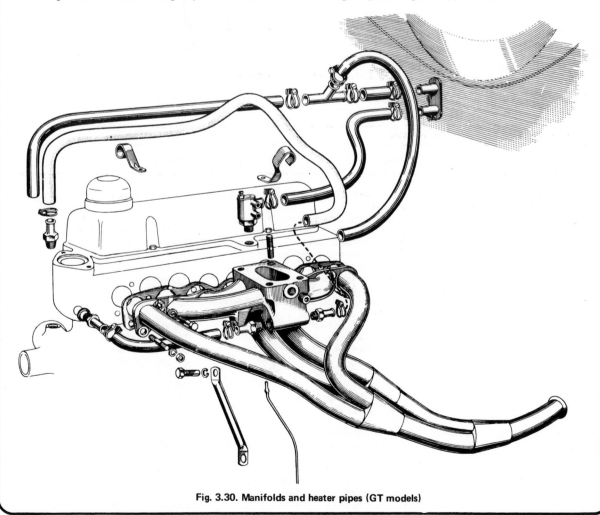

Fig. 3.30. Manifolds and heater pipes (GT models)

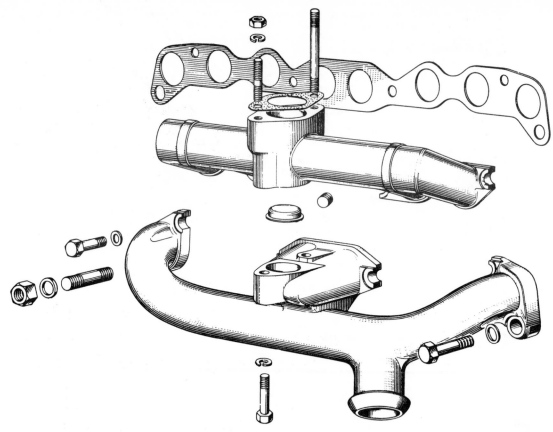

Fig. 3.31. Manifolds (standard models)

12 Tighten the pipe clamp, the manifold flange nuts and the rear suspension strap bolts. Check that the exhaust system will not knock against any part of the vehicle when deflected slightly in a sideways or upward direction.

20 Fault diagnosis - fuel system and carburation

Symptom	Reason/s	Remedy
Fuel consumption excessive	Air cleaner choked and dirty giving rich mixture	Remove, clean and replace air cleaner.
	Fuel leaking from carburettor, fuel pumps, or fuel lines	Check for and eliminate all fuel leaks. Tighten fuel line union nuts.
	Float chamber flooding	Check and adjust float level.
	Generally worn carburettor	Remove, overhaul and replace.
	Distributor condenser faulty	Remove and fit new unit.
	Balance weights or vacuum advance mechanism in distributor faulty	Remove and overhaul distributor.
	Carburettor incorrectly adjusted; mixture too rich	Tune and adjust carburettor.
	Idling speed too high	Adjust idling speed.
	Contact breaker gap incorrect	Check and reset gap.
	Valve clearances incorrect	Check rocker arm to valve stem clearances and adjust as necessary.
	Incorrectly set spark plugs	Re nove, clean and re-gap.
	Tyres under-inflated	Check tyre pressures and inflate if necessary.
	Wrong spark plugs fitted	Remove and replace with correct units.
	Brakes dragging	Check and adjust brakes.
Insufficient fuel delivery or weak mixture due to air leaks	Fuel tank air vent restricted	Clean out air vent pipe.
	Partially clogged filters in pump and carburettor	Remove and clean filters. Remove and clean out float chamber and needle valve assembly.
	Incorrectly seating valves in fuel pump	Remove, and fit new fuel pump.
	Fuel pump diaphragm leaking or damaged	Remove, and fit new fuel pump.
	Gasket in fuel pump damaged	Remove, and fit new fuel pump.

Fuel pump valves sticking due to petrol gumming	Remove and thoroughly clean fuel pump.
Too little fuel in fuel tank (prevalent when climbing steep hills)	Refill fuel tank.
Union joints on pipe connections loose	Tighten joints and check for air leaks.
Split in fuel pipe on suction side of fuel pump	Examine, locate and repair.
Inlet manifold to block or inlet manifold to carburettor gasket leaking	Test by pouring oil along joints - bubbles indicate leak. Renew gasket as appropriate.

Chapter 4 Ignition system

Contents

Specifications

Distributor index nos:
HC 40857
LC 40856
40927 GT

Type ... ... — Single pair contact breaker points, driven from skew gear on camshaft. Mechanical (centrifugal) and vacuum advance.

Static ignition advance setting
1198 cc ... ... — 6° BTDC
1498 cc ... ... — 8° BTDC
1498 cc GT ... ... — 10° BTDC

Centrifugal advance (mechanical)
8.7 : 1 compression ratio (8.3 : 1 Corsair) ... ... — Starts at 1250 rev/min, ends at 5000 rev/min
7.3 : 1 compression ratio (7.0 : 1 Corsair) ... ... — Starts at 1325 rev/min, ends at 5000 rev/min
GT (9.0 : 1) compression ratio ... ... — Starts at 1200 rev/min, ends at 5500 rev/min

Contact breaker points gap ... ... — 0.014 - 0.016 in (0.356 - 0.406 mm)

Coil
Type ... ... — 12 v

Capacitor ... ... — 0.18 to 0.22 microfarad

Spark plugs (14 mm)
Type:
Standard vehicles ... ... — Champion N5 or Autolite AG32
GT models ... ... — Champion N4 or Autolite AG22
Gap ... ... — 0.023 - 0.028 in (0.584 - 0.711 mm)

1 General description

In order that the engine can run correctly it is necessary for an electrical spark to ignite the fuel/air mixture in the combustion chamber at exactly the right moment in relation to engine speed and load. The ignition system is based on feeding low tension voltage from the battery to the coil where it is converted to high tension voltage. This voltage is powerful enough to jump the spark plug gap in the cylinders many times a second under high compression pressure, providing that the system is in good condition, and that all adjustments are correct.

The ignition system is divided into two circuits. The low tension circuit, and the high tension circuit. The low tension circuit consists of the battery, lead to the control box, lead to the ignition switch, ignition switch, lead to the low tension or primary coil windings (coil terminal SW), and the lead from the low tension coil windings (coil terminal CB) to the contact breaker points and condenser in the distributor.

The high tension circuit consists of the high tension or secondary coil windings, the heavy ignition lead from the centre of the coil to the centre of the distributor cap, the rotor arm, and the spark plug leads and spark plugs.

The system functions in the following manner. Low tension voltage is changed in the coil into high tension voltage by the opening and closing of the contact breaker points in the low tension circuit. High tension voltage is then fed to the rotor arm of the distributor. The rotor arm revolves inside the distributor cap and each time it comes in line with one of the four metal segments in the cap, which are connected to the leads and spark plugs, the opening and closing of the contact breaker points causes the high tension voltage to build up, jump the gap from the rotor arm to the appropriate metal segment, and so, via the spark plug or ignition lead, to the spark plug where it finally jumps the spark plug gap before going to earth.

As with the other electrical equipment the circuit is wired on the positive earth system. On some very late models the electrical system was changed to negative earth and where this is the case, the correct polarity must be observed when fitting accessories such as radios and also when using test equipment during servicing of ignition and other electrical components.

The ignition advance is controlled mechanically by a spring-loaded centrifugal governor which advances the spark in relation to piston tdc as the number of revolutions per minute increases.

At the same time there is a vacuum operated control which is influenced by manifold pressures inside the intake manifold under conditions of low pressures, which occur when the throttle is opened only a small amount.

Corrections to spark advance are necessary because of the wide variations in engine speed and load under operating conditions.

When the distributor is stripped down it will be found that the mechanical governor underneath the top plate consists of two weights pivoted in such a way that as they revolve they move outwards from the shaft when the engine speed rises.

In doing so they turn a cam relative to the distributor shaft and this advances the firing point.

The weights are restrained by two springs of differing tensions in order to provide a progressive action.

To maintain smooth operation throughout the engine speed range, the weights follow the contours of fixed cam segments as they move outwards, and this allows the number of moving parts to be kept to a minimum.

Distributors for high and low compression engines are identified by the number 40857 hc or 40856 lc, which is stamped on the distributor body.

Alternatively, the low tension terminal will have a brown washer or marking for the high compression units and a yellow washer or marking for the low compression unit.

2 Contact breaker points - adjustment

1 To adjust the contact breaker gap, first remove the distributor cap (photo) and lift off the rotor arm, and then turn the crankshaft until the heel of the moving point is on the highest point of one of the cam lobes. At this stage, prise the points gently open to examine the condition of their faces. If they are rough, pitted or dirty, it will be necessary to remove them for resurfacing, or for new points to be fitted.

2 Now check the points gap (presuming they do not require resurfacing or renewal) which should be between 0.014 and 0.016 inch (0.3556 and 0.4064 mm) by inserting a feeler gauge so that it will slide gently and easily between the points without pushing away the moving point, or without being loose in the gap.

3 If it is found that this gap is greater or smaller than the required amount, then adjustment is required.

4 In order to carry out the adjustment, slacken the single locking screw which holds the bracket of the adjustable point to the baseplate. The bracket can then be moved by means of the slot in the end until the correct gap indicated by the feeler gauge is obtained, and then the securing screw tightened.

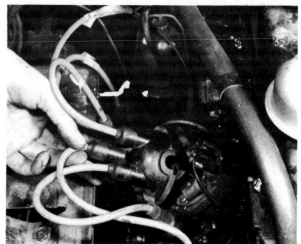

2.1 Removing distributor cap

3 Contact breaker points - removal and refitting

1 From time to time it will be necessary to remove the points in order to smooth the faces and remove the burned areas, or to renew the points if they are badly burned, and this is done by unscrewing the terminal nut and removing the flanged nylon bush together with the primary and condenser leads, noting carefully how these come away. The breaker arm can then be withdrawn. The adjustable contact is removed by unscrewing the single securing screw.

2 To reface the points, rub their faces on a fine oil stone. It is important that the faces are rubbed flat and parallel to each other so that there will be complete face-to-face contact when the points are closed. One of the points will be pitted and the other will have deposits on it. It is necessary to remove completely the built up deposits and the pitting.

3 To replace the points, first position the point with the plate and secure it with the screw and washer. Fit the fibre washer to the terminal and pivot posts and fit the spring or moving point at the pivot post. Fit the nylon bush inside the spring or moving point at the terminal, together with the two small wires. Secure them in position with the large washer and nut. The contact breaker points gap should now be set as previously detailed.

4 When the contacts are replaced, if it is found that the engine will not fire, take particular note of the loose end of the moving arm spring. This may just be touching an adjacent metal part, thus earthing the circuit and preventing the plugs from receiving current.

5 Alternatively, if this spring is incorrectly returned without complete insulation the same condition will arise.

4 Condenser (capacitor) - removal, testing, refitting

1 The purpose of the condenser is to ensure that when the contact breaker points open there is no sparking across them which would waste current.

2 The condenser is fitted in parallel across the contact points, and if it becomes damaged, will cause ignition failure by preventing the points from interrupting the low tension circuit effectively. The condenser cannot be readily checked without special test equipment, but it can be suspected if the engine becomes very difficult to start, starts to miss after several miles running, and the contact breaker points show signs of excessive burning.

3 If the points, with the ignition switched on, are separated by hand and such separation is accompanied by a high flash, this is very suggestive of condenser failure.

4 The condenser is secured to the distributor baseplate by a single screw. When refitting the condenser ensure that the screw is well tightened, also that the condenser lead is positioned with the LT lead tag, **below** the upper insulating nylon bush.

5 Distributor - removal and refitting

1 Detach the HT leads from the spark plug terminals.

2 Disconnect the HT lead from the coil by pulling it from the distributor cap.

3 Disconnect the LT lead from the distributor body terminal.

4 Disconnect the vacuum pipe from the vacuum capsule on the distributor.

5 Unscrew and remove the single clamp plate bolt which holds the distributor to the crankcase.

6 Withdraw the distributor from its recess.

7 Refitting must be carried out in accordance with the procedure described in Section 7 in order to ensure correct timing of the ignition.

6 Distributor - dismantling, servicing, reassembly

1 Before dismantling a distributor, consideration should be given to a factory exchange unit. Undoubtedly if the original unit is well worn due to high mileage, it would be more economical than repairing it.

2 Remove the distributor cap, rotor arm and contact breaker points as previously described.

3 Remove the condenser and then unhook the vacuum capsule spring from the baseplate pin.

4 Remove the two screws and their lockwashers which secure the baseplate assembly to the distributor body. Note the earth wire which is located beneath one of these screws.

5 Slide the LT terminal from its channel in the distributor body and lift out the baseplate assembly.

6 Twist the movable baseplate fully anticlockwise to disengage it from the fixed baseplate component.

7 Unhook the counterweight springs from their cam plate pegs.

8 Unscrew and remove the centre shaft screw which retains the cam and lift the cam clear of the counterweights.

9 Disconnect the springs completely and withdraw the counterweights.

10 If essential, the distributor driving shaft can be further dismantled by driving the retaining pin from the driving collar.

11 Remove the vacuum unit ratchet spring and adjuster nut spring. Do not attempt to dismantle the vacuum capsule.

12 With the distributor now fully dismantled, check the distributor cap for cracks indicated by a thin black line between the segments. Renew the cap if any signs of tracking are found.

13 If the metal portion of the rotor arm is badly burned or loose, renew the arm. If slightly burnt clean the arm with a fine file.

14 Check that the carbon brush moves freely in the centre of the distributor cover.

15 Examine the fit of the breaker plate on the bearing plate and also check the breaker arm pivot for looseness or wear and renew as necessary.

16 Examine the balance weights and pivot pins for wear, and renew the weights or cam assembly if a degree of wear is found.

17 Examine the shaft and the fit of the cam assembly on the shaft. If the clearance is excessive compare the items with new units, and renew either, or both, if they show excessive wear. The correct shaft endfloat is 0.002 to 0.006 inch (0.051 to 0.152 mm).

18 If the shaft is a loose fit in the distributor sleeve and can be seen to be worn, it will be necessary to fit a new bearing sleeve.

19 Examine the length of the balance weight springs and compare them with new springs. If they have stretched they must be renewed.

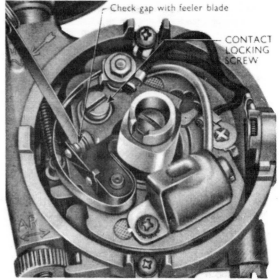

Fig. 4.1. Checking contact breaker points gap

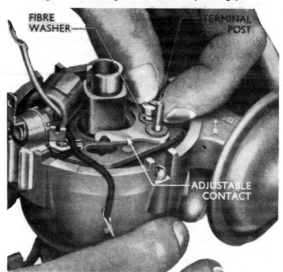

Fig. 4.2. Refitting the adjustable contact breaker arm

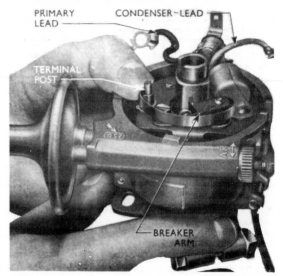

Fig. 4.3. Refitting the movable contact breaker arm

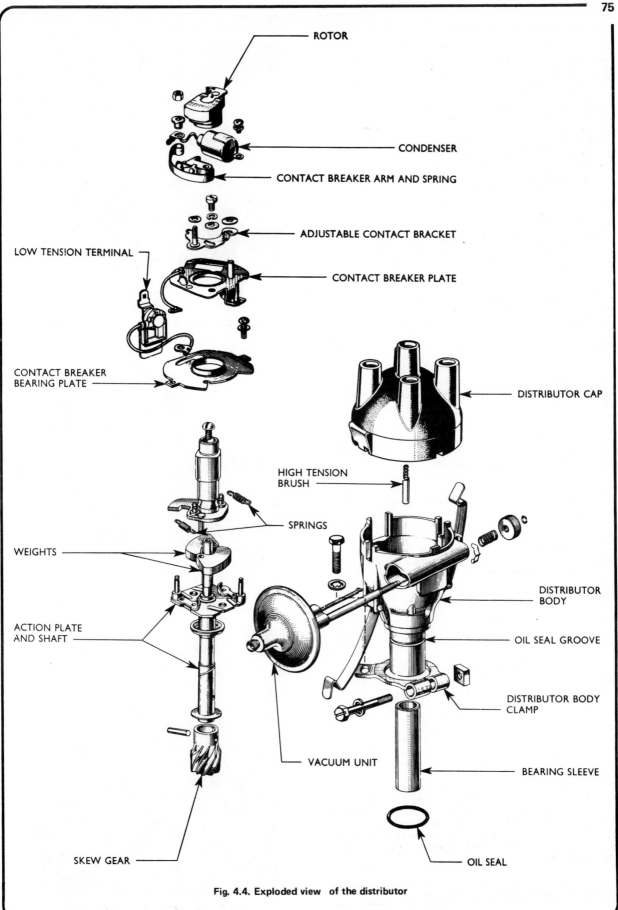

ROTOR

CONDENSER

CONTACT BREAKER ARM AND SPRING

ADJUSTABLE CONTACT BRACKET

LOW TENSION TERMINAL

CONTACT BREAKER PLATE

CONTACT BREAKER BEARING PLATE

DISTRIBUTOR CAP

HIGH TENSION BRUSH

SPRINGS

WEIGHTS

DISTRIBUTOR BODY

ACTION PLATE AND SHAFT

OIL SEAL GROOVE

DISTRIBUTOR BODY CLAMP

VACUUM UNIT

BEARING SLEEVE

SKEW GEAR

OIL SEAL

Fig. 4.4. Exploded view of the distributor

20 Reassembly is a straight reversal of the dismantling process, but there are several points which should be noted in addition to those already given in the section on dismantling.

21 Lubricate with engine oil the balance weights and other parts of the mechanical advance mechanism, the distributor shaft, and the portion of the shaft on which the cam bears, during assembly. Do not oil excessively but ensure these parts are adequately lubricated.

22 Check the action of the weights in the fully advanced and fully retarded positions and ensure they are not binding.

23 Tighten the micrometer adjusting nut to the middle position on the timing scale.

24 Finally, set the contact breaker gap to the correct clearance.

7 Ignition timing

1 The ignition timing marks comprise a notch in the crankshaft pulley and two marks moulded into the timing cover. The mark nearer the engine is the 10° btdc index and the outer (lower) one is the 6° btdc index. A point midway between the two is the 8° btdc index.

2 Apply a ring spanner to the crankshaft pulley bolt and turn the engine until No 1 piston (nearest the radiator) is at tdc. This may be established by either removing No 1 spark plug and feeling the compression being generated or by removing the rocker cover and turning the engine until the valves of No 1 cylinder are both closed.

3 Turn the engine back a few degrees and then turn it in its normal direction of rotation until the notch in the crankshaft pulley is opposite the appropriate mark on the timing cover. Refer to the Specifications for static ignition advance in relation to engine type.

4 Now hold the distributor above its crankcase recess so that the vacuum unit is towards the rear of the engine and parallel to the cylinder block centre line. Turn the rotor arm so that it points to the distributor LT terminal.

5 Push the distributor into its recess and as the drive gears mesh, the rotor arm will rotate and align with No 1 segment in the distributor cap. Tighten the distributor clamp plate bolt to secure the distributor in this position.

6 Turn the vernier adjuster on the vacuum unit until the contact points are just about to open.

7 If the range of adjustment provided by this adjuster is not sufficient, then, if clamp bolt is not already slackened, it will be necessary to slacken it and turn the distributor body slightly. Sufficient adjustment will normally be found available using the distributor micrometer adjuster. Difficulty is sometimes experienced in determining exactly when the contact breaker points open. This can be ascertained most accurately by connecting a 12 volt bulb in parallel with the contact breaker points (one lead to earth and the other from the distributor low tension terminal). Switch on the ignition, and turn the advance and retard adjuster until the bulb lights up indicating that the points have just opened. Eleven clicks of the knurled micrometer adjuster nut represent 1° of timing movement.

8 A better result can sometimes be obtained by making slight re-adjustments under running conditions. First start the engine and allow to warm up to normal temperature, and then accelerate in top gear from 30 to 50 mph, listening for heavy pinking of the engine. If this occurs, the ignition needs to be retarded slightly until just the faintest trace of pinking can be heard under these operating conditions.

9 Since the ignition advance adjustment enables the firing point to be related correctly to the grade of fuel used, the fullest advantage of any change of fuel will only be attained by re-adjustment of the ignition settings. This is done by varying the setting of the index scale on the vacuum advance mechanism one or two divisions, checking to make sure that the best all round result is attained.

8 Ignition system - fault tracing and rectification

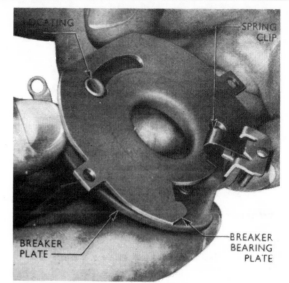

Fig. 4.5. Separating the fixed and movable baseplates

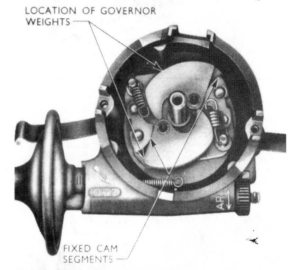

Fig. 4.6. Springs disconnected pending removal of counter-weights

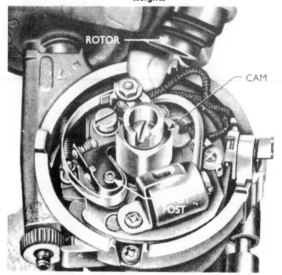

Fig. 4.7. Distributor lubrication points

By far the majority of breakdown and running troubles are caused by faults in the ignition system, either in the low tension or high tension circuits.

Engine fails to start

1 If the engine fails to start and the car was running normally when it was last used, first check there is fuel in the fuel tank. If the engine turns over normally on the starter motor and the battery is evidently well charged, then the fault may be in either the high or low tension circuits. First check the HT circuit. If the battery is known to be fully charged, the ignition light comes on and the starter motor fails to turn the engine, **check the tightness of the leads on the battery terminals** and also the security of the earth lead to its **connection to the body**. It is quite common for the leads to have worked loose, even if they lock and feel secure. If one of the battery terminal posts gets very hot when trying to work the starter motor, this is a sure indication of a faulty connection to that terminal.

2 One of the commonest reasons for bad starting is wet or damp spark plug leads and distributor. Remove the distributor cap. If condensation is visible internally, dry the cap with a rag and also wipe over the leads. Replace the cap.

3 If the engine still fails to start, check that current is reaching the plugs, by disconnecting each plug lead in turn at the spark plug end, and hold the end of the cable about 3/16 inch (4.8 mm) away from the cylinder block. Spin the engine on the starter motor.

4 Sparking between the end of the cable and the block should be fairly strong with a regular blue spark. (Hold the lead with rubber to avoid electric shocks). If current is reaching the plugs, then remove them and clean and regap them. The engine should now start.

Fig. 4.8. Ignition timing marks

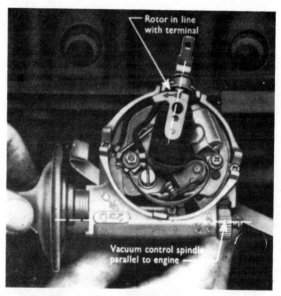

Fig. 4.9. Distributor correctly aligned prior to installation

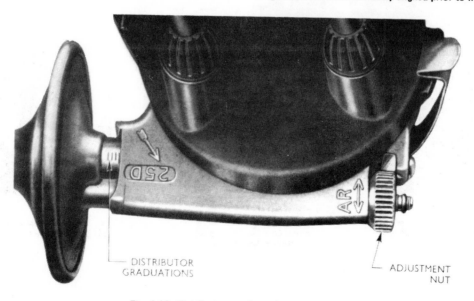

Fig. 4.10. Distributor vernier scale and adjuster

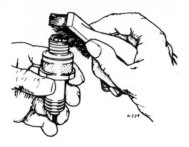

Cleaning deposits from electrodes and surrounding area using a fine wire brush

Checking plug gap with feeler gauges

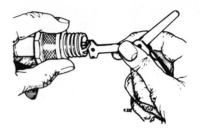

Altering the plug gap. Note use of correct tool

Sparking plug maintenance

White deposits and damaged porcelain insulation indicating overheating

Broken porcelain insulation due to bent central electrode

Electrodes burnt away due to wrong heat value or chronic pre-ignition (pinking)

Excessive black deposits caused by over-rich mixture or wrong heat value

Mild white deposits and electrode burnt indicating too weak a fuel mixture

Plug in sound condition with light greyish brown deposits

Fig. 4.11. Spark plug appearances indicating engine conditions

5 If there is no spark at the plug leads take off the HT lead from the centre of the distributor cap and hold it to the block as before. Spin the engine on the starter once more. A rapid succession of blue sparks between the end of the lead and the block indicate that the coil is in order and that the distributor cap is cracked, the rotor arm faulty, or the carbon brush in the top of the distributor cap is not making good contact with the spring on the rotor arm. Possibly the points are in bad condition. Clean and reset them as described in this Chapter.

6 If there are no sparks from the end of the lead from the coil, check the connections at the coil end of the lead. If it is in order start checking the low tension circuit.

7 Use a 12 v voltmeter or a 12 v bulb and two lengths of wire. With the ignition switch on and the points open, test between the low tension wire to the coil (it is marked SW) and earth. No reading indicates a break in the supply from the ignition switch. Check the connections at the switch to see if any are loose. Refit them and the engine should run. A reading shows a faulty coil or condenser, or broken lead between the coil and the distributor.

8 Take the condenser wire off the points assembly and with the points open, test between the moving contact point and earth. If there now is a reading, then the fault is in the condenser. Fit a new one and the fault is cleared.

9 With no reading from the moving contact point to earth, take a reading between earth and the CB terminal of the coil. A reading here shows a broken wire which will need to be replaced between the coil and distributor. No reading confirms that the coil has failed and must be replaced, after which the engine will run once more. Remember to refit the condenser wire to the points assembly. For these tests it is sufficient to separate the points with a piece of dry paper while testing with the points open.

Engine misfires

10 If the engine misfires regularly run it at a fast idling speed. Pull off each of the plug caps in turn and listen to the note of the engine. Hold the plug cap in a dry cloth or with a rubber glove as additional protection against a shock from the HT supply.

11 No difference in engine running will be noticed when the lead from the defective circuit is removed. Removing the lead from one of the good cylinders will accentuate the misfire.

12 Remove the plug lead from the end of the defective plug and hold it about 3/16 inch (4.8 mm) away from the block. Restart the engine. If the sparking is fairly strong and regular the fault must lie in the spark plug.

13 The plug may be loose, the insulation may be cracked, or the points may have burnt away giving too wide a gap for the spark to jump. Worse still, one of the points may have broken off. Either renew the plug, or clean it, reset the gap, and then test it.

14 If there is no spark at the end of the plug lead, or if it is weak and intermittent, check the ignition lead from the distributor to the plug. If the insulation is cracked or perished, renew the lead. Check the connections at the distributor cap.

15 If there is still no spark, examine the distributor cap carefully for tracking. This can be recognised by a very thin black line running between two or more electrodes, or between an electrode and some other part of the distributor. These lines are paths which now conduct electricity across the cap, thus letting it run to earth. The only answer is a new distributor cap.

16 Apart from the ignition timing being incorrect, other causes of misfiring have already been dealt with under the Section dealing with the failure of the engine to start. To recap - these are that:

- a) The coil may be faulty giving an intermittent misfire
- b) There may be a damaged wire or loose connection in the low tension circuit
- c) The condenser may be short circuiting
- d) There may be a mechanical fault in the distributor (broken driving spindle or contact breaker spring)

17 If the ignition timing is too far retarded, it should be noted

that the engine will tend to overheat, and there will be a quite noticeable drop in power. If the engine is overheating and the power is down, and the ignition timing is correct, then the carburettor should be checked, as it is likely that this is where the fault lies.

9 Spark plugs and leads

1 The correct functioning of the spark plugs is vital for the correct running and efficiency of the engine. The plugs fitted as standard are listed on the Specification page.

2 At intervals of 5000 miles (8000 km) the plugs should be removed, examined, cleaned and, if worn excessively, renewed. The condition of the spark plug will also tell much about the overall condition of the engine.

3 If the insulator nose of the spark plug is clean and white, with no deposits, this is indicative of a weak mixture, or too hot a plug. (A hot plug transfers heat away from the electrode slowly; a cold plug transfers it away quickly.)

4 If the top and insulator nose is covered with hard black looking deposits, then this is indicative that the mixture is too rich. Should the plug be black and oily, then it is likely that the engine is fairly worn, as well as the mixture being too rich.

5 If the insulator nose is covered with light tan to greyish brown deposits, then the mixture is correct and it is likely that the engine is in good condition.

6 If there are any traces of long brown tapering stains on the outside of the white portion of the plug, then the plug will have to be renewed, as this shows that there is a faulty joint between the plug body and the insulator, and compression is being allowed to leak away.

7 Plugs should be cleaned by a sand blasting machine, which will free them from carbon more thoroughly than cleaning by hand. The machine will also test the condition of the plugs under compression. Any plug that fails to spark at the recommended pressure should be renewed.

8 The spark plug gap is of considerable importance, as, if it is too large or too small the size of the spark and its efficiency will be seriously impaired. The spark plug gap should be set to between 0.023 and 0.028 inch (0.584 and 0.711 mm).

10.1 Coil LT terminals and leads

9   To set it, measure the gap with a feeler gauge, and then bend open, or close, the outer plug electrode until the correct gap is achieved. The centre electrode should never be bent as this may crack the insulation and cause plug failure, if nothing worse.

10 When replacing the plugs, remember to use new plug washers if the old ones are flattened, and replace the leads from the distributor in the correct firing order 1 2 4 3, No 1 cylinder being the one nearest the radiator.

11 The plug leads require no routine attention other than being kept clean and wiped over regularly.

10 Coil polarity

1   High tension current should be positive at the spark plug terminals. To ensure this, check the LT connections to the coil are correctly made (photo).

2   The LT wire from the distributor must connect with the positive (+) terminal of the coil.

3   An incorrect connection can cause as much as 60% loss of spark efficiency together with rough idling and misfiring at speed.

4   On some late models with negative earth electrical systems, the LT wire from the distributor connects with the negative (−) terminal of the coil.

Chapter 5 Clutch and actuating mechanism

Contents

Specifications

Type	Single dry plate, hydraulically operated
Release arm free travel	$1/10$ in (2.54 mm)
Master cylinder diameter	0.625 in (15.9 mm)
Operating cylinder diameter	0.75 in (19.0 mm)
Driven plate	
Friction lining outside diameter	7.25 in (189.2 mm)
Friction lining thickness	0.28 in (7.1 mm)
Total friction area	43.28 in^2 (279.2 cm^2)
Pressure plate diameter	7.38 in (187.0 mm)

Torque wrench settings	lb ft	kg m
Clutch to flywheel bolts	12 - 15	1.66 - 2.07
Clutch bellhousing to engine bolts	40	5.53

1 General description

The clutch assembly comprises a steel cover which is bolted
and dowelled to the rear face of the flywheel and contains the
pressure plate, pressure plate springs, release levers, and clutch
disc (driven plate).

The pressure plate, pressure springs, and release levers are all
attached to the clutch assembly cover. The clutch disc is free to
slide along the splined first motion shaft and is held in position
between the flywheel and the pressure plate by the pressure of the
pressure plate springs.

Friction lining material is riveted to the clutch disc and it has
a spring cushioned hub to absorb transmission shocks and to help
ensure a smooth take-off.

The clutch is actuated hydraulically. The pendant clutch
pedal is connected to the clutch master cylinder and hydraulic
fluid reservoir by a short pushrod. The master cylinder and
hydraulic reservoir are mounted on the engine side of the

bulkhead in front of the driver.

Depressing the clutch pedal moves the piston in the master
cylinder forwards, so forcing hydraulic fluid through the clutch
hydraulic pipe to the slave cylinder.

The piston in the slave cylinder moves forward on the entry
of the fluid and actuates the clutch release arm by means of a
short pushrod. The opposite end of the release arm is forked and
is located behind the release bearing.

As this pivoted clutch release arm moves backwards it bears
against the release bearing, pushing it forwards to bear against
the release bearing thrust plate and three clutch release levers.
These levers are also pivoted so as to move the pressure plate
backwards against the pressure of the pressure plate springs, in
this way disengaging the pressure plate from the clutch disc.

When the clutch pedal is released, the pressure plate springs
force the pressure plate into contact with the high friction linings
on the clutch disc, at the same time forcing the clutch disc against
the flywheel and so taking the drive up.

The clutch pedal is of the pendant type and is mounted together with the brake and accelerator pedals on a bracket which is held to the front bulkhead by four bolts. On the engine side of the bulkhead the clutch and brake master cylinders are held in place on these same four bolts by nuts and washers which also serve to hold the bracket against the bulkhead.

Two further bolts hold the top of the bracket to the upper portion of the front bulkhead.

2 Clutch - adjustment

1 A clearance must always be maintained between the end of the slave cylinder operating pushrod and the release arm. The correct clearance is 1/10 inch (2.5 mm).
2 To carry out any necessary adjustment, disconnect the return spring from the clutch release arm and slacken the locknut on the threaded part of the operating rod. Turn the adjusting nut until the specified clearance is obtained. The pushrod should be held stationary by applying a spanner to the flats on its centre section (photo).
3 Tighten the locknut and reconnect the return spring.

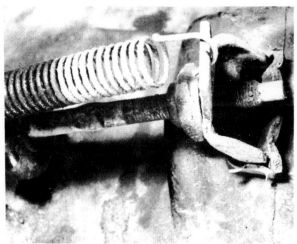

2.2 Clutch slave cylinder push rod, locknut and return spring

3 Master cylinder - removal and refitting

1 Disconnect the pushrod from the clutch pedal by removing the bolt and nut which retains it to the pedal arm.
2 Disconnect the fluid pipe from the master cylinder by unscrewing the union. Plug the line to prevent loss of fluid or the entry of dirt.
3 Unscrew and remove the two nuts which secure the master cylinder to the engine rear bulkhead and withdraw the unit. Drain the reservoir.
4 Refitting is a reversal of removal but bleed the system as described in Section 7.

4 Master cylinder - dismantling and reassembly

1 Peel off the rubber dust excluding boot.
2 Extract the now exposed circlip and withdraw the pushrod complete with retaining washer.
3 The piston and valve assembly will now be ejected from the master cylinder body.
4 Using a small screwdriver, prise up the tag of the piston return spring retainer. The retainer, spring and valve assembly can now be separated from the piston.
5 Dismantle the valve assembly by compressing the spring and moving the retainer to one side which, as it has an offset hole, will allow the valve stem to be released.
6 Remove all rubber seals and discard them.
7 Wash all components in clean hydraulic fluid or methylated spirit.
8 Examine the piston and cylinder bore surfaces for 'bright' wear areas. Where these are evident, renew the master cylinder complete.
9 Obtain a repair kit which will contain all the necessary seals and renewable components.
10 Reassembly is a reversal of dismantling but observe the following points:
11 Fit the new rubber seals using only the fingers to manipulate them into position. Dip all components in clean hydraulic fluid before assembly. Check particularly carefully that the seal chamfers and contours are facing the correct way.

5 Slave cylinder - removal and refitting

1 Disconnect the return spring from the outside of the slave cylinder.
2 Unscrew the union nut and disconnect the fluid line from the cylinder body. Plug the line to prevent entry of dirt.
3 Withdraw the pushrod and rubber dust excluding boot and extract the circlip. The cylinder may now be drawn forward and removed from the clutch bellhousing.
4 Refitting is a reversal of removal but bleed the system as described in Section 7 and check and adjust the clearance as described in Section 2.

6 Slave cylinder - dismantling and reassembly

1 Tap the cylinder on a block of wood to eject the piston and seal. Discard the seal and wash all components in clean hydraulic fluid or methylated spirit.
2 Examine the piston and cylinder bore surfaces for 'bright' wear areas. If these are evident, renew the slave cylinder complete.
3 If necessary unscrew the bleed valve and extract the ball.
4 Obtain a repair kit and fit the new rubber seal using only the fingers to manipulate it onto the piston. The recess in the seal must be furthest from the greatest diameter of the piston.
5 Dip the piston in clean hydraulic fluid and insert it carefully into the cylinder, taking care not to nip or distort the seal lips.
6 Refit the operating rod and new rubber boot.

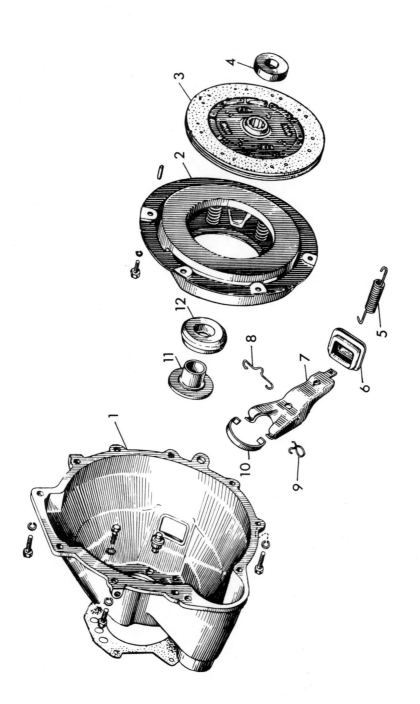

Fig. 5.1. Components of the clutch

1	Bellhousing	4	Spigot bearing	7	Release arm	10	springs (two)
2	Pressure plate assembly	5	Release arm return spring	8	Release arm to fulcrum pin spring	11	Release bearing link
3	Driven plate	6	Dust excluder	9	Release bearing locating	12	Release bearing hub
							Release bearing

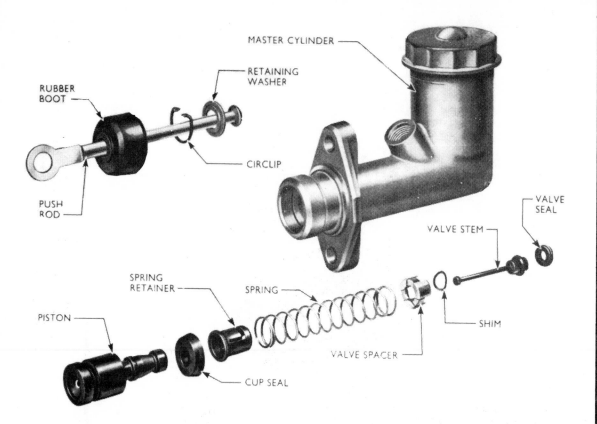

MASTER CYLINDER

RETAINING WASHER

RUBBER BOOT

CIRCLIP

PUSH ROD

VALVE SEAL

VALVE STEM

SPRING RETAINER

SPRING

SHIM

PISTON

VALVE SPACER

CUP SEAL

Fig. 5.2. Exploded view of the clutch master cylinder

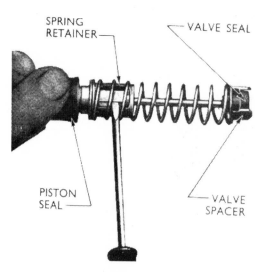

SPRING RETAINER

VALVE SEAL

PISTON SEAL

VALVE SPACER

Fig. 5.3. Prising tag on master cylinder spring retainer

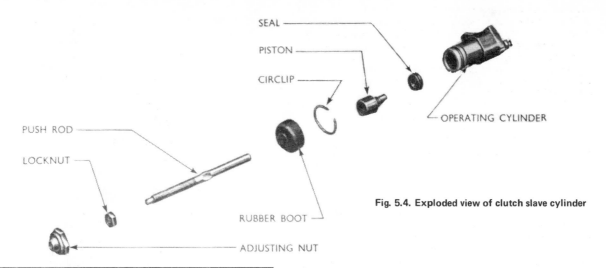

Fig. 5.4. Exploded view of clutch slave cylinder

7 Hydraulic system - bleeding

1 Pour about one inch of clean fluid into a jam jar.
2 Fit a rubber or plastic bleed tube to the bleed nipple on the clutch slave cylinder.
3 Check that the master cylinder reservoir is full, it not top it up with hydraulic fluid which has been stored in an airtight container and has remained unshaken for at least 24 hours.
4 Place the open end of the bleed tube below the level of the fluid in the jar and keep it there throughout the bleeding operation.
5 Open the bleed nipple half a turn with a spanner and then have an assistant depress the clutch pedal fully and slowly. When the pedal reaches the full extent of its travel the foot should be removed quickly so that the pedal returns without the weight of the foot upon it.
6 Repeat the procedure until no more bubbles of air appear from the end of the tube immersed in the fluid in the jar. If more than two or three strokes of the pedal have to be given to eject all the air in the system then the reservoir will have to be topped up again to prevent air being drawn into the system through the reservoir.
7 Tighten the bleed nipple using a spanner of short length when the pedal is in the fully depressed position, or during a pedal downstroke.
8 Discard the fluid in the jar or retain it for further use **in the bleed jar only**. Do not use it for topping up either the clutch or brake hydraulic systems as it will be contaminated with dust and grit.

8 Clutch/brake pedal and bracket - removal and refitting

1 Disconnect the retracting springs from both the clutch and brake pedals.
2 Detach the clutch and brake master cylinder pushrods from their respective pedal arms by unscrewing and removing the bolts and nuts.
3 Withdraw the spring clips, flat and wave washers and slide each pedal from the cross shaft.
4 Disconnect the pedal bracket from the steering column (one bolt) and then remove the clutch master cylinder (Section 3 of this Chapter) and the brake master cylinder (Chapter 9). The bolts which secure these units in position are splined in the pedal bracket.
5 Disconnect the upper leg of the bracket from the bulkhead and withdraw the bracket complete from the car.
6 Check the condition of the pedal bushes and cross shaft and renew if worn.
7 Refitting is a reversal of removal but bleed the clutch and

brake hydraulic systems and check and adjust the clutch clearance, the brake pedal setting (Chapter 9) and the accelerator linkage adjustment (Chapter 3).

9 Clutch - removal

1 Access to the clutch may be gained either by removing the gearbox as described in Chapter 6, or at the time of major engine

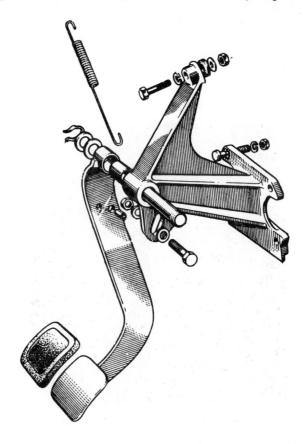

Fig. 5.5. Clutch and brake pedal bracket (brake pedal removed)

overhaul when the engine is removed.

2 Remove the clutch assembly by unscrewing the six bolts which secure the cover plate to the flywheel. Unscrew the bolts in a diagonal sequence - half a turn at a time, until the pressure of the clutch springs has been relieved.

3 Unscrew and remove the bolts completely and withdraw the clutch assembly from the locating dowels catching the driven plate which will fall out.

10 Clutch assembly - inspection and renovation

1 It is not always easy to decide when to go to the trouble of removing the gearbox in order to check the wear on the friction lining. The only positive indication that something needs doing is when it starts to slip or when squealing noises on engagement indicate that the friction lining has worn down to the rivets. In such instances it can only be hoped that the friction surfaces on the flywheel and pressure plate have not been badly worn or scored. A clutch will wear according to the way in which it is used. Much intentional slipping of the clutch while driving - rather than the correct selection of gears - will accelerate wear. It is best to assume, however, that the friction disc will need renewal every 35,000 miles (56,000 km) at least and that it will be worth replacing it after 25,000 miles (40,000 km). The maintenance history of the car is obviously very useful in such cases.

2 Examine the surfaces of the pressure plate and flywheel for signs of scoring. If this is only light it may be left, but if very deep the pressure plate unit will have to be renewed. If the flywheel is deeply scored it should be taken off and advice sought from an engineering firm. Providing it may be machined completely across the face the overall balance of engine and flywheel should not be too severely upset. If renewal of the flywheel is necessary the new one will have to be balanced to match the original.

3 The friction plate lining surfaces should be at least 1/32 inch (0.8 mm) above the rivets, otherwise the disc is not worth putting back. If the lining material shows signs of breaking up or black areas where oil contamination has occurred it should also be renewed. If facilities are readily available for obtaining and

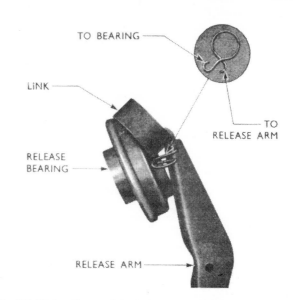

Fig. 5.7. Fitting diagram for clutch release bearing springs and link

fitting new friction pads to the existing disc this may be done but the saving is relatively small compared with obtaining a complete new disc assembly which ensures that the shock absorbing springs and the splined hub are renewed also. The same applies to the pressure plate assembly which cannot be readily dismantled and put back together without specialised tools and balancing equipment. An allowance is usually given for exchange units.

11 Clutch release bearing - renewal

1 To remove the clutch release bearing, disconnect the retracting spring, remove the spring clip securing the gaiter and detach the gaiter. Pull the forked end of the release arm from the spring clips and link of the release bearing hub and disengage the arm from the fulcrum pin. Pull the hub off the main drive gear bearing retainer and withdraw the release arm.

2 The clutch release bearing assembly is a light press fit on the hub and to dismantle, hold the bearing downwards and tap the shoulder of the hub sharply on the bench. Check that the release arm fork spring clips on the rear face of the hub are sound and assemble the new bearing on the hub with the thrust face away from the hub. Press the hub into position, ensuring that it enters squarely into the bearing bore.

3 Pass the clutch release arm through the opening in the side of the clutch housing with the fulcrum pin spring clip facing to the rear and engage the clip around the pin head. Check carefully that the machined sleeve of the gearbox main shaft bearing is free from burrs and dirt, then lightly smear the sleeve with high melting point grease and replace the release bearing assembly, engaging the fork in the end of the release arm with the spring clips and link on the hub. Check the movement on the outer end of the clutch release arm.

12 Clutch spigot bearing - inspection and renewal

Before refitting the clutch assembly, examine the spigot bush in the centre of the crankshaft rear flange upon which the flywheel is mounted. If the bush requires renewal, a thread should be tapped into it and a bolt screwed in to extract it. Tap the new bush into position making sure it enters squarely. The bush is impregnated with lubricant during manufacture and requires no attention in service.

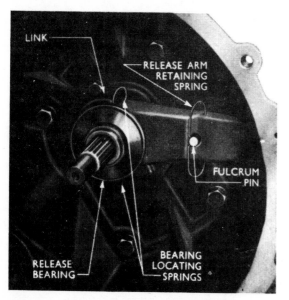

Fig. 5.6. Clutch release bearing mechanism

13 Clutch - refitting

1 It is important that no oil or grease gets on the clutch disc friction linings, or the pressure plate and flywheel faces. It is advisable to replace the clutch with clean hands and to wipe down the pressure plate and flywheel faces with a clean, dry rag before assembly begins.

2 Place the clutch disc against the flywheel with the shorter end of the hub, which is the end with the chamfered splines, facing the flywheel. On no account should the clutch disc be replaced with the longer end of the centre hub facing the flywheel as on reassembly it will be found quite impossible to operate the clutch in this position.

3 Replace the clutch cover assembly loosely on the three dowels. Replace the six bolts and spring washers and tighten them finger tight so that the clutch disc is gripped but can still be moved.

4 The clutch disc must now be centralised so that when the engine and gearbox are mated the gearbox input shaft splines will pass through the splines in the centre of the driven plate hub.

5 Centralisation can be carried out quite easily by inserting a round bar or old gearbox input shaft through the hole in the centre of the clutch so that the end of the bar rests in the small hole in the end of the crankshaft containing the input shaft bearing bush.

6 Using the input shaft bearing bush as a fulcrum, moving the bar sideways or up and down will move the clutch disc in whichever direction is necessary to achieve centralisation.

7 Centralisation is easily judged by removing the bar and viewing the driven plate hub in relation to the hole in the release bearing. When the hub appears exactly in the centre of the release bearing hole all is correct.

8 Tighten the clutch bolts in a diagonal sequence to ensure that the cover plate is pulled down evenly and without distortion of the flange. (Tightening torque 12 to 15 lb ft/1.6 to 2.0 kg m).

9 Mate the engine and gearbox and check that the clutch is operating properly.

14 Clutch faults

There are four main faults to which the clutch and release mechanism are prone. They may occur by themselves or in conjunction with any of the other faults. They are: clutch squeal; slip; spin; and judder, and reference should be made to the following chart to establish the cause of such symptoms.

15 Fault diagnosis - clutch

Symptom	Reason/s	Remedy
Judder when taking up drive	Loose engine or gearbox mountings	Tighten and inspect rubber insulators for deterioration.
	Badly worn friction surfaces or contaminated with oil	Renew driven plate and rectify oil leakage, probably crankshaft rear oil seal or input shaft oil seal.
	Worn splines on gearbox input shaft or driven plate hub	Renew component.
	Worn input shaft spigot bush in flywheel	Extract old and fit new bush.
Clutch spin (failure to disengage) so that gears cannot be meshed	Incorrect release bearing to pressure plate clearance	Adjust clearance at slave cylinder pushrod.
	Driven plate sticking on input shaft splines due to rust. May occur after vehicle standing idle for long period	As temporary remedy, engage top gear, apply handbrake, depress clutch and start engine. If driven plate badly stuck, engine will not turn. When engine running, rev up and slip clutch until normal clutch disengagement is possible. Renew driven plate at earliest opportunity.
	Damaged or misaligned pressure plate assembly	Renew pressure plate assembly.
Clutch slip (increase in engine speed does not result in increase in vehicle road speed - particularly on gradients)	Incorrect release bearing to pressure plate clearance	Adjust clearance at slave cylinder pushrod.
	Friction surfaces worn out or oil contaminated	Renew driven plate and rectify oil leakage.
Noise evident on depressing clutch pedal	Dry, worn or damaged release bearing	Renew bearing.
	Insufficient pedal free travel	Adjust.
	Weak or broken pedal return spring	Renew.
	Weak or broken clutch release lever return spring	Renew.
	Excessive play between driven plate hub splines and input shaft splines	Renew both components.
Noise evident as clutch pedal released	Distorted driven plate	Renew.
	Broken or weak driven plate cushion coil springs	Renew driven plate as an assembly.
	Insufficient pedal free travel	Adjust.
	Weak or broken clutch pedal return spring	Renew.
	Weak or broken release lever return spring	Renew.
	Distorted or worn input shaft	Renew input shaft (see Chapter 6) and driven plate if necessary.
	Release bearing loose on retainer hub	Renew hub and bearing.
	Friction surfaces worn down to rivets	Renew driven plate.

Chapter 6 Gearbox and automatic transmission

Contents

Specifications

Manual gearbox

Type	Constant mesh; four forward speeds and reverse; synchromesh on all forward gears
Gear selection methods (see Section 1)	Direct floor mounted lever Steering column lever Remote control (floor mounted)

Gear ratios:

	Standard and GT	Overall	
		Standard	GT
First	3.543 : 1	14.615 : 1	13.818 : 1
Second	2.396 : 1	9.883 : 1	9.344 : 1
Third	1.412 : 1	5.824 : 1	5.507 : 1
Fourth	1.0 : 1	4.125 : 1	3.900 : 1
Reverse	3.963 : 1	16.347 : 1	15.456 : 1

Tolerances

Countershaft gear endfloat	0.008 - 0.020 in (0.203 - 0.508 mm)
First and second gear endfloat	0.005 - 0.010 in (0.127 - 0.254 mm)
Third gear endfloat	0.005 - 0.016 in (0.127 - 0.406 mm)

Main drive gear circlip availability

0.0870 - 0.0899 in (2.210 - 2.284 mm)	Green
0.0900 - 0.0929 in (2.286 - 2.36 mm)	Black
0.0930 - 0.0959 in (2.362 - 2.436 mm)	Blue
0.0960 - 0.0989 in (2.438 - 2.512 mm)	Orange

Oil capacity	1.75 pints (1 litre)

Automatic transmission

Type	Borg-Warner 35

Ratios:

First	2.39 : 1
Second	1.45 : 1
Third	1 : 1
Reverse	2.09 : 1

Shift speeds (mph):

	1 – 2	2 – 3	3 – 2	3 – 1	2 – 1
D selected					
Minimum throttle	6	13	6	–	2
Full throttle	20	40	15	2	2
'Kickdown'	31	55	45	25	25
L selected	–	–	8	8	8

Fluid capacity	11¾ pints (6.7 litres)
Fluid operating temperature	100 - 115°C (212 - 240°F)

Torque wrench settings

	lb ft	kg m
Manual gearbox		
Gearbox filler and drain plugs	25 - 30	3.46 - 4.15
Mainshaft retaining nut	20 - 25	2.76 - 3.46
Extension housing to gearbox bolts	20 - 25	2.76 - 3.46
Bellhousing to gear casing bolts	40 - 45	5.53 - 6.22
Abutment housing to extension housing (gearchange cables)	15 - 18	2.07 - 2.49
Clutch bellhousing to engine	40	5.53
Automatic transmission		
Torque converter to driveplate	25 - 30	3.46 - 4.14
Converter housing to transmission casing	10	1.38
Extension housing to transmission casing	10	1.38
Oil pan to transmission casing	10	1.38
Filler tube sleeve nut	18	2.48
Stoneguard bolts	18	2.48
Torque converter housing to engine	30	4.15
Driveplate to crankshaft flange	50	6.91

Part 1: Manual Gearbox

1 General description (manual gearbox)

The gearbox fitted to all models is similar except for variations in gearchange and selector mechanisms. Standard Cortina models have a 'direct' floor mounted gearchange lever.

Standard and deluxe Corsair models have a steering column gearshift and this is optionally available on the deluxe versions of the Cortina.

GT versions of the Cortina and Corsair have a remote type floor control and this is optionally available on deluxe Corsair models.

The gearbox is of constant mesh type having four forward speeds and reverse. Synchromesh is provided on all forward speeds.

2 Gearbox (floor gearchange - 'direct' type) - removal and refitting

1 Drain the oil from the gearbox.
2 Disconnect the lead from the battery positive terminal.
3 Disconnect the lead from the starter motor terminal.
4 Unscrew and remove the starter motor bolts and withdraw the starter motor.
5 Unscrew and remove the bolts which secure the clutch bellhousing to the engine. Note the earth strap which is located beneath one of the upper bolts and the engine rear plate is secured by the three lower bolts.
6 Remove the clutch operating cylinder assembly from its bellhousing location as described in the preceding Chapter. There

is no need to disconnect the hydraulic pipe if care is taken not to displace the piston from the cylinder.
7 Unscrew the bolt from the speedometer cable retainer on the gearbox extension housing and withdraw the speedometer cable.
8 Mark the edges of the propeller shaft rear flange and the rear axle pinion driving flange and then remove the four bolts. Pull the propeller shaft slightly forward to separate the two flanges and then lower the rear of the shaft and withdraw it rearwards so that the front sleeve is drawn off the gearbox mainshaft splines.
9 Inside the car, place the gearchange lever in the neutral position and remove the four self-tapping screws which secure the retainer and gearlever gaiter in position. Push the gaiter up the lever, unscrew the cap and lift the lever from the gearbox.
10 Support the engine sump with a jack and a block of wood and unless the car is over a pit or standing on ramps, the rear should be jacked up and supported on stands or blocks to provide clearance to withdraw the gearbox from below and to the rear of the car.
11 Using a jack, preferably of the trolley type, support the gearbox and then remove the gearbox rear mounting from both the gearbox and the bodyframe (photo).
12 Carefully lower the engine and gearbox jacks until the gearbox bellhousing will clear the lower edge of the engine compartment rear bulkhead and then withdraw the gearbox to the rear. Do not allow the weight of the gearbox to hang upon the input shaft while it is still engaged with the splines of the driven plate or damage to the clutch mechanism will result.
13 Refitting is a reversal of removal. Centralise the clutch driven plate if the clutch assembly has been disturbed, as described in Chapter 5.
14 Adjust the clutch release arm free movement as described in Chapter 5.

2.11 Gearbox rear mounting

15 Refill the gearbox with the correct quantity and grade of oil.
16 When reconnecting the propeller shaft and pinion drive flanges, align the marks made on removal.

3 Gearbox (column gearchange type) - removal and refitting

1 Carry out operations 1 to 8 as described in the preceding Section.
2 Support the engine sump with a jack and a block of wood and unless the car is standing over a pit or on ramps, jack up the rear and support on stands or blocks to provide clearance to withdraw the gearbox from below and to the rear of the car.
3 Support the gearbox, preferably on a trolley type jack, and remove the rear gearbox mounting from both the gearbox and the body frame.
4 Inside the car, remove the inspection plate from the transmission tunnel.
5 Lower the gearbox and engine support jacks slightly and withdraw the four bolts which secure the cable abutment housing to the top of the gearbox extension. One bolt acts as a breather, check that it is clear.
6 Slacken and remove the gearchange cable rear collar nuts and their locknuts.
7 Lift out the cable abutment housing, easing the cables clear of the selector shafts. Place the housing to one side of the gearbox.
8 Carry out operation 12 described in the preceding Section.
9 Refitting is a reversal of removal but if the clutch driven plate has been disturbed it must be centralised as described in Chapter 5. Special attention must also be given to the selector cable mechanism as described in the following paragraphs.
10 Ensure that the forward collar nuts and their locknuts on the cable adjustment housing end of the cables are screwed in to their fullest extent.
11 Locate the cable abutment housing so that the rear clears the ends of the gearchange shaft forks. Check that the threaded ends of the cables enter the forks.
12 Bolt the cable abutment housing to the gearbox extension and then push all the cables forward towards the gate housing.
13 The rubber plug must now be removed from the gate housing and a special Ford adjustment setting tool obtained (No 7115). Check that the scribed line on the tool is at the top and apply slight hand pressure to it.
14 Pull each cable in turn rearward until the stop can be felt at the gauge. Commence operations on the left hand cable and when all the cables are correctly positioned, push the gauge fully home.
15 Fit the rear collar nuts and locknuts to the ends of the cables. Screw all the collar nuts (both front and rear) up to the shaft forks finger tight and then unscrew them between ½ and 1

flat each.
16 Tighten the locknuts and using feeler gauges, check the clearance between the faces of the collar nuts and the shaft forks. This should be between 0.006 and 0.012 inch (0.152 and 0.305 mm).
17 Remove the setting tool and refit the rubber plug.
18 Carry out the remainder of the refitting procedure including those items contained in paragraphs 14, 15 and 16 of Section 2.
19 Refit the cable abutment housing cover (two bolts) and secure the transmission tunnel inspection plate.

4 Gearbox (floor gearchange - remote type) - removal and refitting

1 Removal of this type of unit is similar to that described in Section 2 except that the remote control mechanism must first be removed.
2 Withdraw both front seats to the rear as far as possible.
3 Remove the screw from the lower rear corner of each heater outlet panel and the two countersunk headed screws from the rear of the console.
4 Unscrew the gear lever knob and raise the rear of the console until it clears the gear lever. Now pull it to the rear and to the right to remove it from contact with the remote control housing. If it is wished to remove the console completely then the instrument connecting wires will have to be disconnected noting the position of the leads carefully for correct reconnection.
5 Remove the bracket (two screws) from the rear of the draught excluder and withdraw the carpet from the remote control housing. Remove the draught excluder retainer.
6 Place the gear lever in the neutral position and unscrew and remove the four bolts which secure the remote control housing to the gearbox extension housing. Note that one of the bolts serves as a breather which should be checked to see that it is clear.
7 Unhook the handbrake secondary cable from the lower end of the relay lever and disengage it from the eyelet on the gearbox mounting crossmember.
8 Refitting is a reversal of removal but any special attention to refitting the remote control gearchange as described in the following paragraphs.
9 Lift the gear lever against its spring over the reverse stop and engage the selector arm with the slot in the reverse gear relay lever. The gearbox must be in neutral.

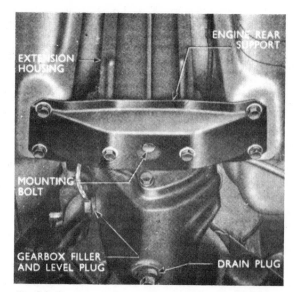

Fig. 6.1. Gearbox rear mounting and location of drain and filler plugs

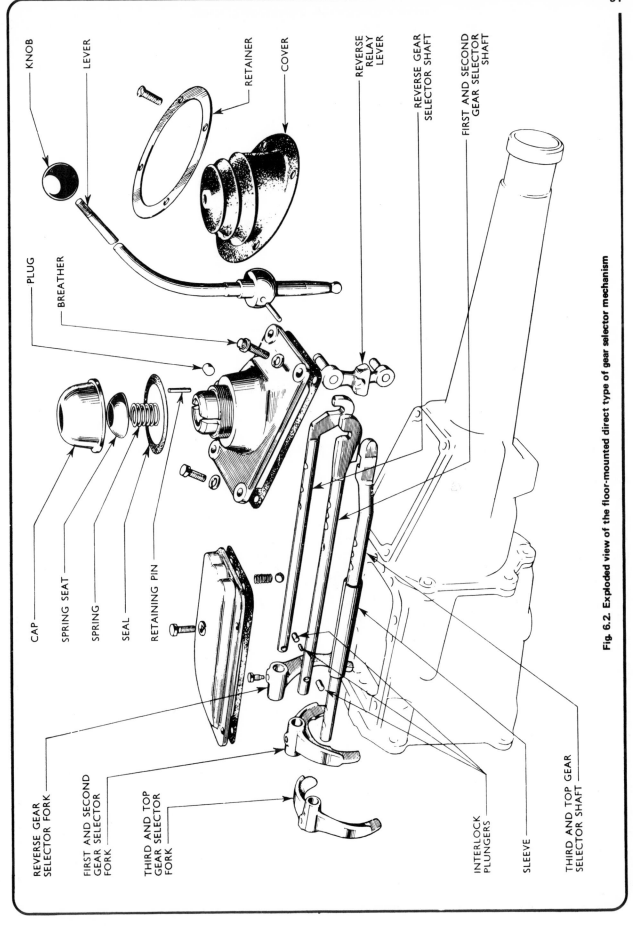

Fig. 6.2. Exploded view of the floor-mounted direct type of gear selector mechanism

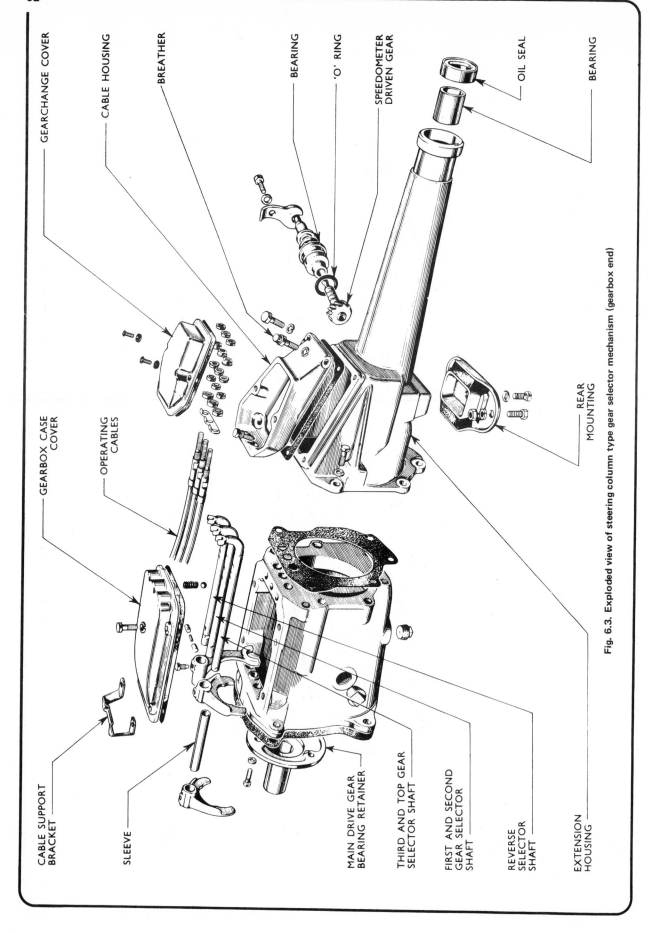

GEARCHANGE COVER

CABLE HOUSING

BREATHER

BEARING

'O' RING

SPEEDOMETER DRIVEN GEAR

OIL SEAL

BEARING

GEARBOX CASE COVER

OPERATING CABLES

REAR MOUNTING

CABLE SUPPORT BRACKET

SLEEVE

MAIN DRIVE GEAR BEARING RETAINER

THIRD AND TOP GEAR SELECTOR SHAFT

FIRST AND SECOND GEAR SELECTOR SHAFT

REVERSE SELECTOR SHAFT

EXTENSION HOUSING

Fig. 6.3. Exploded view of steering column type gear selector mechanism (gearbox end)

10 Fit a new gasket to the extension housing and holding the selector arm in the previously set position, fit the remote control housing so that the relay lever engages with the reverse gear selector shaft.

11 Screw in the four securing bolts, ensuring that the breather bolt is fitted to the left rear position. Tighten them evenly.

12 Refit the draught excluder, console and carpet, making sure that the instrument leads are correctly reconnected.

5 Gearbox - dismantling

1 It must be emphasised that before commencing to dismantle the gearbox, the correct tools and extractors must be to hand. Where these are not available, then operations should be limited to removal of the main sub assemblies (mainshaft and countershaft).

2 Remove the release bearing and operating mechanism as described in the preceding Chapter.

3 Unscrew and remove the four bolts which secure the clutch bellhousing to the gearbox casing.

4 With direct floor-mounted gearchange lever gearboxes only, remove the gear lever housing (four bolts) noting that the rear left hand bolt acts as a breather. If the reverse relay lever must be removed from the gear lever housing, invert the housing and tap it on a piece of wood to extract the dowel which retains the lever.

5 Remove the gearbox top cover (four bolts), lifting it carefully as the selector shaft locking springs are normally stuck in the holes in the cover.

6 Extract the balls from their locations in the holes in the casing top face.

7 Ensure that the gearbox is in the neutral mode and then cut and remove the locking wire from the taper bolts which secure the selector forks to their shafts.

8 Withdraw the third/fourth selector shaft to the rear, at the same time supporting the sleeve which is fitted to the shaft.

9 Withdraw the first/second selector shaft, at the same time removing the pin from the drilling at the forward end of the shaft. Turn the shaft through 90° and withdraw it from the gearbox casing.

10 Withdraw the reverse selector shaft to the rear, turning it through 90° to prevent it from fouling the extension housing.

11 Lift the selector forks from their gear grooves and then extract the two interlock plungers from the front face of the gearbox casing.

12 Unscrew the five bolts which secure the extension housing to the gearbox casing.

13 Remove the speedometer driven gear and the gear bearing from the extension housing.

14 Withdraw the extension housing and at the same time mark the sandwich plate and gearbox casing to facilitate mating on reassembly.

15 Using a brass drift, drive the countershaft towards the rear of the gearbox until it is no longer in contact with the front face of the gearbox.

16 Using a longer drift to act as a dummy countershaft, push the countershaft out of the rear of the gearbox. With the dummy countershaft still in position through the centre of the thrust washers, countershaft gear and needle rollers, the countershaft gear assembly can lie at the bottom of the gearbox casing until the mainshaft is withdrawn.

17 The mainshaft may now be withdrawn towards the rear and during removal, take off the top gear blocker ring; also extract the thirteen needle rollers from inside the main drive gear.

18 Unscrew and remove the three bolts from the main drive gear bearing retainer - which is located on the front face of the gearbox. Wind masking tape over the main drive gear splines so that, as the retainer is withdrawn, the oil seal will not be damaged.

19 Extract the main drive gear bearing outer circlip and tap out the main drive gear.

20 Lift the countershaft gear and the two thrust washers from the bottom of the gearbox casing. The dummy countershaft will still be in position in the assembly at this stage and it may now be withdrawn to release the twenty needle rollers at each end of the countershaft cluster gear. Note the washer used at each end to retain the needle rollers.

21 Withdraw the reverse idler shaft by screwing a 5/16 inch 24 UNF 2 bolt into the tapped hole in its end face and then using a nut, washer and a piece of tube as a distance piece, extract the shaft by tightening the nut.

22 The gearbox has now been dismantled into its major components and further work should not be attempted (as described in Section 7) unless the necessary press and support plates are available. Carry out the inspection described in the next Section and if necessary take the mainshaft and main drive gear to your Ford dealer for the removal of any worn components and the fitment of replacements.

Fig. 6.4. Location of cable setting tool (steering column gearchange)

Fig. 6.5. Cable adjustment nuts at gearbox end (steering column gearchange)

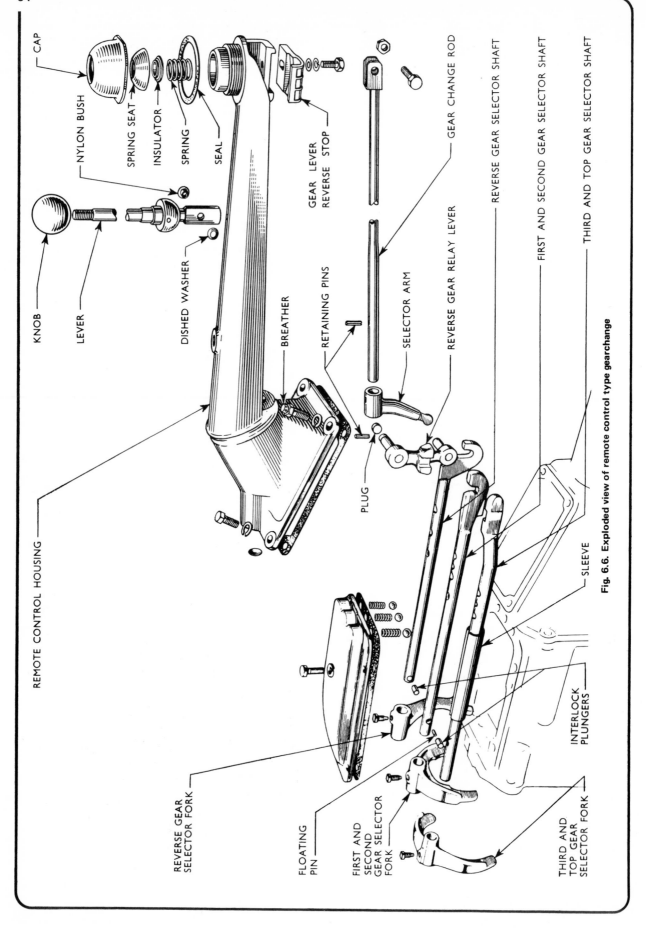

CAP

NYLON BUSH

SPRING SEAT

INSULATOR

SPRING

SEAL

GEAR LEVER REVERSE STOP

GEAR CHANGE ROD

REVERSE GEAR SELECTOR SHAFT

FIRST AND SECOND GEAR SELECTOR SHAFT

THIRD AND TOP GEAR SELECTOR SHAFT

KNOB

LEVER

DISHED WASHER

BREATHER

RETAINING PINS

SELECTOR ARM

REVERSE GEAR RELAY LEVER

PLUG

REMOTE CONTROL HOUSING

SLEEVE

REVERSE GEAR SELECTOR FORK

FLOATING PIN

FIRST AND SECOND GEAR SELECTOR FORK

THIRD AND TOP GEAR SELECTOR FORK

INTERLOCK PLUNGERS

Fig. 6.6. Exploded view of remote control type gearchange

6 Gearbox - inspection

1   Inspect each component for wear, chipped or worn teeth or splines and renew as appropriate.
2   Check the ball races for shake or wear also the needle rollers and thrust washers.
3   Check the synchromesh units for wear, although, if these are worn, their condition would have been noticed through poor gear changing when operating the vehicle prior to gearbox dismantling.
4   Examine the gearbox casing for cracks particularly around shaft, bearing and bolt holes.
5   With the gearbox completely dismantled, renew the front and rear extension oil seals as a matter of course.

7 Mainshaft and main drive gear - dismantling and reassembly

1   It will be found that there is a thrust washer machined on the mainshaft which abuts the second gear on one side, so that

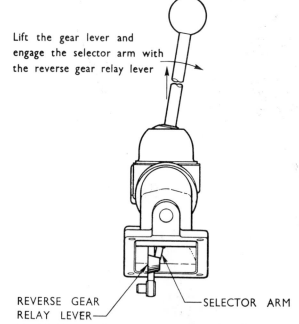

Lift the gear lever and engage the selector arm with the reverse gear relay lever

REVERSE GEAR RELAY LEVER — SELECTOR ARM

Fig. 6.7. Engaging the remote control type of gear lever

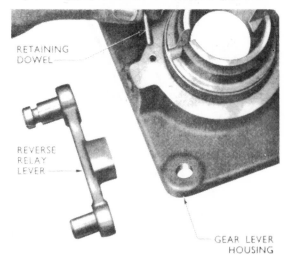

RETAINING DOWEL

REVERSE RELAY LEVER

GEAR LEVER HOUSING

Fig. 6.8. Reverse relay lever and retaining dowel (direct floor-mounted type gearchange housing)

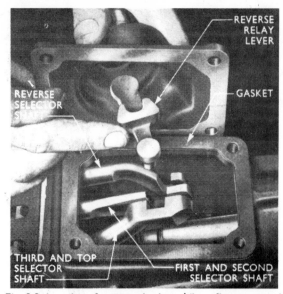

REVERSE RELAY LEVER

GASKET

REVERSE SELECTOR SHAFT

THIRD AND TOP SELECTOR SHAFT

FIRST AND SECOND SELECTOR SHAFT

Fig. 6.9. Location of reverse relay lever (direct floor-mounted gearchange)

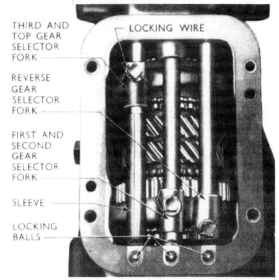

THIRD AND TOP GEAR SELECTOR FORK

REVERSE GEAR SELECTOR FORK

FIRST AND SECOND GEAR SELECTOR FORK

SLEEVE

LOCKING BALLS

LOCKING WIRE

Fig. 6.10. Gear selector shafts, forks and locking balls

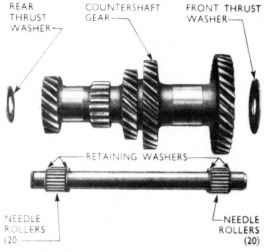

REAR THRUST WASHER

COUNTERSHAFT GEAR

FRONT THRUST WASHER

RETAINING WASHERS

NEEDLE ROLLERS (20)

NEEDLE ROLLERS (20)

Fig. 6.11. Countershaft gear components

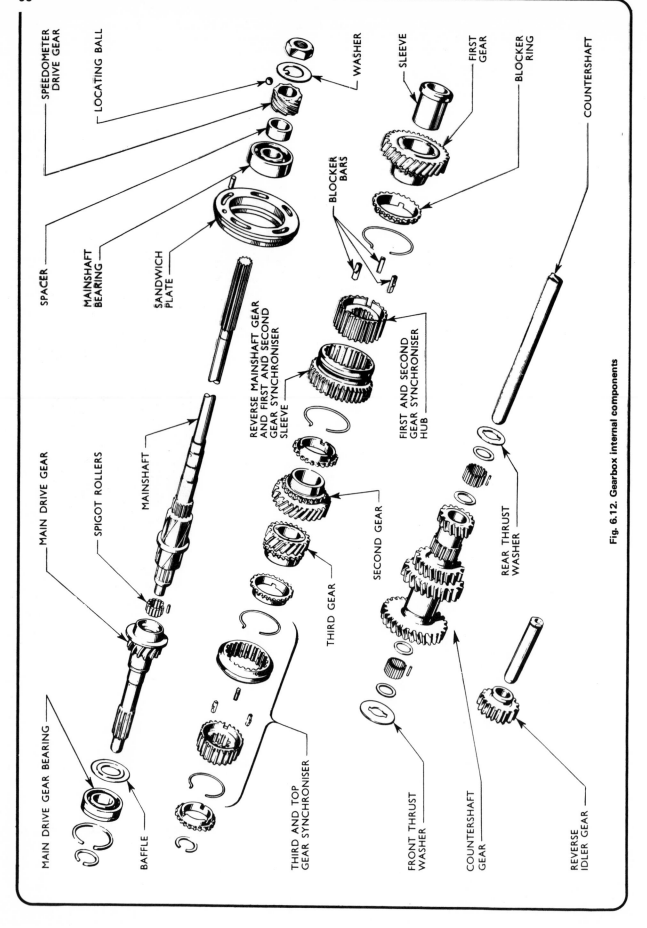

Fig. 6.12. Gearbox internal components

SPEEDOMETER DRIVE GEAR

LOCATING BALL

WASHER

SLEEVE

FIRST GEAR

BLOCKER RING

COUNTERSHAFT

BLOCKER BARS

SPACER

MAINSHAFT BEARING

SANDWICH PLATE

REVERSE MAINSHAFT GEAR AND FIRST AND SECOND GEAR SYNCHRONISER SLEEVE

FIRST AND SECOND GEAR SYNCHRONISER HUB

MAIN DRIVE GEAR

SPIGOT ROLLERS

MAINSHAFT

SECOND GEAR

REAR THRUST WASHER

THIRD GEAR

MAIN DRIVE GEAR BEARING

BAFFLE

THIRD AND TOP GEAR SYNCHRONISER

FRONT THRUST WASHER

COUNTERSHAFT GEAR

REVERSE IDLER GEAR

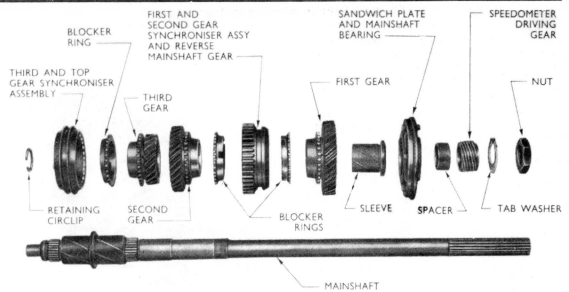

Fig. 6.13. Exploded view of the mainshaft

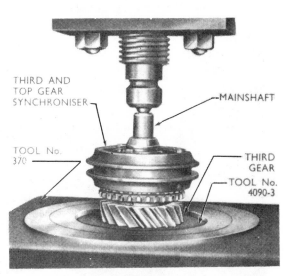

Fig. 6.14. Pressing off third gear from the mainshaft

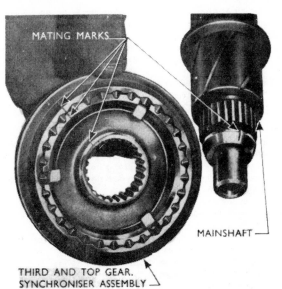

Fig. 6.15. Synchro unit and mainshaft mating marks

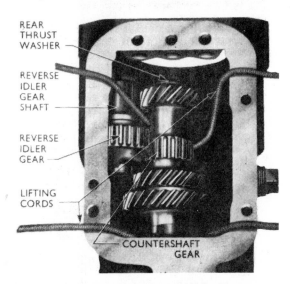

Fig. 6.16. Supporting the countershaft gear with a piece of cord

Fig. 6.17. Fitting the main drive bearing retainer

providing the correct tools are available, it is possible to remove the gears from one side of this thrust washer without disturbing the cluster of gears on the opposite side.

2 Release the tab washer and unscrew the nut securing the speedometer drive gear and then extract the locating ball and remove the spacer.

3 Now remove the third gear and the third and top synchroniser assembly, remove the small circlip from the forward end of the mainshaft.

4 Using semi-circular adaptor plates (Ford tool P.4090-3) located behind the rear face of third gear, press the mainshaft from the synchroniser unit, the latter being supported to prevent it from dropping.

5 Next, locate the same tool around the front face of the second gear in order to press the mainshaft bearing together with the sandwich plate, first and second gears and the synchronisers on the mainshaft.

6 It will be found that the synchroniser hubs and sleeves are mated together and also to the mainshaft, and mating marks are provided on the splines of the hub and sleeve and near the hub and mainshaft splines.

7 The synchroniser and hub assembly are serviced as a unit and must be fitted as such.

8 Dismantle the main drive gear by extracting the circlip and then supporting the rear face of the bearing inner track, press the drive gear from the bearing.

9 Commence reassembly of the mainshaft by fitting second gear so that the dog teeth are towards the rear. Fit the blocker ring onto the cone face.

10 The first and second gear synchroniser unit is then fitted over the hub, making certain that the mating marks are in line, and then locate a blocker bar in each of the three slots in the hub.

11 Now fit a blocker bar spring in one bar, then note the direction of rotation of the spring and fit the other spring to the opposite face of the unit, making sure that the spring tag locates in the same blocker bar as the first spring inserted, but with this second spring running in the opposite direction. The other end of each spring is left free.

12 Next, locate the first and second gear synchroniser on the mainshaft with the selector fork groove to the rear and with the mating splines of the hub and shaft corresponding.

13 Fit a blocker ring in the synchroniser so that the cut-outs in this ring locate over the blocker bars.

14 Locate the hardened steel bush in the first gear with the shoulder of the bush away from the dog teeth, and then fit this assembly onto the mainshaft so that the dog teeth are adjacent to the blocker ring of the first and second gear synchroniser.

15 Position the sandwich plate on the mainshaft with the dowel hole to the rear and fit the mainshaft bearing, and then ease the sandwich plate towards the rear in order to fit it over the bearing.

16 Using a press and suitable support plates, ensure that the cut-outs in the second gear blocker ring are in line with the blocker bars in the first and second gear synchroniser, and that the mating marks on the mainshaft and hub are still in line before gently pressing the mainshaft down until the bearing and the first and second gear synchroniser are home.

17 Make sure that the first and second gears are free to rotate.

18 Next slide the third gear onto the shaft with the dog teeth away from the thrust collar and locate the blocker ring on the taper face of the gear. Locate the third and top gear synchroniser hub on the mainshaft with the long boss toward the front, and make sure that the mating marks are in line. Support the third and top gear synchroniser hub on the support tool and press the hub home on the shaft and then fit the circlip in its groove.

19 Fit the synchroniser sleeve on the hub, locate the blocker bar in each of the three cut-out slots in the hub, install one blocker bar spring so that the tag end locates in a blocker bar with the other end of the spring left free. Note the direction of rotation of this spring and then fit the other spring at the front face of the synchroniser with the tag of this spring locating in the same blocker bar as the first spring fitted, but running in the opposite direction.

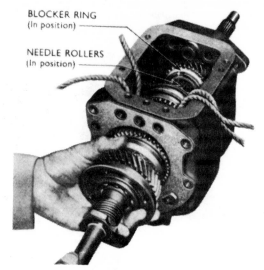

Fig. 6.18. Installing the mainshaft

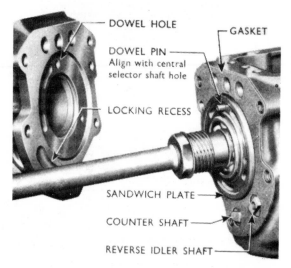

Fig. 6.19. Refitting the gearbox extension housing

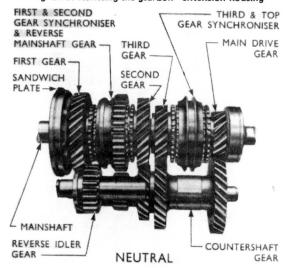

Fig. 6.20. Gears set in neutral mode

20 Slide the spacer onto the mainshaft, install the locating ball for the speedometer drive and fit the gear with the shoulder towards the rear. Fit a new tab washer over the shaft and locate the tab on the inner diameter into the groove on the inside of the drive gear. Screw on the nut and tighten to a torque of 20 lb ft (2.765 kg m).

21 On early models, install the oil slinger in the main drive gear so that the outer edge is dished towards the gear. On later models an oil slinger is not fitted.

22 Position the main drive gear bearing on the gear with the circlip groove away from the gear, support the assembly on the tool adaptors and press the bearing home on the gear. Fit the circlip in the groove and then check the clearance between the inner race and the circlip, which should be 0.002 inch (0.0508 mm). If the clearance is greater, then a thicker circlip should be used.

8 Gearbox - reassembly

1   Reassemble the countershaft in the reverse order to dismantling and position the countershaft assembly in the gearbox, passing two pieces of cord around the ends of this shaft to assist refitting.

2   Fit the main drive gear into the gearbox with the large circlip in its locating groove in the bearing and then fit the bearing retainer in the reverse order to dismantling.

3   Next install the reverse idler gear and its shaft and then install the thirteen needle rollers over the taper face of the top gear.

4   Position the blocker ring over the taper face of the top gear, and place the gasket in position before passing the mainshaft assembly through the rear of the gearbox.

5   Locate the spigot of the mainshaft on the needle rollers in the bore of the main drive, and note particularly that, as the mainshaft is gently tapped in, the sandwich plate will fit into the recess machined in the gearbox.

6   The countershaft can now be fitted in position with the aid of the pieces of cord which allow the gear to be lifted into mesh with the mainshaft gears. Take care that the thrust washers are not disturbed as the shaft is fitted.

7   Finally, refit the extension housing making sure that the dowel in the sandwich plate locates in the hole provided in the housing. Use a new gasket.

8   It is an advantage to apply a sealer to all the bolts which penetrate through the gearbox casing in order to prevent oil leakage.

9   Refit and bolt-up the clutch bellhousing.

10 Check that all gears slide easily and can be obtained and then set the gears in the neutral mode.

11 Assemble the clutch release mechanism as described in Chapter 5.

12 Now refit the selector mechanism by first ensuring that the interlock plungers are correctly located in the front face of the gearbox. If they have been withdrawn then the plug will have to be removed from the right hand side of the gearbox. Use a rod as a guide and insert the three plungers into their correct positions in the gearbox casing cross drillings. Always fit a new expansion plug.

13 Locate the selector forks on the gears, check that the gears are still in neutral and install the reverse selector shaft and then turn it through 90º.

14 Install first/second selector shaft, turning it through 90º to prevent it impinging on the extension housing. Before pushing this shaft fully home, ensure that the floating pin is located in the shaft and then set the shaft in the neutral position. Align the hole in the shaft with the bolt hole in the selector fork and screw in the taper bolt. Tighten it fully and lock it with wire.

15 Repeat the foregoing operation with the reverse selector fork.

16 Install third/top selector shaft, remembering to install the sleeve on the shaft before pushing it through the fork. Fit and tighten the taper bolt and lock with wire.

17 Locate a new gasket on the top face of the gearbox and insert

the selector shaft locking balls and springs. Fit the cover plate, ensuring that the springs are correctly retained by the cover plate drillings.

18 With floor-mounted type gearchange lever gearboxes, locate the spigot end of the reverse relay lever in its hole in the lever housing. Align the groove in this spigot with the dowel pin hole in the gear lever housing and insert the dowel pin until it is flush with the machined face of the gear lever housing. Using a new gasket, fit the gear lever housing to the extension housing, making sure that the reverse relay lever engages with the reverse selector fork.

19 With steering column change and remote control type gearboxes, refit the gearchange mechanism as described in Sections 3 or 4 after the gearbox has been installed.

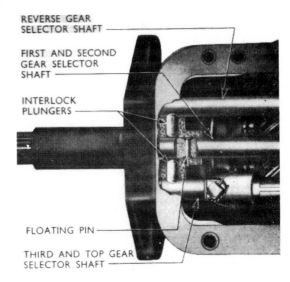

Fig. 6.21. Cut-away view of interlock plungers

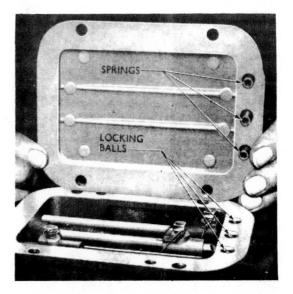

Fig. 6.22. Gearbox top cover, selector shaft locking balls and springs

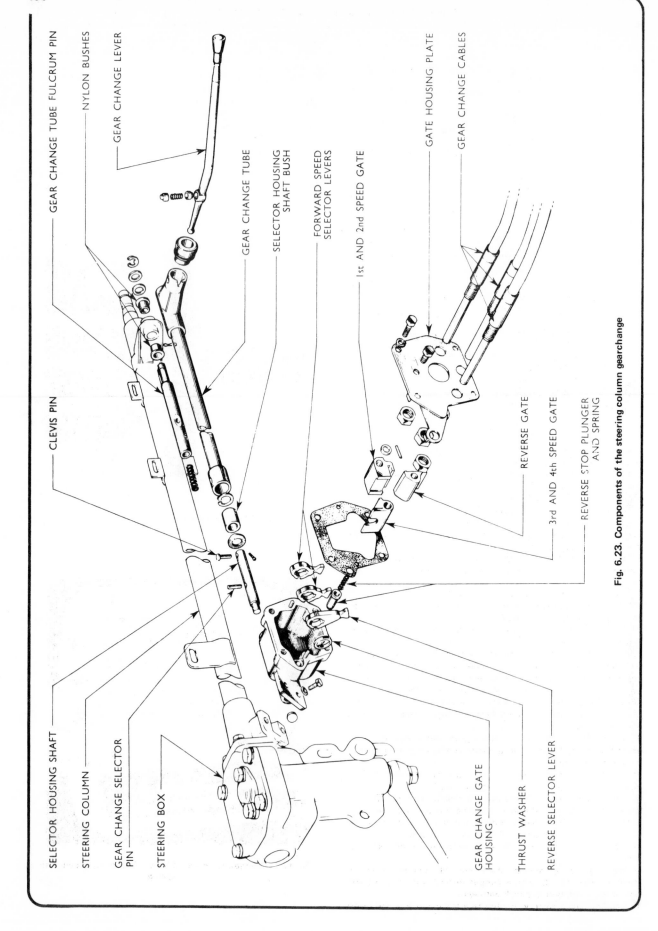

SELECTOR HOUSING SHAFT

STEERING COLUMN

GEAR CHANGE SELECTOR PIN

STEERING BOX

CLEVIS PIN

GEAR CHANGE TUBE FULCRUM PIN

NYLON BUSHES

GEAR CHANGE LEVER

GEAR CHANGE TUBE

SELECTOR HOUSING SHAFT BUSH

FORWARD SPEED SELECTOR LEVERS

1st AND 2nd SPEED GATE

GATE HOUSING PLATE

GEAR CHANGE CABLES

REVERSE GATE

3rd AND 4th SPEED GATE

REVERSE STOP PLUNGER AND SPRING

GEAR CHANGE GATE HOUSING

THRUST WASHER

REVERSE SELECTOR LEVER

Fig. 6.23. Components of the steering column gearchange

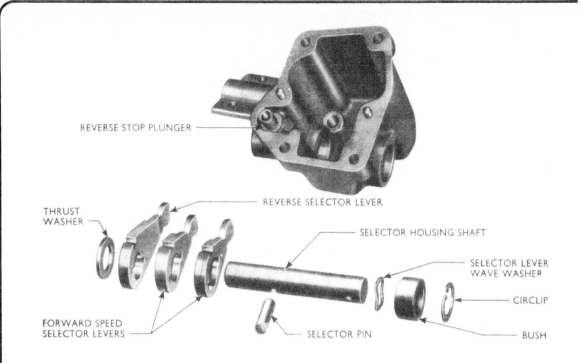

REVERSE STOP PLUNGER

THRUST WASHER

REVERSE SELECTOR LEVER

SELECTOR HOUSING SHAFT

SELECTOR LEVER WAVE WASHER

CIRCLIP

BUSH

FORWARD SPEED SELECTOR LEVERS

SELECTOR PIN

Fig. 6.24. Steering column gearchange selector levers and gate housing

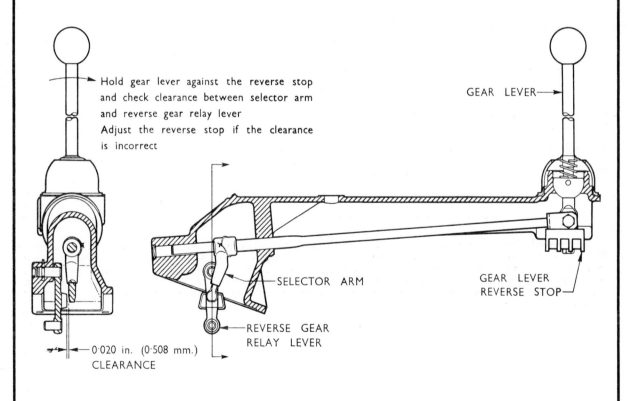

Hold gear lever against the reverse stop and check clearance between selector arm and reverse gear relay lever

Adjust the reverse stop if the clearance is incorrect

GEAR LEVER

SELECTOR ARM

GEAR LEVER REVERSE STOP

REVERSE GEAR RELAY LEVER

0·020 in. (0·508 mm.) CLEARANCE

Fig. 6.25. Reverse stop adjustment diagram (remote type gearchange control)

9 Steering column gearchange linkage - servicing

1 To remove the gearchange cable assembly, first release the handbrake and disconnect its cable by withdrawing the clevis from the relay lever slot.
2 Disconnect the selector housing shaft from the gearchange tube by withdrawing the split pin and clevis pin.
3 Remove the gate housing at the bottom of the steering column (two bolts).
4 Lift the gearchange tube clear of the selector housing shaft by depressing the gear lever beyond the reverse stop plunger and then lifting it right back.
5 Support the gearbox on a jack and remove the gearbox mounting and support crossmember.
6 Inside the car, remove the inspection plate from the transmission tunnel.
7 Lower the gearbox sufficiently to give access to the bolts which secure the cable abutment housing to the top of the gearbox extension housing.
8 Remove the collar nuts and locknuts from the rear ends of the cables.
9 Withdraw the assembly by removing the gate housing, the cables and the abutment housing from the engine compartment.
10 Commence dismantling by removing the gate housing plate (four bolts).
11 If the gates must be removed from their cables then drift out the tension pins.
12 Extract the circlip from the rear end of the selector shaft and remove the reverse stop plunger and spring from the gate housing.
13 Withdraw the shaft rearwards together with the selector pin.
14 Remove the housing shaft bush, the lever retaining washer and the three selector levers. Pick out the thrust washer from the recess in the housing.
15 Reassembly is a reversal of dismantling but note the following points. The selector lever slots face the cover plate. The larger (reverse) selector is located at the front.
16 On lhd vehicles, the reverse gearchange cable is longer than the other two.
17 During reassembly apply lithium based grease to the change gates and selector levers.
18 Adjust the cables as described in Section 3, paragraphs 10 to 19.

10 Remote control gearchange - servicing

1 Remove the remote control assembly as described in Section 4.
2 Remove the gear lever reverse stop (one bolt).
3 Disconnect the gear lever from the gearchange rod by removing the clevis nut and bolts. Retain the dished washer and nylon bush.
4 Unscrew the gearlever ball cap and remove the gear lever, cap, spring seat, insulator and spring.
5 Detach the locking wire and drive out the pin which retains the selector arm to the rod. Slide the rod out of the housing towards the rear.
6 If the reverse gear relay lever must be removed, extract the retaining pin from the remote control mounting flange and withdraw the lever.
7 Reassembly is a reversal of dismantling but observe the following points. Always use new retaining pins. Check that the reverse stop adjustment is as specified in Fig 6.25.
8 Refit the remote control assembly as described in Section 4.

11 Fault diagnosis - manual gearbox

Symptom	Reason/s	Remedy
Ineffective synchromesh	Worn baulk rings or synchro hubs	Dismantle and renew.
Jumps out of one or more gears (on drive or over-run)	Weak detent springs or worn selector forks or worn gears	Dismantle and renew.
Noisy, rough, whining and vibration	Worn bearings and/or thrust washers (initially) resulting in extended wear generally due to play and backlash	Dismantle and renew.
Noisy and difficult engagement of gears	Clutch fault	Examine clutch operation.

It is sometimes difficult to decide whether it is worthwhile removing and dismantling the gearbox for a fault which may be nothing more than a minor irritant. Gearboxes which howl, or where the synchromesh can be 'beaten' by a quick gear change, may continue to perform for a long time in this state. A worn gearbox usually needs a complete rebuild to eliminate noise because the various gears, if re-aligned on new bearings will continue to howl when different wearing surfaces are presented to each other.
The decision to overhaul therefore must be considered with regard to time and money available, relative to the degree of noise or malfunction that the driver has to suffer.

Part 2: Automatic Transmission

12 General description (automatic transmission)

Borg-Warner automatic transmission is fitted.

The automatic transmission system comprises two main components: a three-element hydrokinetic torque converter coupling capable of torque multiplication at an infinitely variable ratio between 2 : 1 and 1 : 1 and a torque speed responsive and hydraulically operated epicyclic gearbox comprising a planetary gear set providing three forward ratios and reverse ratio.

Due to the complexity of the automatic transmission unit, if performance is not up to standard, or overhaul is necessary, it is imperative that this is undertaken by Ford main agents who will have special equipment for accurate fault diagnosis and rectification.

The content of the following sections is therefore solely general and servicing information.

13 Maintenance

1 Maintain the fluid level as described in the Routine Maintenance Section at the front of this manual.
2 Keep the exterior of the unit free from mud and oil, also the stoneguards on the converter housing to prevent overheating.

14 Automatic gearbox - removal and refitting

1 Any suspected faults must be referred to the main agent before unit removal as with this type of transmission its fault must be confirmed using special equipment before it is removed from the car.
2 As the automatic transmission is relatively heavy it is best if the rear of the car is raised from the ground on ramps but it is possible to remove the unit if the car is placed on high axle stands.
3 Disconnect the battery.
4 Disconnect the downshift cable from the throttle linkage at the side of the carburettor.
5 Remove the dipstick from its guide tube.
6 Detach the exhaust downpipe from the manifold. Release the support clip from the support bracket.
7 Undo the bolt securing the engine earth cable to the torque converter.
8 Place a suitably large container under the transmission unit oil pan and remove the drain screw. When all the fluid has drained, refit the drain screw.
9 Disconnect the speed selector linkage at the universal joint which is located in the cross shaft which runs between the transmission unit selector rod and the body side frame. Disconnection is carried out by removing the split pins and clevis pins from the universal joint yokes.
10 Note the leads which are attached to the terminals of the starter inhibitor/reverse light switch and then disconnect them. The terminals at 45° angle are for the reversing lights.
11 Unscrew and remove the upper filler/dipstick tube support bracket bolt and then unscrew the lower union nut and withdraw the filler/dipstick tube plugging the hole in the transmission unit with a piece of rag to prevent the ingress of dirt.
12 With a scriber or file mark the propeller shaft and rear axle flanges so that they may be refitted in their original positions.
13 Undo and remove the four locknuts and bolts that secure the two flanges together.
14 Pull the propeller shaft slightly forward to separate the flanges and then withdraw it to the rear so that the sliding sleeve is disconnected from the splines on the transmission extension shaft.
15 Disconnect the speedometer cable from the extension housing.
16 Unhook the handbrake secondary cable from the lower end

of the relay lever and also disengage it from the rear mounting support.
17 Unscrew the starter motor bolts and withdraw the starter, letting it rest on the engine splash shield.
18 Unscrew each of the bolts which secure the drive plate to the torque converter. These are accessible, one at a time, through the starter motor aperture and the engine will have to be turned to bring each bolt into view by applying a spanner to the crankshaft pulley bolt. Mark the relative position of the drive plate to the torque converter so that it can be refitted in exactly the same place.
19 Unscrew and remove the bolts which secure the blanking plate to the front of the clutch bellhousing. The engine support bracket will be released by this operation.
20 Place a jack under the engine sump and a second one (preferably of the trolley type) under the transmission oil pan. Use pieces of wood between the jack and the sump and oil pan to prevent damage to these components.
21 Lower the two jacks together so that the transmission can be withdrawn to the rear and from beneath the car. During withdrawal, the engine rear plate will probably fall from its locating dowels and some transmission fluid will be discharged from the torque converter.
22 Installation is a reversal of removal but observe the following points:
23 Secure the engine rear plate to its dowels before offering up the transmission.
24 Should the torque converter have been partially displaced forward during removal of the transmission, ensure that it is pushed fully rearward and its tangs are engaged with the oil pump drive.
25 Do not let the weight of the transmission unit hang upon the main input shaft while it is still engaged with the bush in the crankshaft rear driving flange.
26 Align the drive plate and torque converter mating marks and tighten the bolts to a torque of between 25 and 30 lb ft (3.6 to 4.14 kg m).
27 Check the adjustment of the selector linkage (Section 15).
28 Check the adjustment of the downshift cable (Section 16).
29 Refill the unit with the correct grade and quantity of fluid.

15 Selector linkage - adjustment

1 It is essential that the selector linkage is correctly adjusted to prevent malfunction of the transmission.
2 With the steering wheel speed selector indicator in any one of its five positions, the operating lever on the side of the transmission should be in the centre of its corresponding detent without any tendency to be overridden by the pull or push effect of the steering column selector downshaft.
3 To carry out any necessary adjustment, slacken the locknut on the adjuster pin which is located next to the selector downshaft bracket. Place the steering column lever in the 'D' position. Have an assistant hold the lever in this position and then from underneath the vehicle, place the operating lever on the side of the transmission unit in the 'D' detent. This is one 'click' from its fully depressed position. Tighten the locknut on the adjuster pin and then test all selector positions. Any slight correction to synchronise the pointer on the quadrant indicator may be carried out by removing the top half of the steering column shroud and using a small screwdriver, adjusting the grub screw on the pointer linkage.

16 Downshift valve cable - adjustment and renewal

1 The downshift cable (kick-down facility) is preset during production by means of the crimped collar.
2 Periodically, check the cable setting but first ensure that the accelerator linkage is correctly adjusted as described in Chapter 3.
3 Correct adjustment of the downshift cable is indicated when there is a clearance of 0.015 inch (0.3810 mm) between the end

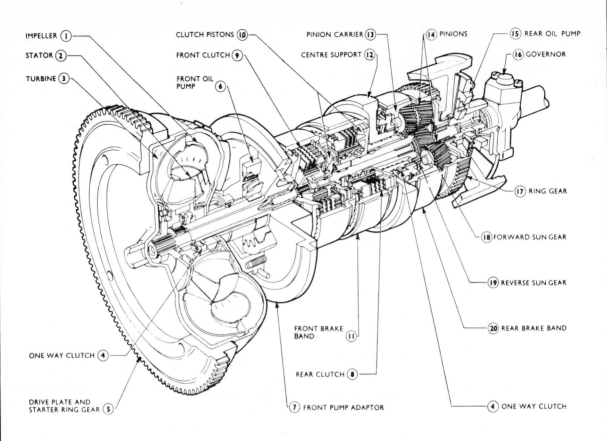

IMPELLER ①
STATOR ②
TURBINE ③
FRONT OIL PUMP ⑥
CLUTCH PISTONS ⑩
FRONT CLUTCH ⑨
PINION CARRIER ⑬
CENTRE SUPPORT ⑫
⑭ PINIONS
⑮ REAR OIL PUMP
⑯ GOVERNOR
⑰ RING GEAR
⑱ FORWARD SUN GEAR
⑲ REVERSE SUN GEAR
⑳ REAR BRAKE BAND
④ ONE WAY CLUTCH
ONE WAY CLUTCH ④
DRIVE PLATE AND STARTER RING GEAR ⑤
FRONT BRAKE BAND ⑪
REAR CLUTCH ⑧
⑦ FRONT PUMP ADAPTOR

Fig. 6.26. Cut-away view of the automatic transmission

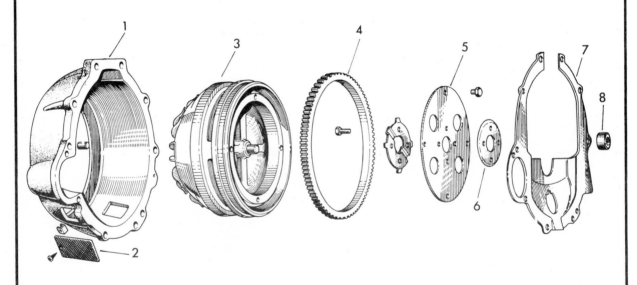

Fig. 6.27. Exploded view of the torque converter

1 *Converter housing*	3 *Converter assembly*	5 *Driveplate*	7 *Engine rear plate*
2 *Stoneguard*	4 *Starter ring gear*	6 *Crankshaft flange plate*	8 *Spigot bush*

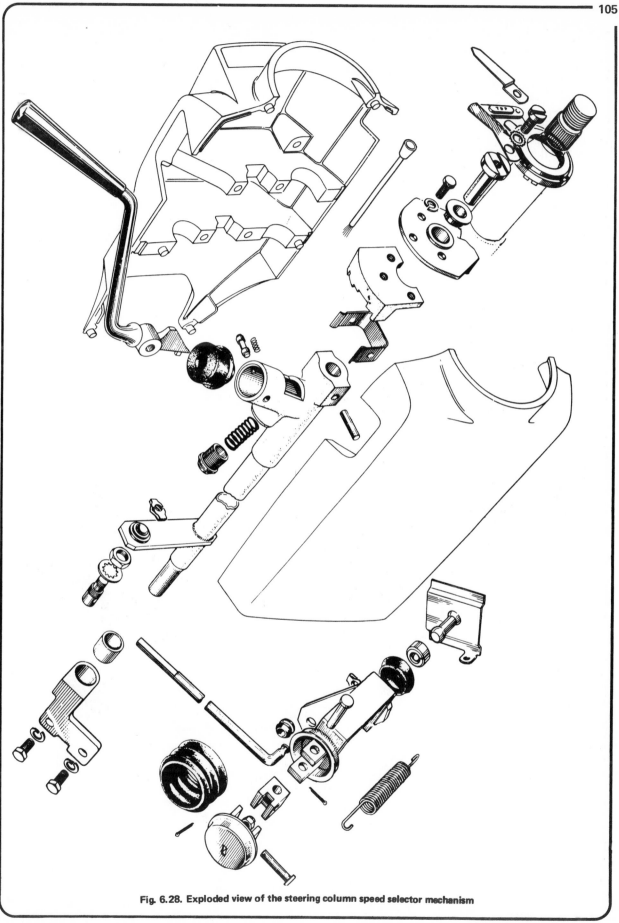

Fig. 6.28. Exploded view of the steering column speed selector mechanism

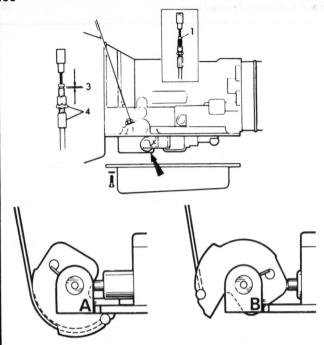

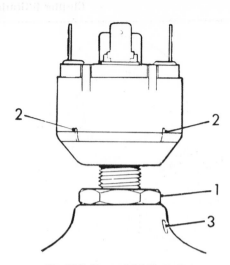

Fig. 6.30. Starter inhibitor switch

1 Locknut
2 Setting marks on switch body
3 Alignment mark on transmission case

Fig. 6.29. Downshift cable setting diagram

1	Crimped collar	(A)	Position of downshift
3	Clearance (crimped collar		cable at engine idling
	to adjuster sleeve)	(B)	'Kickdown' position
4	Locknut on outer cable		

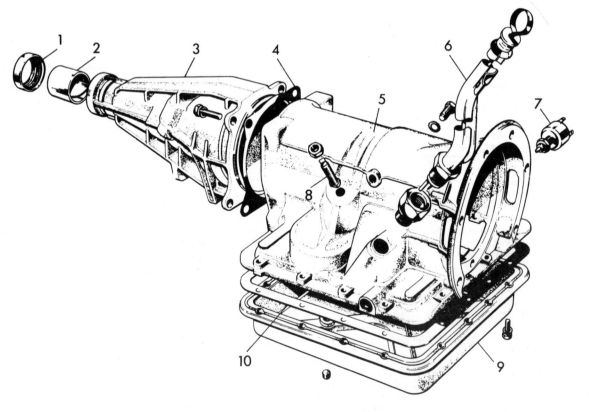

Fig. 6.31. External components of the automatic transmission

1	Rear oil seal	4	Gasket		breather tube		adjuster
2	Bush	5	Transmission casing	7	Starter inhibitor switch	9	Oil pan
3	Extension housing	6	Combined filler/dipstick/	8	Rear brake band	10	Gasket

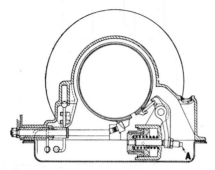

Fig. 6.32. Sectional view of front brake band (A) adjuster screw

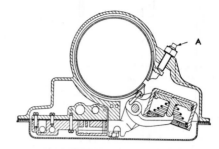

Fig. 6.33. Sectional view of rear brake band (A) adjuster screw

of the threaded cable adjuster sleeve and the crimped stop. Use a feeler blade to check this and if necessary slacken the cable adjuster locknut and rotate the threaded sleeve until the clearance is correct.

4   In the event of the cable having to be renewed or the crimped stop having been displaced then cable renewal and adjustment will have to be carried out in the following way. New downshift cables are supplied with the stop loose on the cable for later crimping when it has been fitted and set.

5   Drain the transmission fluid into a suitable container. If it is to be used for replenishing, keep the fluid clean and free from dirt.

6   Remove the oil pan from the transmission unit.

7   With the cable correctly connected to the downshift valve within the transmission and to the carburettor linkage at its upper end, the valve cam should appear as shown in 'A' (Fig 6.29) with the throttle at rest in the idling position. Adjust the length of the outer cable by means of its threaded adjuster sleeve until any slack in the inner cable has been removed.

8   Depress the accelerator pedal fully to the 'kick-down' position and check that the valve cam is in the position shown in 'B'.

9   Release the accelerator pedal, tighten the locknut on the outer cable adjuster sleeve. If a new cable has been fitted, crimp the stop onto the inner cable so that there is a clearance of 0.015 inch (0.3810 mm) between it and the end face of the adjuster sleeve.

10 Fit the oil pan using a new gasket and fill the transmission with the correct quantity of fluid.

17   Starter inhibitor/reversing lamp switch - adjustment

1   Select 'D' or 'L'. Identify the leads to the inhibitor switch and disconnect them.

2   Connect a battery and test lamp across the (smaller) starter inhibitor switch terminals and another set across the two larger (angled) reverse lamp terminals.

3   Slacken the switch locknut and unscrew the switch about two turns. Slowly screw in the switch until the test lamp across the reverse lamp terminals goes out. Mark the relative position of the switch body to the transmission case by putting a mark on both components.

4   Continue to screw in the switch until the test lamp across the starter inhibitor terminals lights up. Mark the transmission casing opposite the mark previously made on the switch body.

5   Unscrew the switch until the mark on its body is exactly halfway between the two marks made on the transmission casing. Tighten the locknut.

6   Reconnect the leads to the switch terminals and check that the starter motor operates only when the selector lever is in the 'N' or 'P' positions. Also check that the reversing lamps (where fitted) operate only when the selector lever is in the 'R' position.

7   If the switch operates incorrectly, it should be renewed.

18   Extension housing oil seal - renewal

1   The most likely component to require attention after a high mileage is the oil seal fitted to the rear of the extension housing.

2   Where there is continual need for topping up of the transmission

fluid and the area of floor pan under the vehicle is saturated with fluid then carry out the following operations:

3   Remove the propeller shaft as previously described in Section 14. Remove the filler/dipstick tube upper bracket bolt.

4   Support the oil pan of the transmission unit on a jack and a block of wood as an insulator and disconnect the rear mounting and support. Lower the jack just enough to enable the extension housing to transmission casing bolts to be withdrawn.

5   Withdraw the extension housing fully to the rear so that it clears the transmission shaft and governor and can be lifted away. Remove the gasket and obtain a new one.

6   Support the extension housing on its narrower end using a block of wood suitably drilled to accept the old seal as it is drifted out. Use a long rod inserted from the larger end of the extension housing and drift the oil seal from its location. Take great care not to damage the bush at the rear of the housing during this operation.

7   Tap the new seal into position first having coated its outer diameter surface with jointing compound.

8   Refitting is a reversal of removal using a new gasket (fitted the correct way round). Tighten the extension housing bolts to a torque of 10 lb ft (1.382 kg m) only.

19   Front brake band - adjustment

1   Adjustment of the front or rear brake bands must not be considered as routine maintenance but only to be carried out in the event of fault symptoms occurring which might be attributed to these two components.

2   Incorrect adjustment of the front brake band could cause slip on first to second upshift or on third to second downshift with 'kick-down' in operation.

3   To adjust, remove the oil pan as described in Section 16. The front servo is now exposed.

4   Slacken the locknut on the servo lever and move the lever until a flat bar ¼ inch (6.35 mm) thick can be inserted between the servo piston pin and the adjuster screw. Tighten the adjuster screw to a torque of 10 lb in (0.14 kg m). If a torque screwdriver is not available for this setting, use a right-angled cranked screwdriver and spring balance attached to the screwdriver shaft at a distance of 1 inch (25.4 mm) from the centre of the adjuster screw. When 10 lb force is registered on the scale of the spring balance, hold the screw and tighten the locknut to a torque of 20 lb ft (2.8 kg m). Remove the flat bar used as a gauge.

5   Refit the oil pan and refill the unit.

20   Rear brake band - adjustment

1   Adjustment of the rear brake band may be required in the event of no drive when the selector is in 'R' and no engine braking with the selector in 'L'.

2   To carry out the adjustment, remove the plug or plate from the right hand side of the transmission tunnel within the vehicle interior.

3   Slacken the locknut on the now exposed rear band adjuster screw and tighten the screw to a torque of 10 lb ft (1.38 kg m). Unscrew the adjuster screw one complete turn and tighten the locknut.

21 Fault diagnosis - automatic transmission

Stall test procedure

The function of a stall test is to determine that the torque converter and gearbox are operating satisfactorily.

1 Check the condition of the engine. An engine which is not developing full power will affect the stall test readings.

2 Allow the engine and transmission to reach correct working temperatures.

3 Connect a tachometer to the vehicle.

4 Check the wheels and apply the handbrake and footbrake.

5 Select L or R and depress the throttle to the 'kickdown' position. Note the reading on the tachometer which should be 1800 rev/min. If the reading is below 1000 rev/min suspect the converter for stator slip. If the reading is down to 1200 rev/min the engine is not developing full power. If the reading is in excess of 2000 rev/min suspect the gearbox for brake band or clutch slip.

Note: Do not carry out a stall test for a longer period than 10 seconds, otherwise the transmission will overheat.

Converter diagnosis

Inability to start on steep gradients, combined with poor acceleration from rest and low stall speed (1000 rev/min), indicates that the converter stator uni-directional clutch is slipping. This condition permits the stator to rotate in an opposite direction to the impeller and turbine, and torque multiplication cannot occur.

Poor acceleration in third gear above 30 mph (48 kph) and reduced maximum speed, indicates that the stator uni-directional clutch has seized. The stator will not rotate with the turbine and impeller and the 'fluid flywheel' phase cannot occur. This condition will also be indicated by excessive overheating of the transmission although the stall speed will be correct.

Symptom	Reason/s	Remedy
Engine will not start in N or P	Faulty starter or ignition circuit	Check and repair.
	Incorrect linkage adjustment	Adjust.
	Incorrectly installed inhibitor switch	Adjust.
Engine starts in selector positions other than N or P	Incorrect linkage adjustment	Adjust.
	Incorrectly installed inhibitor switch	Adjust.
Severe bump when selecting D or R and excessive creep when handbrake released	Idling speed too high	Check and adjust.
	Downshift valve incorrectly adjusted	Check and adjust.
Poor acceleration and low maximum speed	Incorrect oil level	Check and fill.
	Incorrect linkage adjustment	Adjust.

Chapter 7 Propeller shaft and universal joints

Contents

Specifications

Type ... ...   Tubular steel; with two universal joints and a sliding sleeve at front end

Torque wrench setting

	lb ft	kg m
Rear flange to drive pinion bolts	18	2.49

1 General description

Drive is transmitted from the gearbox to the rear axle by means of a finely balanced tubular propeller shaft. Fitted at each end of the shaft is a universal joint which allows for vertical movement of the rear axle. Each universal joint comprises a four legged centre spider, four needle roller bearings and two yokes.

Fore and aft movement of the rear axle is absorbed by a sliding spline in the front of the propeller shaft which slides over a mating spline on the rear of the gearbox mainshaft. A supply of oil through very small oil holes from the gearbox lubricates the splines. On early models a grease nipple is fitted to each universal joint for regular lubrication. On later models sealed type universal joints are fitted which require no lubrication or maintenance.

2 Propeller shaft - removal and refitting

1   Jack up the rear of the car, or position the rear of the car over a pit or on a ramp.
2   If the rear of the car is jacked up supplement the jack with support blocks so that danger is minimised should the jack collapse.
3   If the rear wheels are off the ground, place the car in gear or put the handbrake on to ensure that the propeller shaft does not turn when an attempt is made to loosen the four nuts securing the propeller shaft to the rear axle.
4   Unscrew and remove the four self-locking nuts, bolts and securing washers which hold the flange on the propeller shaft to the flange on the rear axle.
5   The propeller shaft is carefully balanced to fine limits and it is important that it is replaced in exactly the same position it was in prior to its removal. Scratch a mark on the propeller shaft and rear axle flanges to ensure accurate mating when the time comes for reassembly.
6   Slightly push the shaft forward to separate the two flanges, and then lower the end of the shaft and pull it rearwards to disengage the gearbox mainshaft splines.
7   Place a large can or a tray under the rear of the gearbox extension to catch any oil which is likely to leak through the spline lubricating holes, when the propeller shaft is removed.
8   Replacement of the propeller shaft is a reversal of the above procedure. Ensure that the mating marks scratched on the propeller shaft and rear axle flanges line up.

3 Universal joints - inspection and repair

1   Wear in the needle roller bearings is characterised by vibration in the transmission, 'clonks' on taking up the drive, and in extreme cases of lack of lubrication, metallic squeaking, and ultimately grating and shrieking sounds as the bearings break up.
2   It is easy to check if the needle roller bearings are worn with the propeller shaft in position, by trying to turn the shaft with one hand, the other hand holding the rear axle flange when the rear universal is being checked, and the front half coupling when the front universal is being checked. Any movement between the propeller shaft and the front and the rear half couplings is indicative of considerable wear. If worn, the old bearings and spiders will have to be discarded and a repair kit, comprising new universal joint spiders, bearings, oil seals, and retainers, purchased. Check also by trying to lift the shaft and noticing any movement in the joints.
3   Examine the propeller shaft splines for wear. If worn it will be necessary to purchase a new front half coupling, or if the yokes are badly worn, an exchange propeller shaft. It is not possible to fit oversize bearings and journals to the trunnion bearing holes.

4 Universal joints - dismantling

1   Clean away all traces of dirt and grease from the circlips located on the ends of the spiders and remove the circlips by

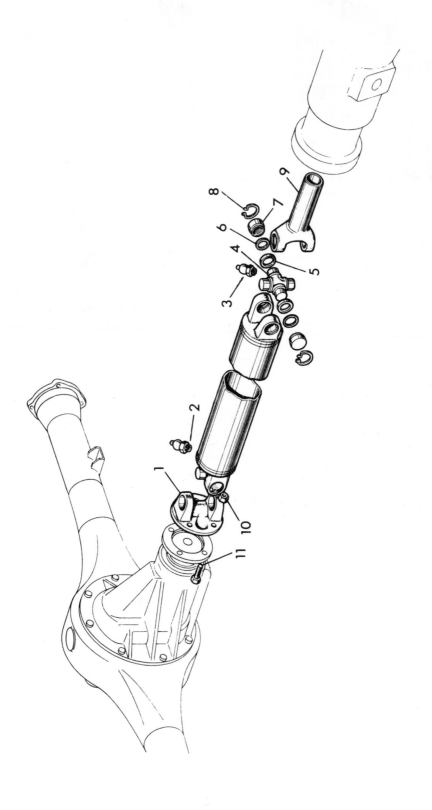

Fig. 7.1. Exploded view of the propeller shaft and universal joints

1 Drive shaft flange yoke
2 Grease nipple
3 Grease nipple

4 Spider
5 Oil seal retainer
6 Oil seal

7 Needle roller bearing
  and cap
8 Retaining circlip

9 Universal joint knuckle
10 Nut
11 Bolt

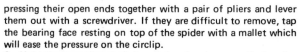

Fig. 7.2. Rear universal joint showing correct location of flange bolt heads and mating marks made prior to dismantling

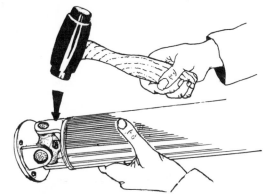

Fig. 7.3. Extracting a universal joint bearing cup

Fig. 7.4. Separating a universal joint

pressing their open ends together with a pair of pliers and lever them out with a screwdriver. If they are difficult to remove, tap the bearing face resting on top of the spider with a mallet which will ease the pressure on the circlip.

2   Hold the propeller shaft in one hand and remove the bearing cups and needle rollers by tapping the yoke at each bearing with a copper or hide faced hammer. As soon as the bearings start to emerge they should be gripped in a vice or a pair of mole grips and twisted out of the trunnion holes.

3   With the bearings removed it is relatively easy to extract the spiders from their yokes. If the bearings and spider journals are thought to be badly worn this can easily be ascertained visually

with the universal joints dismantled.

5 Universal joints - reassembly

1   Thoroughly clean out the yokes and journals.

2   Fit new oil seals and retainers on the spider journals, place the spider on the propeller shaft yoke, and assemble the needle rollers in the bearing races with the assistance of some thin grease.

3   Refit the bearing cups on the spider and tap (or press, using a vice) the bearings home so that they lie squarely in position.

4   Replace the circlips and liberally lubricate the bearings with a lithium based grease.

6 Fault diagnosis - propeller shaft and universal joints

Symptom	Reason/s	Remedy
Vibration when vehicle running on road	Out of balance or distorted propeller shaft	Renew.
	Backlash in splined shaft	Renew components.
	Loose flange securing bolts	Tighten nuts.
	Worn universal joint bearings	Renew joints or complete propeller shaft assembly.

Chapter 8 Rear axle

Contents

Specifications

Type	Semi-floating hypoid	
Axle ratio (except GT)	4.125 : 1	
Axle ratio (GT)	3.9 : 1	
Number of pinion teeth (4.125 : 1 ratio)	8	
Number of crownwheel teeth (4.125 : 1 ratio)	33	
Number of pinion teeth (3.9 : 1 ratio)	10	
Number of crownwheel teeth (3.9 : 1 ratio)	39	
Oil capacity	2 pints (1.1 litres)	

Torque wrench settings	lb ft	kg m
Brake backplate to axle housing flange	18	2.49
Differential unit to axle casing	18	2.49
Halfshaft bearing retainer plate bolts	18	2.49

1 General description

The rear axle is of the semi-floating type, having the crownwheel and pinion mounted in a differential carrier which in turn is bolted to the front face of a 'banjo' type casing.

When it is necessary to execute major repairs and the replacement of worn parts to the rear axle it is more practical to remove the complete axle and have the work undertaken at a Ford dealer service workshop which is equipped with the special tools and gauges essential to carry out the adjustments for bearing preload and meshing of gears.

It is recommended that servicing is limited to the operations described in the following Sections.

2 Rear axle - removal and refitting

1   Jack up the rear of the vehicle and securely support the bodyframe under the jacking points.
2   Remove the road wheels and place a jack under the differential ('banjo') casing.
3   Disconnect the propeller shaft from the rear axle pinion driving flange as described in the preceding chapter.
4   Disconnect the handbrake cable at the left hand operating link by withdrawing the split pin and clevis pin.
5   Remove the clevis and pull the rubber boot from the cable. Remove the spring clip which retains the conduit to the large clevis and withdraw the conduit and inner handbrake cable from the clevis.
6   Disconnect the shock absorbers at their lower mountings.

7   Unscrew the flexible brake pipe at its bracket above the rear axle casing. Plug the fluid lines to prevent loss of fluid and the ingress of dirt.
8   Unscrew and remove the self-locking nuts from the road spring 'U' bolts and withdraw the road spring locating plates from below the axle casing. The axle is supported by the centrally located jack during this operation.
9   The axle may now be withdrawn through the wheel arch on the right hand side of the vehicle.
10 Refitting is a reversal of removal but tighten the 'U' bolt nuts evenly to between 20 and 25 lb ft (2.76 and 3.46 kg m); bleed the brakes and adjust the handbrake linkage as described in Chapter 9.

3 Halfshaft - removal and refitting

1   Jack up the axle and the rear bodyframe and support securely on axle stands or blocks.
2   Remove the road wheel and release the handbrake.
3   Unscrew and remove the countersunk screws which retain the brake drum and withdraw it. If the drum is stuck, slacken the brake shoe adjuster and tap the drum off using a hammer and hardwood block. Do not strike the brake drum directly with a hammer or it may fracture.
4   Remove the four bolts and spring washers which secure the axle shaft bearing retainer to the axle casing end flange. The bolts are accessible through the holes in the axle shaft flange.
5   Attach a slide hammer to the axle wheel nut studs by means of the wheel nuts and withdraw the halfshaft. It is quite useless,

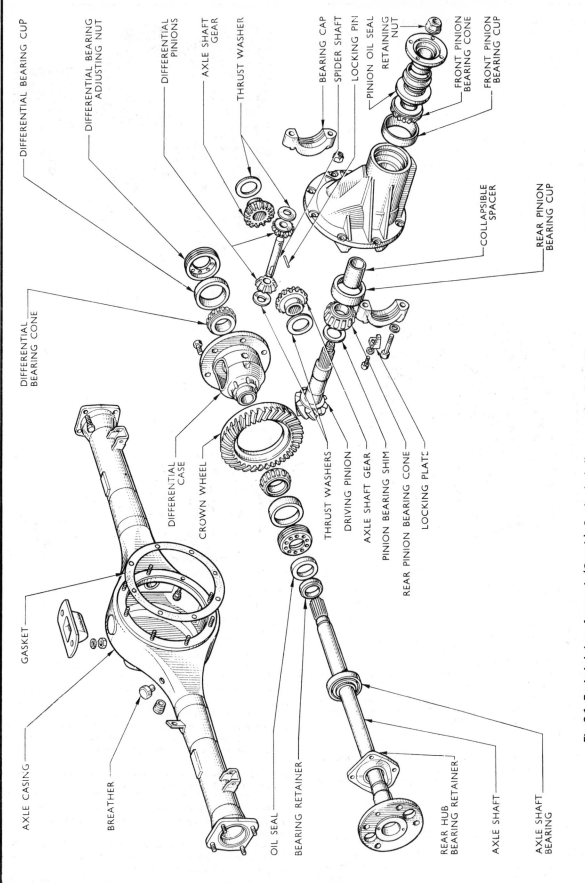

Fig. 8.1. Exploded view of rear axle (Corsair). Cortina is similar except for slight differences in axle casing and halfshaft flanges

in the absence of a slide hammer, to try and pull the axle shaft from the axle casing, you will only succeed in pulling the car off the stands. An alternative method of removal is to bolt on an old road wheel and strike it simultaneously at two opposite points on its inside rim.

6   Refitting commences by inserting the splined end of the axle shaft very carefully through the oil seal in the outer end of the axle casing.

7   Keep the halfshaft horizontal until the splines can be felt to engage with those in the differential gear, then tap the shaft fully home into the axle casing.

8   The rest of the refitting procedure is a reversal of removal but remember to adjust the brake if the adjuster was slackened off prior to removal of the brake drum.

Fig. 8.2. Location of halfshaft bearing retainer plate bolts (four)

4   Axle shaft oil seals and bearings - renewal

1   Withdraw the axle halfshaft as previously described in Section 3.

2   Removal and refitting of a halfshaft bearing is not within the scope of the home mechanic as the bearing is an interference fit

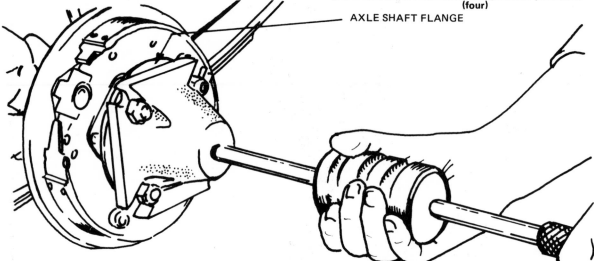

Fig. 8.3. Using a slide hammer to withdraw a halfshaft

on the shaft and a press will be required to press the shaft from the bearing and its retaining collar and to press the new components onto the shaft. It is therefore preferable to take the shaft to your Ford dealer for this work to be carried out.

3   Renewal of the halfshaft oil seals is an operation which is likely to occur more frequently than bearing renewal and this the owner can accomplish easily.

4   After withdrawal of the halfshaft, use a claw type extractor as would be employed to remove bearing outer tracks. Insert the extractor into the end of the axle casing and engage the claws behind the metal rim of the oil seal. Extract the oil seal by either attaching the puller to a slide hammer or by using a bar as a bridge piece across the brake backplate and screwing in the extractor bolt.

5   Drive the new oil seal squarely into position using a piece of copper or plastic tubing as a fitting tool.

6   When inserting the halfshaft, take great care not to damage the lips of the oil seal with the splines.

5   Differential unit - removal and refitting

1   Drain the oil from the rear axle and jack up the rear of the car and fit axle stands under the axle casing. Later models are not fitted with a drain plug and the oil will have to be caught in

a bowl as the differential is withdrawn.

2   Withdraw both halfshafts as described in Section 3.

3   Disconnect the propeller shaft at its rear flange as described in Chapter 7.

4   Unscrew the circle of eight self-locking nuts which secure the differential unit to the axle casing.

5   Pull the unit forward off the studs and remove it.

6   The differential unit may now be exchanged for a factory reconditioned unit or a good replacement obtained from a car breaker. Without the necessary tools and gauges it is not practicable to attempt to dismantle and re-adjust the unit.

7   Refitment is a reversal of removal procedure but always use a new sealing gasket and tighten the nuts in a diagonal sequence to a torque of 18 lb ft (2.49 kg m).

6   Pinion oil seal - renewal (axle in situ)

The pinion oil seal can be renewed with the axle in position in the car provided the following operations are carefully followed.

1   Jack up the rear of the car and support the axle on stands.

2   Mark the edges of the propeller shaft and pinion coupling flanges to ensure exact replacement.

3   Remove the four coupling bolts, detach the propeller shaft at

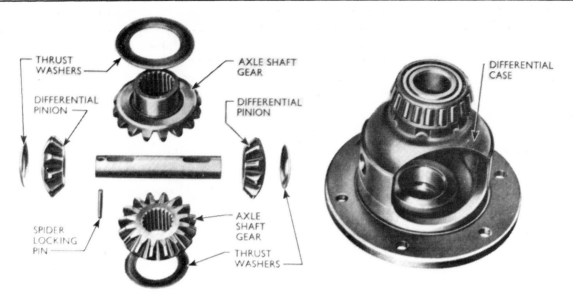

Fig. 8.4. Components of the differential unit

the axle pinion flange and tie the propeller shaft to one side.

4 Remove both rear road wheels and brake drums to eliminate any drag.

5 Wind a cord round the pinion flange coupling and exerting a steady pull note the reading on a spring balance required to rotate the flange. The spring balance reading indicates the pinion bearing pre-load.

6 Mark the coupling in relation to the pinion splines for exact replacement.

7 Hold the pinion coupling flange by placing two 2 inch (50.8 mm) long bolts through two opposite holes, bolting them up tight, undo the self-locking nut whilst holding a large screwdriver or tyre lever between the two bolts as a lever.

8 Remove the defective oil seal by drifting in one side of the seal as far as it will go to force the opposite side of the seal from the housing.

9 Refit the new oil seal first having greased the mating surfaces of the seal and the axle housing. The lips of the oil seal must face inwards. Using a piece of brass or copper tubing of suitable diameter, carefully drive the new oil seal into the axle housing recess until the face of the seal is flush with the housing. Make sure that the end of the pinion is not knocked during this operation.

10 Refit the coupling to its original position on the pinion splines after first having located the dust cover.

11 Fit a new pinion nut and holding the coupling still with the screwdriver or tyre lever, **tighten the nut until the pinion end float only just disappears. Do not overtighten.**

12 Rotate the pinion to settle the bearing and then check the pre-load using the cord and spring balance method previously described and by slight adjustment of the nut and rotation of the pinion obtain a spring balance pre-load figure to match that which applied before dismantling.

13 On no account overtighten the pinion nut as it cannot be slackened without introducing end-float caused by over compressing the collapsible spacer shown. Should this happen, withdraw the pinion nut, coupling, oil seal, taper roller bearing and the collapsible spacer. Fit a new spacer and reassemble the other components and tighten the pinion nut until a force of between 14 and 16 lb on the spring balance is needed to rotate the coupling flange. Tighten the nut only a fraction of a turn at a time once the pinion endfloat has disappeared.

14 Remove the two holding bolts and refit the propeller shaft making sure to align the mating marks. Refit the brake drums and road wheels and lower the car.

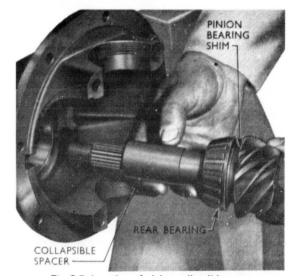

Fig. 8.5. Location of pinion collapsible spacer

Location of rear axle breather

7 Fault diagnosis - rear axle

Symptom	Reason/s	Remedy
Noisy operation	Low oil level Worn components	Top up. Renew or exchange differential unit.
Oil leakage	Worn axle shaft or pinion oil seals Choked breather (photo)	Renew. Clean.
'Clonk' on taking up drive or on overrun	Worn halfshaft splines Worn universal joints Road wheels loose on studs	Renew. Repair. Tighten or if wheel holes are elongated, renew.
Vibration at speed	Worn universal joints Propeller shaft out of balance	Renew. Rotate position or have re-balanced.

Chapter 9 Braking system

Contents

Specifications

Cortina standard and de luxe up to October 1964

System type	Four wheel drum, hydraulically operated. Mechanically operated handbrake to rear wheels only
Brake design:	
Front	Two leading shoe
Rear	Leading and trailing shoe
Master cylinder bore diameter	0.625 in (15.9 mm)
Front drum diameter	8.00 in (203.2 mm)
Lining:	
Length	6.26 in (159.0 mm)
Width	1.75 in (44.5 mm)
Thickness	0.187 in (47.7 mm)
Total friction lining area (front wheels)	43.98 in2 (283.74 cm2)
Front wheel cylinder diameter	0.75 in (19.05 mm)
Rear drum diameter	8.00 in (203.2 mm)
Lining length	6.26 in (159.0 mm)
Lining width	1.5 in (38.1 mm)
Thickness	0.188 in (47.7 mm)
Total friction lining area (rear wheels)	37.70 in2 (243.25 cm2)
Rear wheel cylinder diameter	0.75 in (19.05 mm)

Cortina standard and de luxe after October 1964

System type	Front disc, rear drum, hydraulically operated. Mechanically operated handbrake to rear wheels only

Front brakes

Disc diameter	9.50 in (241.3 mm)
Disc thickness	0.375 in (95.25 mm)
Disc run-out (maximum)	0.002 in (0.051 mm)
Caliper piston diameter	1.892 in (48.1 mm)
Total pad lining area	15.70 in2 (101.27 cm2)

Rear brakes

Drum diameter	8.00 in (203.20 mm)

Lining:
    Length   ... ...   6.26 in (159.0 mm)
    Width   ... ...   1.50 in (38.1 mm)
    Thickness   ... ...   0.188 in (47.7 mm)
Total friction lining area 37.70 in2 (243.25 cm2)
Rear wheel cylinder diameter   ... ...   0.75 in (19.1 mm)
Master cylinder bore   ... ...   0.625 in (15.9 mm)

Corsair and GT models

Front brakes   ... ...   Specification as for Cortina standard and de luxe after October 1964, except for pad area 17.94 in2 (115.74 cm2)

Rear brakes
Drum diameter   ... ...   9.00 in (228.6 mm)
Lining:
    Length   ... ...   8.46 in (214.9 mm)
    Width   ... ...   1.75 in (44.5 mm)
    Thickness   ... ...   0.194 in (492.8 mm)
Total lining area (rear wheels)... ... ...   57.60 in2 (371.61 cm2)
Rear wheel cylinder diameter   ... ...   0.70 in (17.8 mm)
Master cylinder bore   ... ...   0.75 in (19.1 mm)

Servo (GT only)
    Type   ... ...   Suspended vacuum
    Boost ratio   ... ...   2.78 : 1

Torque wrench settings	lb ft	kg m
Brake caliper to stub axle carrier	45	6.22
Brake disc to hub	34	4.70
Rear brake backplate to axle flange	18	2.49
Front brake backplate to stub axle carrier	22	3.04

1 General description

Up until October 1964 the Cortina standard and de luxe models were fitted with four wheel drum brakes. After this date, disc front brakes were installed.

All GT and Corsair models are fitted with front discs and rear drum brakes.

All GT versions have vacuum servo assistance.

The braking system is hydraulically operated with a mechanically operated handbrake operating on the rear wheels only.

On GT models, the vacuum servo unit is connected to the inlet manifold of the engine.

2 Drum brakes - adjustment

1   The position of the brake shoes within the drums must be adjusted periodically to compensate for wear of the friction linings.

2   There are two square headed adjusters on each of the front brake backplates (one for each shoe). Jack up the front wheels clear of the ground and then turn one adjuster anticlockwise to bring the lining away from the drum. Now turn the other adjuster of the same drum clockwise until the drum is locked; then, back it off sufficiently to prevent the brake from binding. Screw the first adjuster in a clockwise direction until the drum is locked again and then back it off until the wheel rotates without binding. Always fit a close fitting spanner or a proper brake adjuster to the square headed shoe adjusters in order to preserve their heads.

3   Repeat the operation on the opposite front drum.

4   On rear brakes, only one adjuster is fitted. Release the handbrake, chock the front wheels and raise the rear wheels clear of the ground.

5   Turn the adjuster on one rear backplate until the shoes are locked. Slacken the adjuster two audible clicks and check the wheel for free rotation.

6   Repeat the operation on the opposite wheel, lower the jack, apply the handbrake and remove the chocks.

7   The method of adjusting the rear brakes applies where front disc type (non-adjustable) brakes are fitted.

8   Adjustment of the rear brakes will adjust the handbrake at the same time automatically. Where the handbrake cable has stretched however or if the linkage has been dismantled, refer to Section 18.

9   If difficulty is experienced (during the adjustment procedure) in eliminating brake drag, check the shoe return springs for security and to ensure that they have not stretched or broken. Also bleed the system as described in Section 17 to eliminate any air which may be trapped within the fluid lines or wheel cylinders. Check that the handbrake cable has been correctly set (Section 18).

3 Front disc brake pads - inspection, removal and refitting

1   The front brake disc pads are self-adjusting but they should be checked for wear at regular intervals.

2   Jack up the front of the vehicle and remove the road wheels.

3   Inspect the thickness of the friction pad material (excluding backing plate). When the thickness has been reduced to between 1/16 and 1/8 inch (1.59 and 3.18 mm) the pads must be renewed in the following manner:

4   Withdraw the spring clips from the pad retaining pins and then withdraw the pins from the caliper units.

5   Withdraw the two friction pads and anti-squeal shims, using pliers to grip the pad backing plates if necessary.

6   Using a flat bar of wood or metal, insert it through the caliper unit and press each of the pistons into its housing in order to make room for the thicker replacement pads. During this operation the fluid level in the hydraulic fluid reservoir will rise and may overflow. In order to avoid this, as the caliper pistons are depressed, unscrew the caliper bleed nipple to allow displaced fluid to be ejected. Tighten the nipple.

7   Insert the new pads with their shims at the rear and with the location arrow or cut-out correctly positioned.

8   Refit the retaining pins and their spring clips.

9   Apply the brake pedal hard three or four times and then top up the reservoir if necessary.

10 Replace the road wheel and lower the vehicle.

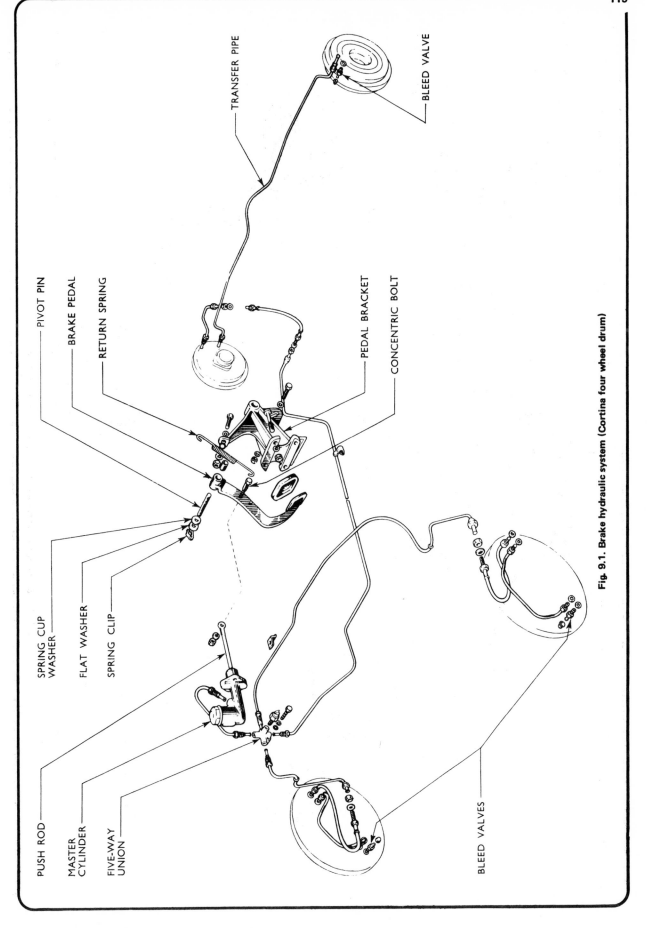

TRANSFER PIPE

BLEED VALVE

PIVOT PIN

BRAKE PEDAL

RETURN SPRING

PEDAL BRACKET

CONCENTRIC BOLT

SPRING CUP
WASHER

FLAT WASHER

SPRING CLIP

PUSH ROD

MASTER
CYLINDER

FIVE-WAY
UNION

BLEED VALVES

Fig. 9.1. Brake hydraulic system (Cortina four wheel drum)

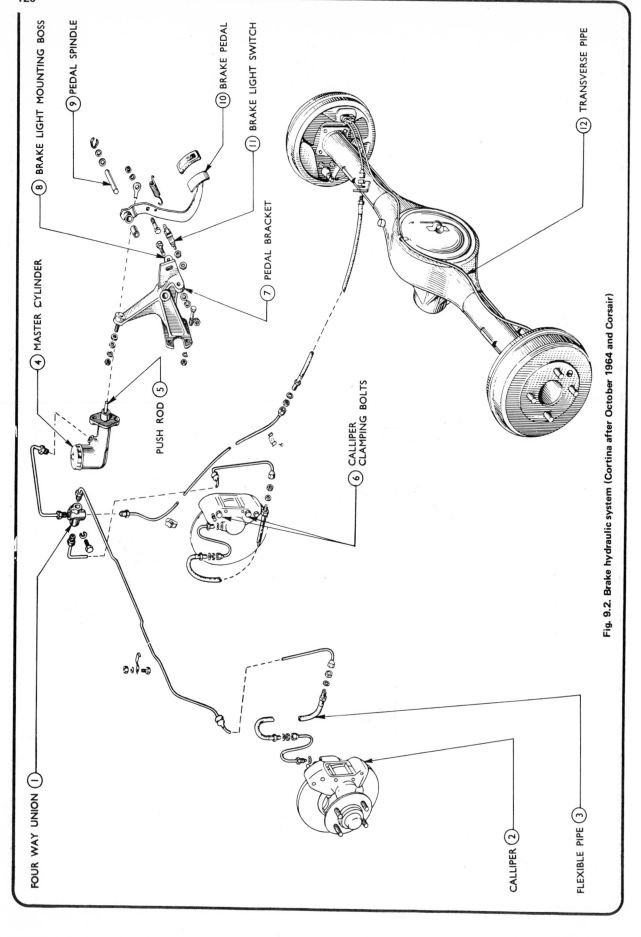

8 BRAKE LIGHT MOUNTING BOSS

9 PEDAL SPINDLE

10 BRAKE PEDAL

11 BRAKE LIGHT SWITCH

12 TRANSVERSE PIPE

4 MASTER CYLINDER

7 PEDAL BRACKET

PUSH ROD 5

6 CALLIPER CLAMPING BOLTS

FOUR WAY UNION 1

CALLIPER 2

FLEXIBLE PIPE 3

Fig. 9.2. Brake hydraulic system (Cortina after October 1964 and Corsair)

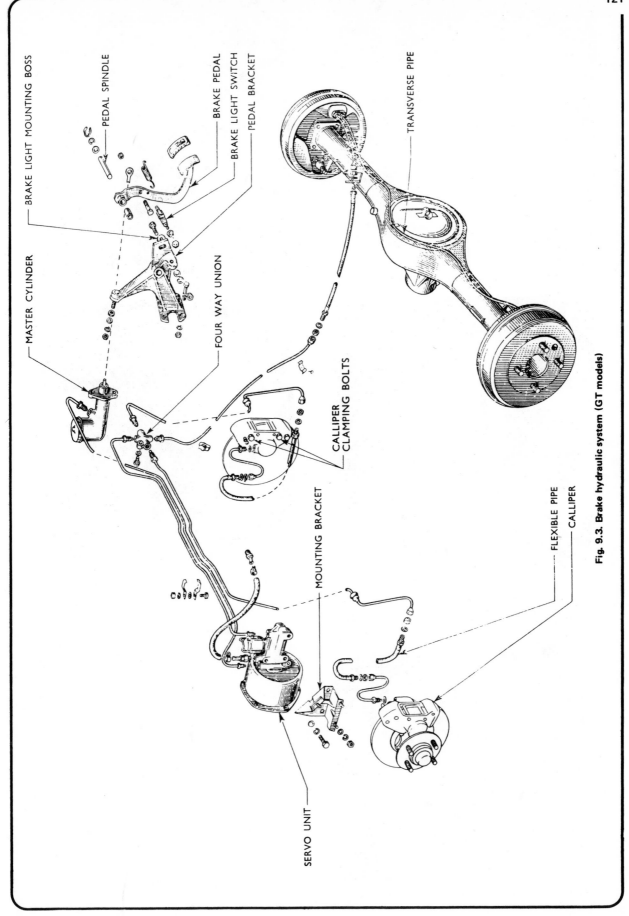

BRAKE LIGHT MOUNTING BOSS

PEDAL SPINDLE

BRAKE PEDAL

BRAKE LIGHT SWITCH

PEDAL BRACKET

TRANSVERSE PIPE

MASTER CYLINDER

FOUR WAY UNION

CALLIPER
CLAMPING BOLTS

MOUNTING BRACKET

FLEXIBLE PIPE

CALLIPER

SERVO UNIT

Fig. 9.3. Brake hydraulic system (GT models)

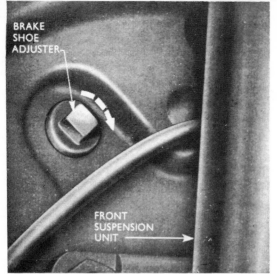

Fig. 9.4. One of two front drum brake shoe adjusters

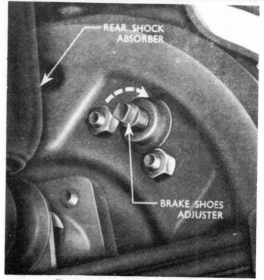

Fig. 9.5. A rear brake shoe adjuster

Fig. 9.6. Front brake caliper

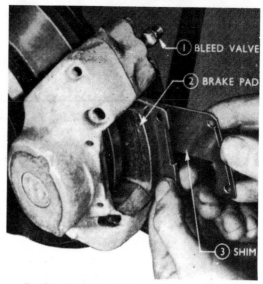

Fig. 9.7. Removing brake pads from a caliper unit

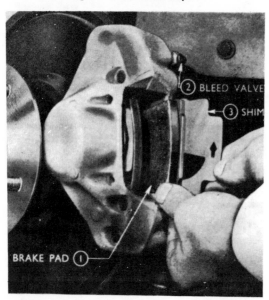

Fig. 9.8. Modified front caliper (GT and Corsair models)

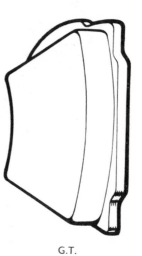

G.T.

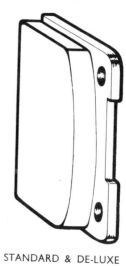

STANDARD & DE-LUXE

Fig. 9.9. Cortina brake pad identification

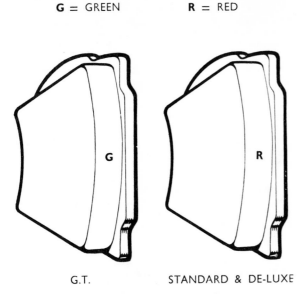

G = GREEN   **R** = RED

G.T.   STANDARD & DE-LUXE

Fig. 9.10. Corsair brake pad identification

4 Front drum brake shoes - inspection and renewal

1 Jack up the front of the car under the front bodyframe crossmember and remove the road wheel.
2 Prise the dust cap from its location at the end of the hub. Slacken off completely the brake adjuster screws.
3 With the hub nut now exposed, withdraw the split pin, the castellated nut and the thrust washer.
4 Pull the brake drum off the stub axle, catching the outer taper roller bearing as it is withdrawn.
5 Brush the linings and the drum interiors free of dust and examine the wear of the linings. If they are worn down to within 1/32 inch (0.79 mm) of the rivet heads renew the brake shoes on an exchange basis. It seldom proves satisfactory to renew the linings yourself.
6 Mark or sketch the position of the shoes with regard to leading and trailing edges, also note the shoe web holes in which the return springs are engaged. Remove the shoe steady clips and spindles.
7 Pull the tapered end of one shoe away from its wheel cylinder piston and then disengage the other end of the same shoe from the slot in the opposing cylinder. Release the shoe slightly and pull it towards you so that it is pulled by the action of the return springs, towards the stub axle. The second shoe can now be released from the wheel cylinders and the two shoes complete with their return springs (still connected) removed from the brake backplate.
8 Position the new shoes flat on the bench with leading and trailing ends correctly located. Engage the shoe return springs in their respective holes in the shoe webs. Apply a trace of high melting point grease to the slots and sliding surfaces of the pistons.
9 Exerting slight tension outwards on the shoes to retain the return springs in their holes, locate the lower shoe web ends with the pistons and then prise the upper shoe against the tension of the return springs into position on the pistons.
10 Fit the shoe steady springs and spindles.
11 Refit the hub/drum assembly, the taper bearing, thrust washer and nut. Tighten the nut to a torque of 30 lb ft (4.148 kg m) at the same time rotating the drum. Back off the nut between two and two and a half flats and fit a new split pin. Refit the dust cap and road wheel.
12 With the vehicle still jacked up, adjust the brake shoes as described in Section 2.
13 Repeat the operations in the opposing front brake.
14 Lower the jack.

5 Rear drum brake shoes - inspection and renewal

1 The procedure is similar to that described in the preceding Section for front brake shoes but observe the following points. The drum is secured by a single countersunk screw (photo).
2 The shoe steady arrangement is of post and dished washer type. To release this kind of steady, depress the washer with a pair of pliers and then turn it through 90° and release it (photo).
3 The shoe return springs are of unequal length. When refitting note that the one with the two sets of coils is located adjacent to the wheel cylinder.

6 Front drum brake wheel cylinders - removal and refitting

1 Remove the brake shoes as described in Section 4.
2 Remove the cap from the brake fluid reservoir and place a piece of thin polythene sheeting over the reservoir opening. Screw on the cap. This action will create a partial vacuum and prevent loss of fluid when the fluid lines are disconnected.
3 Disconnect the flexible brake hose at its union with the rigid line. Plug the rigid line (a bleed nipple dust cap is useful for this purpose) and then unscrew the flexible hose from the upper wheel cylinder.
4 The bridge pipe which runs between the upper and lower wheel cylinders may now be removed and the individual cylinders unbolted from the backplate. It is easier if the backplate is removed complete from the stub axle flange and then the wheel cylinders and bridge pipe detached. A rubber seal is fitted between each cylinder and the backplate.
5 Refitting is a reversal of removal but always screw the end of the flexible hose into the wheel cylinder before connecting it to the rigid line.
6 On completion of reassembly, adjust the hub as described in Section 4, adjust the brake shoes and bleed the hydraulic system (after having removed the polythene sheeting from the top of the fluid reservoir).

7 Front wheel cylinder - servicing

1 Peel off the rubber boot and extract the piston, seal and return spring. This can be carried out by tapping the cylinder on a piece of wood or by applying air from a tyre pump at the fluid entry port.
2 Unscrew and remove the bleed screw.
3 Wash all components in methylated spirit or clean hydraulic fluid and discard the rubber seals and other components.
4 Examine the piston and cylinder bore surfaces for 'bright' wear areas. If these are evident, renew the wheel cylinder complete.
5 Obtain a repair kit which will contain all necessary renewable components.
6 Fit the seal using only the fingers to manipulate it into position.
7 Dip the piston/seal assembly in clean hydraulic fluid and insert it carefully into the cylinder.
8 Fit a new rubber boot and backplate sealing ring.

8 Rear wheel cylinder - removal and refitting

1 Jack up the rear of the vehicle and remove the road wheel.
2 Remove the fluid reservoir cap and place a piece of thin polythene sheeting over the reservoir opening and screw on the cap. This action will help to create a partial vacuum and so prevent loss of hydraulic fluid when the fluid lines are disconnected.
3 Unscrew the rigid fluid line from the wheel cylinder and cap the line to prevent loss of fluid or ingress of dirt (a bleed nipple dust cap is useful for this purpose).
4 Disconnect the handbrake linkage at the handbrake operating link.
5 Remove the brake shoes as described in Section 5.

5.1 Rear drum securing screw

5.2 Removing a rear brake shoe steady spring

5.3 Handbrake cable adjuster

6 Remove the wheel cylinder from the brake backplate by either extracting the retainer and retainer springs (Cortina standard and de luxe) or the two securing bolts (Corsair and GT models).

7 Refitting is a reversal of removal according to type.

8 Bleed the hydraulic system and adjust the brakes as described in Sections 17 and 2 of this Chapter (in that order).

9 Rear wheel cylinder - servicing

1 Servicing a rear wheel cylinder is similar to that described for front wheel cylinders in Section 7 but observe the following points:

2 The bolt-on type cylinder (Corsair and GT) has two pistons and a separate handbrake expander.

3 Only the left hand wheel cylinder is fitted with a bleed nipple, the right hand one having two rigid pipe connections, one from the master cylinder and another to the left hand wheel cylinder.

10 Front brake caliper - removal and refitting

1 The caliper units fitted to the Cortina standard and de luxe models differ slightly in design from those fitted to Corsair and GT models but the procedure for removal and refitting is identical.

2 Jack up the front of the vehicle and remove the road wheel.

3 Disconnect the fluid line at its union with the caliper unit. Cap the line to prevent loss of fluid or the ingress of dirt.

4 Remove the friction pads as described in Section 3.

5 Bend back the lockplate tabs and unscrew the two caliper unit mounting bolts (not the bolts which secure the two halves of the caliper together, these must never be touched). Lift the caliper away.

6 Refitting is a reversal of removal but use a new locking plate and tighten the securing bolts to a torque of between 45 and 50 lb ft (6.22 and 6.91 kg m).

7 Bleed the hydraulic system on completion.

11 Front brake caliper (Cortina standard and de luxe) - dismantling and reassembly

1 Remove the dust cover retaining circlips and detach the dust covers.

2 Apply air from a tyre pump at the fluid entry port on the caliper unit and carefully eject both pistons.

3 Extract the sealing rings from both cylinder bores taking care not to scratch the bore surfaces when removing them.

4 Discard the rubber components and wash the other parts in clean hydraulic fluid or methylated spirit.

5 Examine the piston and cylinder bore surfaces for 'bright' wear areas. If these are evident, renew the complete caliper unit.

6 Obtain a repair kit which will contain all the necessary components which must be renewed at a major overhaul.

7 Fit a new seal to the groove in each cylinder. Use the fingers only to manipulate them into position.

8 Dip each piston in clean brake fluid and insert it (crown first) into its respective cylinder, pushing it to the limit of its travel.

9 Engage the dust covers over the pistons and then secure them to the caliper body with the retainers.

12 Front brake caliper (Corsair and all GT models) - dismantling and reassembly

1 The procedure is similar to that described in the preceding Section but no retainers are used to secure the rubber bellows type dust covers.

2 Partially eject the pistons in order to disengage the bellows

Fig. 9.11. Front hub (drum type brakes)

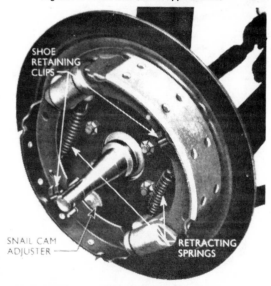

Fig. 9.12. Cortina front drum type brake assembly

Fig. 9.13. Rear drum brake assembly

from the piston skirt recesses. Remove the pistons completely and then disengage the bellows from the grooves in the cylinder bores.

13 Front brake disc - examination, removal and refitting

1   When the friction pads are inspected for wear also check the condition of the discs. If they are badly scored or grooved they must be renewed.

2   Disc run-out (out of true) should not normally require checking unless there has been some damage to the steering or hubs. A dial gauge should be used to check the run-out which must not exceed 0.002 inch (0.051 mm).

3   To renew a disc, jack up the front of the vehicle, remove the road wheel and caliper.

4   Knock the dust cap from the end of the hub, withdraw the split pin, nut retainer, adjusting nut and thrust washer.

5   Pull the hub/disc assembly towards you and catch the outer taper roller bearing. Remove the hub/disc assembly.

6   Bend back the locking plate tabs from the bolts which secure the disc to the hub and separate the two components.

7   Reassembly is a reversal of dismantling but use new bolt locking plates and tighten the bolts to a torque of between 30 and 34 lb ft (4.15 to 4.70 kg m).

8   Refitting is a reversal of removal but tighten the hub adjusting nut to a torque of 28 lb ft (3.85 kg m) whilst rotating the hub in its forward direction of rotation. Slacken the nut 90° and fit the nut retainer and a new split pin.

9   Refit the dust cap, the caliper unit and the road wheel and lower the jack.

14 Master cylinder - removal, servicing and refitting

1   The master cylinder is located on the engine compartment rear bulkhead.

2   Disconnect the master cylinder pushrod from the pedal by unscrewing the bolt from the pedal arm.

3   Disconnect the fluid pipe from the master cylinder body by unscrewing the union nut. Plug the line.

4   Unscrew the nuts from the securing studs and lift the master cylinder from its location.

5   Empty the fluid from the master cylinder integral reservoir and depress the pushrod two or three times to expel the fluid from the cylinder.

6   Pull off the rubber boot, detach the circlip and withdraw the pushrod.

7   Withdraw the piston and valve assembly from the cylinder.

8   Dismantle the assembly by lifting the tab which engages under the piston shoulder and withdrawing the piston. Compress the spring with the fingers and move the retainer to one side, this will allow the valve stem to pass through the larger hole of the retainer. Slide the spacer and shim from the valve stem.

9   Discard all rubber seals and wash the components in methylated spirit or clean brake fluid.

10 Examine the surfaces of the piston and cylinder bore for 'bright' wear areas. If these are evident, renew the master cylinder complete.

11 Obtain a repair kit which will contain all the necessary seals and other parts which must be renewed at a major overhaul.

12 Fit the new seals using the fingers only to manipulate them into position. Reassembly and refitment are reversals of the dismantling and removal procedures. Dip components in clean brake fluid before assembling.

15 Flexible hoses - inspection, removal and refitting

1   Inspect the condition of the flexible hydraulic hoses leading from under the front wings to the brackets on the front suspension unit, and also the single hose on the rear axle casing. If they are swollen, damaged or chafed, they must be renewed.

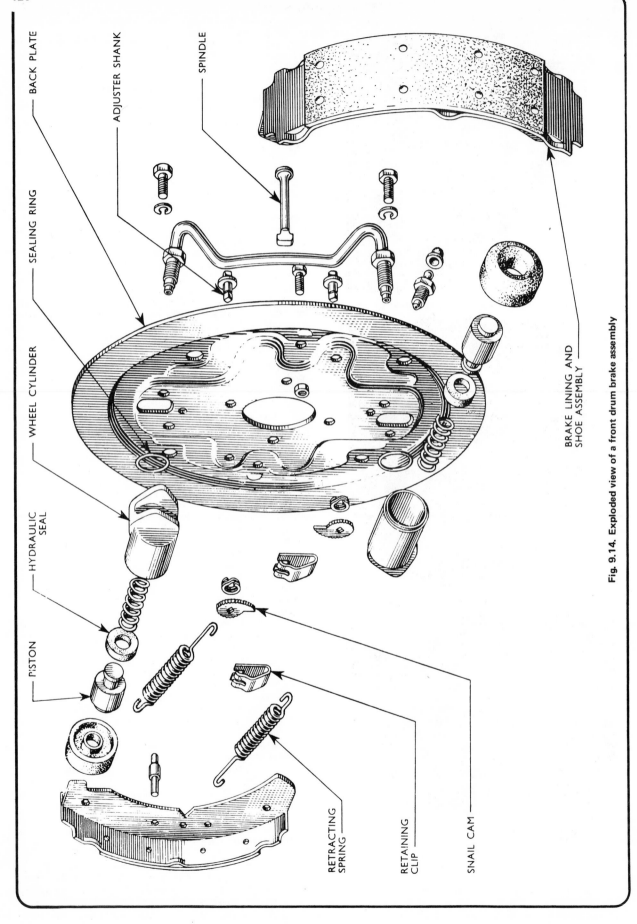

BACK PLATE

ADJUSTER SHANK

SPINDLE

SEALING RING

WHEEL CYLINDER

HYDRAULIC SEAL

PISTON

RETRACTING SPRING

RETAINING CLIP

SNAIL CAM

BRAKE LINING AND SHOE ASSEMBLY

Fig. 9.14. Exploded view of a front drum brake assembly

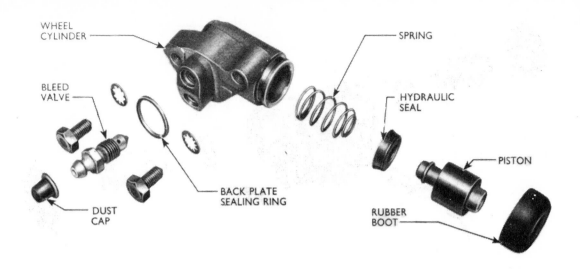

WHEEL CYLINDER

SPRING

BLEED VALVE

HYDRAULIC SEAL

PISTON

DUST CAP

BACK PLATE SEALING RING

RUBBER BOOT

Fig. 9.15. Exploded view of a front wheel cylinder

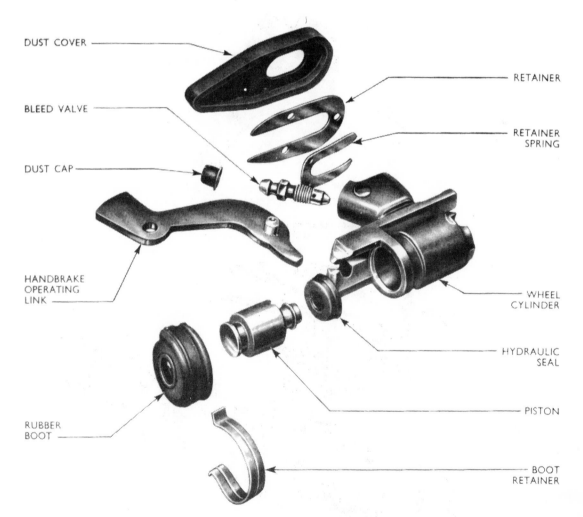

DUST COVER

RETAINER

BLEED VALVE

RETAINER SPRING

DUST CAP

HANDBRAKE OPERATING LINK

WHEEL CYLINDER

HYDRAULIC SEAL

PISTON

RUBBER BOOT

BOOT RETAINER

Fig. 9.16. Exploded view of a rear wheel cylinder (Cortina standard and de-luxe)

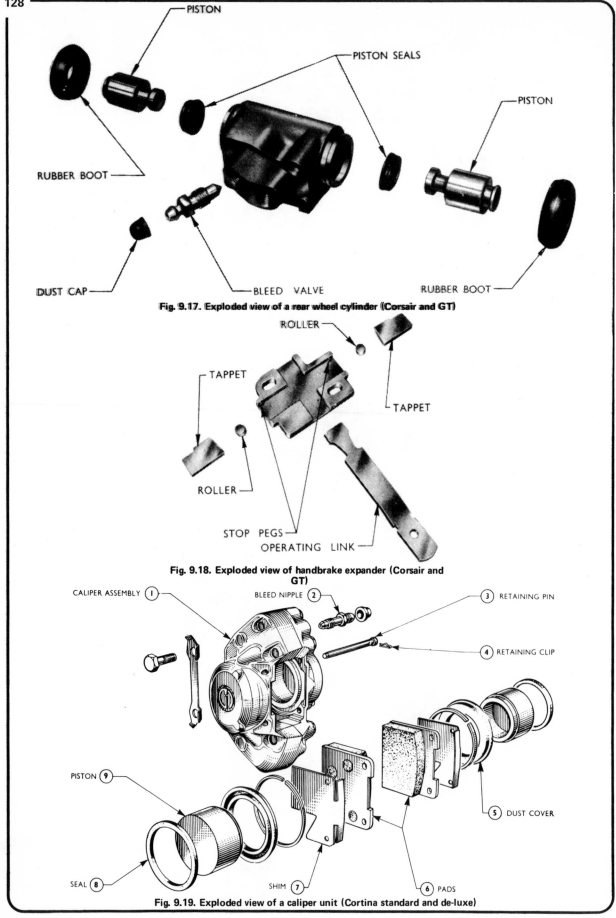

Fig. 9.17. Exploded view of a rear wheel cylinder (Corsair and GT)

Fig. 9.18. Exploded view of handbrake expander (Corsair and GT)

Fig. 9.19. Exploded view of a caliper unit (Cortina standard and de-luxe)

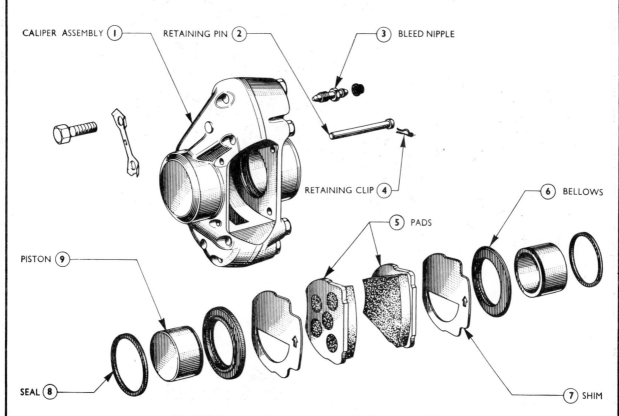

CALIPER ASSEMBLY ① RETAINING PIN ② ③ BLEED NIPPLE

RETAINING CLIP ④

⑤ PADS

⑥ BELLOWS

PISTON ⑨

SEAL ⑧

⑦ SHIM

Fig. 9.20. Exploded view of a caliper unit (Corsair and GT)

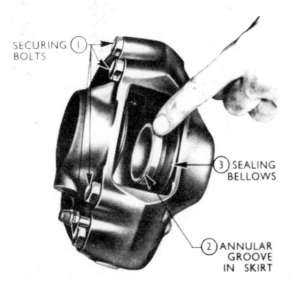

SECURING ① BOLTS

③ SEALING BELLOWS

② ANNULAR GROOVE IN SKIRT

Fig. 9.21. Assembling the sealing bellows (Corsair/GT caliper)
On no account unscrew bolts (1)

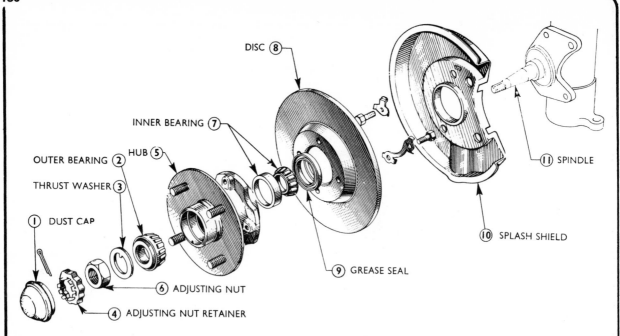

DISC ⑧
INNER BEARING ⑦
OUTER BEARING ② HUB ⑤
THRUST WASHER ③
① DUST CAP
⑥ ADJUSTING NUT
④ ADJUSTING NUT RETAINER
⑪ SPINDLE
⑩ SPLASH SHIELD
⑨ GREASE SEAL

Fig. 9.22. Exploded view of front hub/disc assembly

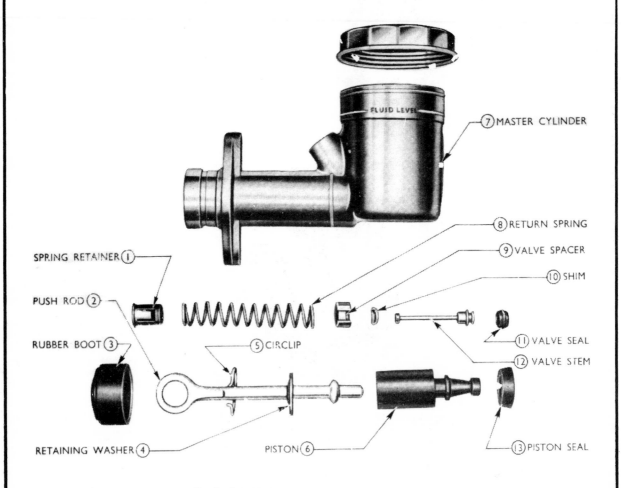

FLUID LEVEL
⑦ MASTER CYLINDER
⑧ RETURN SPRING
⑨ VALVE SPACER
⑩ SHIM
SPRING RETAINER ①
PUSH ROD ②
RUBBER BOOT ③
⑤ CIRCLIP
⑪ VALVE SEAL
⑫ VALVE STEM
RETAINING WASHER ④
PISTON ⑥
⑬ PISTON SEAL

Fig. 9.23. Exploded view of the brake master cylinder

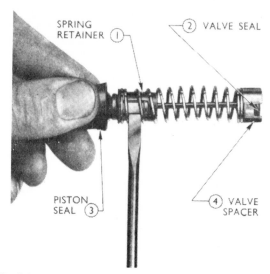

Fig. 9.24. Disengaging the master cylinder spring retainer tab

2 Undo the locknuts at both ends of the flexible hoses and then holding the hexagon nut on the flexible hose steady undo the other union nut and remove the flexible hose and washer.

3 Replacement is a reversal of the removal procedure, but carefully check all the securing brackets are in a sound condition and that the locknuts are tight. Bleed the hydraulic system (Section 17).

16 Rigid brake lines - inspection, removal and refitting

1 At regular intervals, wipe the steel brake pipes clean and examine them for signs of rust or denting caused by flying stones.

2 Examine the securing clips. Bend the tongues of the clips if necessary to ensure that they hold the brake pipes securely without letting them rattle or vibrate.

3 Check that the pipes are not touching any adjacent components or rubbing against any part of the vehicle. Where this is observed, bend the pipe gently away to clear.

4 Any section of pipe which is rusty or chafed should be renewed. Brake pipes are available to the correct length and fitted with end unions from most Ford dealers and can be made to pattern by many accessory suppliers. When installing the new pipes use the old pipes as a guide to bending and do not make any bends sharper than is necessary.

5 The system will of course have to be bled when the circuit has been reconnected.

17 Bleeding the hydraulic system

1 Removal of all the air from the hydraulic system is essential to the correct working of the braking system, and before undertaking this, examine the fluid reservoir cap to ensure that both vent holes, one on top and the second underneath but not in line, are clear; check the level of fluid and top up if required.

2 Check all brake line unions and connections for possible seepage, and at the same time check the condition of the rubber hoses, which may be perished.

3 If the condition of the wheel cylinders is in doubt, check for possible signs of fluid leakage.

4 If there is any possibility of incorrect fluid having been put into the system, drain all the fluid out and flush through with methylated spirit. Renew all piston seals and cups since these will be affected and could possibly fail under pressure.

5 Gather together a clean jam jar, a length of tubing which fits tightly over the bleed nipples, and a tin of the correct brake fluid.

6 To bleed the system clean the areas around the bleed valves, and start on the front brakes first by removing the rubber cup over the bleed valve, if fitted, and fitting a rubber tube in position.

7 Place tne end of the tube in a clean glass jar containing sufficient fluid to keep the end of the tube underneath during the operation.

8 Bleed the front brakes first and then the rear (one bleed nipple only).

9 Open the bleed valve with a spanner and quickly press down the brake pedal. After slowly releasing the pedal, pause for a moment to allow the fluid to recoup in the master cylinder and then depress again. This will force air from the system. Continue until no more air bubbles can be seen coming from the tube. At intervals make certain that the reservoir is kept topped up, otherwise air will enter at this point again. Use only new fluid for topping up which has been stored in an airtight container and has remained unshaken for at least 24 hours.

10 Tighten the bleed screws when the pedal is in the fully depressed position.

11 If a vacuum servo unit is fitted, always depress the brake pedal several times to destroy the vacuum before bleeding the system.

18 Handbrake linkage - adjustment

1 As previously explained, the handbrake is automatically adjusted at the same time as the rear brakes are adjusted. Due to cable stretch after high mileages or after dismantling of the linkage the following supplementary adjustment procedure may be required.

2 Release the handbrake lever fully.

3 Turn each of the rear brake adjusters clockwise until the shoes are locked against the drums.

4 Slacken the locknut on the threaded sleeve of the handbrake outer cable. This is located in the propeller shaft tunnel under the car (Cortina standard and de luxe) (photo).

5 Turn the adjusting nut until all slack is removed from the handbrake cable. Tighten the locknut.

6 Slacken each of the backplate adjusters until the road wheels rotate without any binding of the linings.

7 When correctly adjusted, the handbrake should be full on after moving through four or five notches of the ratchet at the hand control.

8 On GT and Corsair models the handbrake adjustment procedure is similar except that the adjuster sleeve and nuts are located at the rear of the rear axle.

19 Handbrake cable - renewal (Cortina standard and de luxe)

1 Disconnect the cable from the relay lever (bottom end) in the case of facia mounted handles. With floor mounted handbrake levers, disconnect the cable from the handbrake lever.

2 Unscrew the locknut which secures the outer cable to the bracket within the propeller shaft tunnel. Pull the adjuster sleeve to the rear and slide the inner cable out of the bracket.

3 Remove the 'U' clip which retains the outer cable to the long clevis.

4 Disconnect the inner cable at the slotted hole on each brake backplate clevis. Remove the cable.

5 The handbrake lever can be removed after unscrewing the eight self-tapping screws from the gaiter retainer inside the vehicle and then withdrawing the two handbrake lever securing bolts.

6 Installation of the new cable is a reversal of removal, adjust the linkage as described in the preceding Section.

20 Handbrake cable - renewal (GT and Corsair)

1 Fully release the handbrake lever.

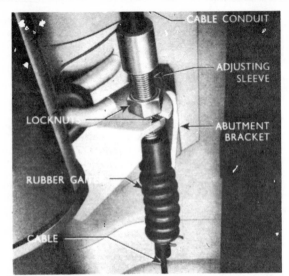

Fig. 9.25. Location of handbrake cable adjuster sleeve (Cortina standard and de-luxe)

2 Within the engine compartment, unhook the primary cable from the relay lever.

3 Inside the car, disconnect the facia mounted handbrake control.

4 Push the rubber boot, cable and grommet through the bulkhead into the engine compartment after having disconnected the cable from the handbrake control.

5 Disconnect the secondary cable from the clevis at the lower end of the relay lever (photo).

6 Unhook the cable from the guide bracket on the gearbox mounting support.

7 Remove the 'U' clip which retains the brake outer cable to the bracket within the propeller shaft tunnel.

8 Pull the outer cable to the rear and slide the inner cable from the bracket.

9 At the left hand backplate disconnect the cable nipple from the clevis.

10 Slacken both adjuster nuts on the equaliser brackets and screw them right back and then remove the cable from the vehicle.

11 Installation is a reversal of removal but adjust the linkage as described in Section 18.

20.5 Handbrake relay lever connection

21 Brake pedal - removal and refitting

The procedure for removing and refitting the brake pedal is described in conjunction with the clutch pedal in Chapter 5.

22 Brake pedal stop light switch - adjustment

1 The stop light switch is of mechanical type and its plunger is in contact with the brake pedal arm.

2 The brake pedal has a 'built-in' free movement of 3/16 inch (4.75 mm) which is provided by the retained type pushrod.

3 As the brake pedal is depressed, the switch plunger extends through the free movement dimension and should only then actuate the stop lights during the following brake operating distance which varies according to the state of brake shoe adjustment but is nominally 7/16 inch (11.11 mm).

4 Carry out any adjustment to the switch by loosening the locknut and varying the effective length of the plunger until with the ignition switched on, the stop lights illuminate as specified in the preceding paragraph (photo).

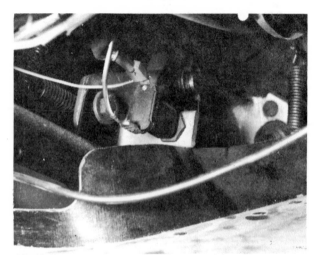

22.4 Stop lamp switch and locknut

23 Vacuum servo unit (booster) - description

1 A vacuum servo unit is fitted into the brake hydraulic circuit in series with the master cylinder, to provide assistance to the driver when the brake pedal is depressed. This reduces the effort required by the driver to operate the brakes under all braking conditions.

2 The unit operates by vacuum obtained from the induction manifold and comprises basically a booster diaphragm and check valve. The servo unit and hydraulic master cylinder are connected together so that the servo unit piston rod acts as the master cylinder pushrod. The driver's braking effort is transmitted through another pushrod to the servo unit piston and its built-in control system. The servo unit piston does not fit tightly into the cylinder, but has a strong diaphragm to keep its edges in constant contact with the cylinder wall, so assuring an air tight seal between the two parts. The forward chamber is held under vacuum conditions created in the inlet manifold of the engine and, during periods when the brake pedal is not in use, the controls open a passage to the rear chamber, so placing it under vacuum conditions as well. When the brake pedal is depressed, the vacuum passage to the rear chamber is cut off and the chamber opened to atmospheric pressure. The consequent rush of air pushes the servo piston forward in the vacuum chamber and operates the main pushrod to the master cylinder.

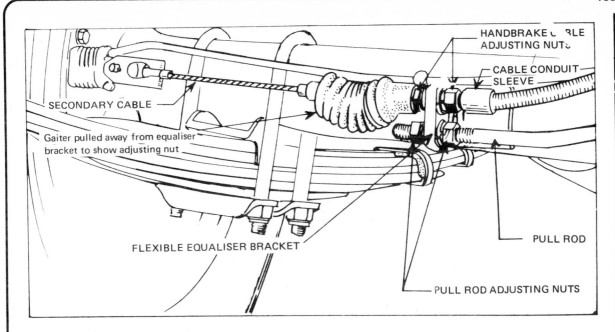

Fig. 9.26. Location of handbrake cable adjuster nuts (Corsair and GT)

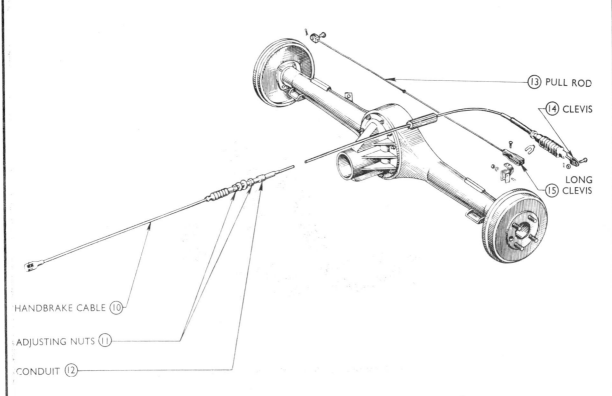

Fig. 9.27. Layout of handbrake linkage (Cortina standard and de-luxe)

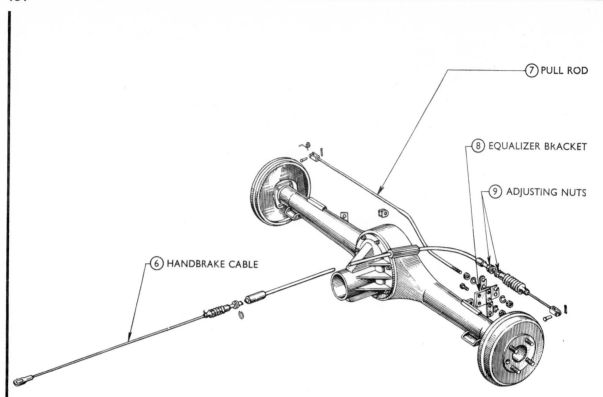

⑦ PULL ROD

⑧ EQUALIZER BRACKET

⑨ ADJUSTING NUTS

⑥ HANDBRAKE CABLE

Fig. 9.28. Layout of handbrake linkage (Corsair and GT)

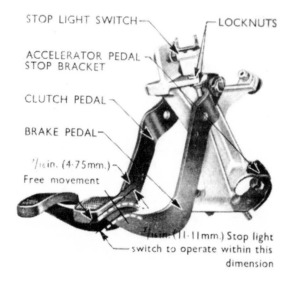

STOP LIGHT SWITCH — LOCKNUTS

ACCELERATOR PEDAL STOP BRACKET

CLUTCH PEDAL

BRAKE PEDAL

$^7/_{16}$in. (4·75mm.) Free movement

$^7/_{16}$in. (11·11mm.) Stop light switch to operate within this dimension

Fig. 9.28a Brake pedal and stop light switch

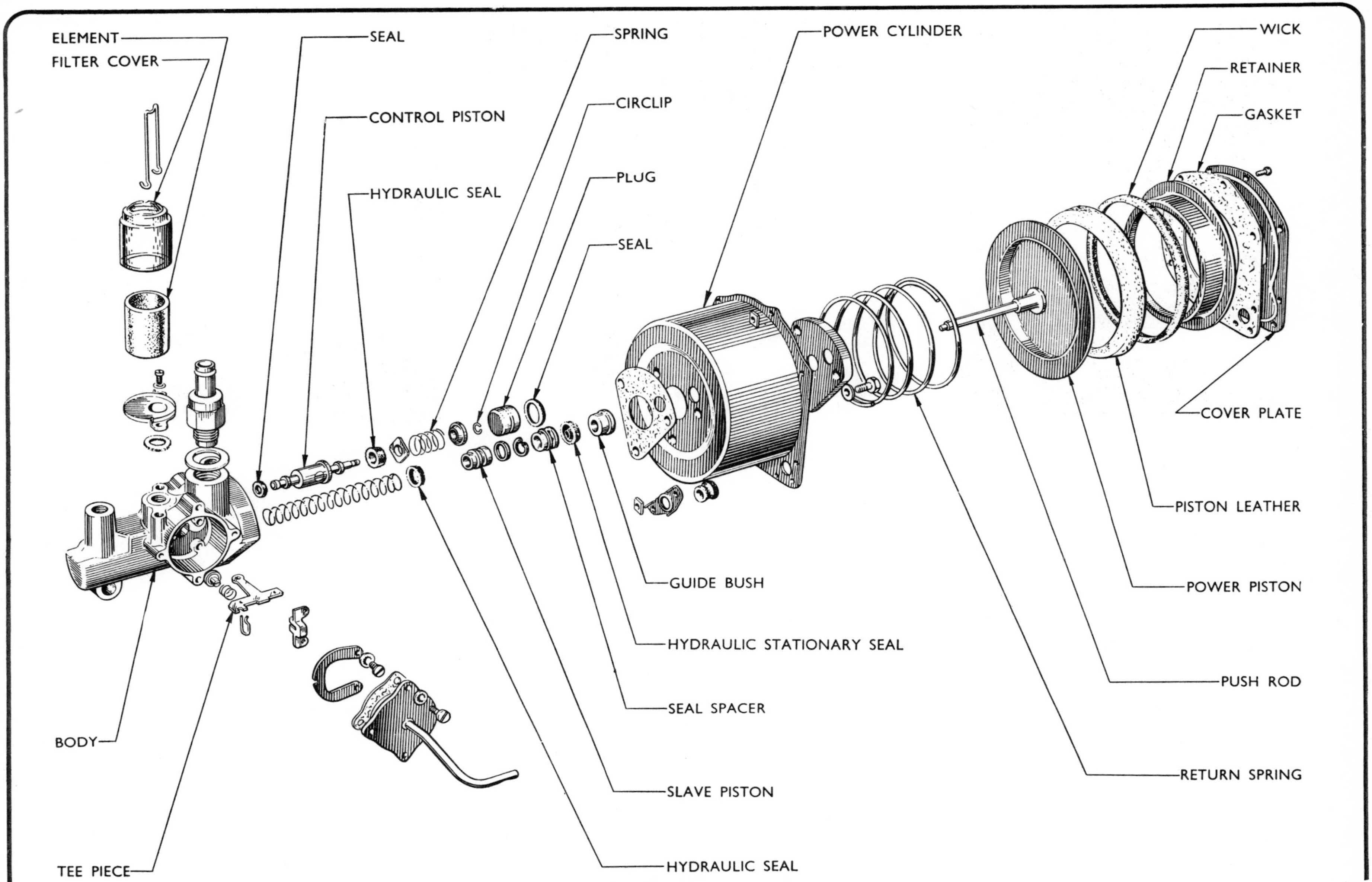

Fig. 9.29. Exploded view of the vacuum servo unit

WICK
RETAINER
GASKET
COVER PLATE
PISTON LEATHER
POWER PISTON
PUSH ROD
RETURN SPRING
POWER CYLINDER
GUIDE BUSH
HYDRAULIC STATIONARY SEAL
SEAL SPACER
SLAVE PISTON
HYDRAULIC SEAL
SPRING
CIRCLIP
PLUG
SEAL
SEAL
CONTROL PISTON
HYDRAULIC SEAL
ELEMENT
FILTER COVER
BODY
TEE PIECE

3 The controls are designed so that assistance is given under all conditions and, when the brakes are not required, vacuum in the rear chamber is established when the brake pedal is released. All air from the atmosphere entering the rear chamber is passed through a small air filter.

4 Under normal operating conditions the vacuum servo unit is very reliable and does not require overhaul except at very high mileages. In this case it is far better to obtain a service exchange unit, rather than repair the original unit.

24 Vacuum servo unit - removal and refitting

1 Disconnect the vacuum pipe from the servo unit.
2 Disconnect the two hydraulic pipelines from the servo unit. Fit bleed nipple dust caps to the open ends of the pipes to prevent ingress of dirt.
3 Unscrew and remove the three bracket bolts also the three bolts which secure the bracket to the servo unit. Withdraw the unit from the engine compartment.
4 Refitting is a reversal of removal but note that the pipe from the master cylinder connects with the tapped hole immediately adjacent to the vacuum power cylinder.
5 When installation is complete, bleed the hydraulic system (Section 17).

25 Vacuum servo unit - dismantling and reassembly

1 Remove the spring clip, filter cover and filter element.
2 Carefully unscrew the eight screws from the power cylinder cover, at the same time restricting the action of the internal return spring which will be forcing the cover off. Two of the screws connect to air/vacuum transfer pipe to the vacuum power cylinder casing.
3 Withdraw the power cylinder cover, gasket and piston assembly.
4 Secure the cast part of the servo unit in a vice fitted with jaw protectors. With the power cylinder uppermost, remove the bolts and washers securing it to the servo body.
5 Remove the reinforcement plate and the screws which retain the air vacuum transfer tube to the valve chest. Remove the opposite end of this pipe from the rubber grommet located on the vacuum power cylinder flange.
6 Remove the vacuum power cylinder, the pushrod guide bush and the gasket from the slave cylinder.
7 Remove the two screws which secure the bridge piece and valve spring to the valve chest.
8 Depress the plug at the end of the vacuum power cylinder end of the control piston, with the thumb to release the two valves and tee-piece.
9 Detach the spring clips which retain the valves to the tee-piece.
10 Remove the hydraulic (stationary) seal from the slave cylinder bore.
11 Remove the nylon seal spacer and then the circlip in the slave cylinder bore. To facilitate the latter operation, depress the slave piston and retain it in the depressed position by making up a wire tool as shown in Fig 9.36.
12 Remove the retaining washer, slave piston and return spring from the bore.
13 Remove the plug/seal assembly from the power cylinder end of the control cylinder bore.
14 Remove the control piston complete with return spring. If essential, the control piston may be dismantled by removing the circlip, spring seats and spring. Renew the seals.
15 Remove the secondary piston, using air pressure from a tyre pump to eject it after having blanked off the end of the control cylinder bore with the palm of the hand.
16 The power piston should not be dismantled beyond the fitting of a new rubber wick.
17 Clean all components in methylated spirit or clean hydraulic fluid. Renew all seals. In some instances, only the complete

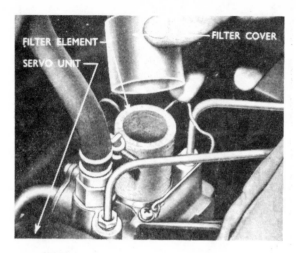
Fig. 9.30. Removing the servo unit filter cover and element

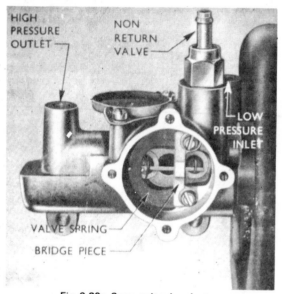
Fig. 9.30a. Servo unit valve chest

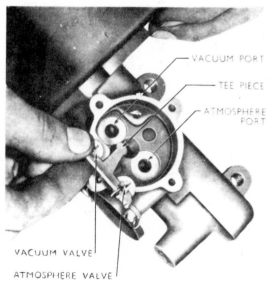
Fig. 9.31. Removing servo unit 'tee' piece

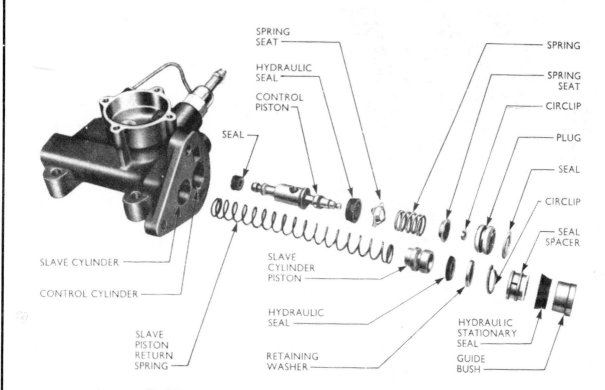

SPRING SEAT

HYDRAULIC SEAL

CONTROL PISTON

SEAL

SPRING

SPRING SEAT

CIRCLIP

PLUG

SEAL

CIRCLIP

SEAL SPACER

SLAVE CYLINDER

CONTROL CYLINDER

SLAVE PISTON RETURN SPRING

SLAVE CYLINDER PISTON

HYDRAULIC SEAL

RETAINING WASHER

HYDRAULIC STATIONARY SEAL

GUIDE BUSH

Fig. 9.32. Exploded view of the servo unit slave cylinder and control unit

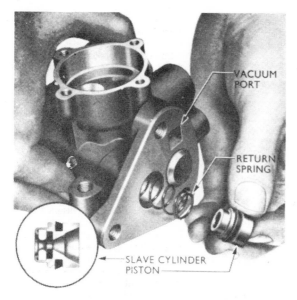

VACUUM PORT

RETURN SPRING

SLAVE CYLINDER PISTON

Fig. 9.33. Removing the servo unit slave cylinder piston

PISTON

RETAINER

RUBBER WICK

Fig. 9.34. The servo unit power piston

Fig. 9.35. Fitting the nylon seal spacer to the servo unit slave cylinder

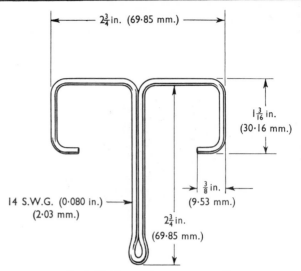

Fig. 9.36. Slave spring compressor diagram

piston/seal assembly is available as a replacement.

18 Dip each component in hydraulic fluid prior to reassembly.

19 Reassembly is a reversal of dismantling but observe the following.

20 Check that the transverse hole in the primary control piston aligns with the drilling in the valve chest.

21 The recess in the arm of the air/vacuum valve tee-piece must be located at the opposite side of the valve chest to the two

valve mechanism securing screw holes.

22 Fit a new gasket between the valve chest and the air/vacuum transfer tube.

23 Ensure that the reinforcement plate and valve body chamber holes are in alignment.

24 Tighten the three bolts which secure the vacuum power cylinder and reinforcement plate to a torque of between 10 and 12 lb ft (1.38 to 1.66 kg m).

26 Fault diagnosis - braking system

Symptom	Reason/s	Remedy
Pedal travels almost to floorboards before brakes operate	Brake fluid level too low	Top up master cylinder reservoir. Check for leaks.
	Caliper leaking	Dismantle caliper, clean, fit new rubbers and bleed brakes.
	Master cylinder leaking (bubbles in master cylinder fluid)	Dismantle master cylinder, clean and fit new rubbers. Bleed brakes.
	Brake flexible hose leaking	Examine and fit new hose if old hose leaking. Bleed brakes.
	Brake line fractured	Replace with new brake pipe. Bleed brakes.
	Brake system unions loose	Check all unions in brake system and tighten as necessary. Bleed brakes.
	Pad or shoe linings over 75% worn	Fit replacement pads or shoes.
	Brakes badly out of adjustment	Jack up car and adjust brakes.
Brake pedal feels springy	New linings not yet bedded-in	Use brakes gently until springy pedal feeling leaves.
	Brake discs or drums badly worn or cracked	Fit new brake discs or drums.
	Master cylinder securing nuts loose	Tighten master cylinder securing nuts. Ensure spring washers are fitted.
Brake pedal feels spongy and soggy	Caliper or wheel cylinder leaking	Dismantle caliper or wheel cylinder, clean, fit new rubbers and bleed brakes.
	Master cylinder leaking (bubbles in master cylinder reservoir)	Dismantle master cylinder, clean and fit new rubbers and bleed brakes. Replace cylinder if internal walls scored.
	Brake pipe line or flexible hose leaking	Fit new pipeline or hose.
	Unions in brake system loose	Examine for leaks, tighten as necessary.
Excessive effort required to brake car	Pad or show linings badly worn	Fit replacement brake shoes and linings.
	New pads or shoes recently fitted — not yet bedded-in	Use brakes gently until braking effort normal.
	Harder linings fitted than standard causing increase in pedal pressure	Remove pads or shoes and replace with normal units.
	Linings and brake drums contaminated with with oil, grease or hydraulic fluid	Rectify source of leak, clean brake drums, fit new linings.

Brakes uneven and pulling to one side	Linings and discs or drums contaminated with oil, grease or hydraulic fluid	Ascertain and rectify source of leak, clean discs or drums, fit new pads or shoes.
	Tyre pressures unequal	Check and inflate as necessary.
	Radial ply tyres fitted at one end of the car only	Fit radial ply tyres of the same make to all four wheels.
	Brake caliper loose	Tighten backplate securing nuts and bolts.
	Brake pads or shoes fitted incorrectly	Remove and fit correct way round.
	Different type of linings fitted at each wheel	Fit the pads or shoes specified by the manufacturer all round.
	Anchorages for front suspension or rear suspension loose	Tighten front and rear suspension pick-up points including spring anchorage.
	Brake discs or drums badly worn, cracked or distorted	Fit new brake discs or drums.
Brakes tend to bind, drag or lock-on	Brake linings adjusted too tightly	Slacken off brake shoe adjusters.

Chapter 10 Electrical system

Contents

Specifications

System	12 volt; positive earth

Battery

Capacity	
Standard	38 amp/hr (9 plates per cell)
Optional heavy duty	51 amp/hr (11 plates per cell)
Specific gravity (charged)	1.275 to 1.290
Electrolyte capacity	
Standard	4.5 pints (2.5 litres)
Heavy duty	6.4 pints (3.6 litres)

Dynamo

Type	12 volt 2 brush
Speed (ratio to engine)	1.50 : 1
Minimum brush length	5/16 in (8.0 mm)
Total fan belt deflection	½ in (13.0 mm)
Rated output	
Standard	22 amps
Heavy duty	25 amps

Starter motor

Type	12 volt 4 pole
Number of brushes	4 (2 earthed)
Number of ring gear teeth	110

Number of pinion teeth	9	
Gear ratio	12.22 : 1	

	Wattage	
Bulbs and sealed beam units	**Cortina**	**Corsair**
Headlamp sealed beam	60/45	60/45
Side lamp	–	6
Side lamp and front direction indicator	6/21	–
Front direction indicator	–	24
Rear direction indicator	21	24
Tail and stop	6/21	6/24
Number plate	6	6
Interior lamp	3	6
Instrument panel and warning...	2.2	2.2

1 General description

The electrical system is of the 12 volt type and the major components comprise: a 12 volt 38 amp/hour battery with the positive terminal earthed; a voltage regulator and cut-out; a 12 volt two brush dynamo driven by the fan belt and the starter motor.

The 12 volt battery positioned on the right hand side of the engine compartment supplies a steady supply of current for the ignition, lighting, and other electrical circuits, and provides a reserve of electricity when the current consumed by the electrical equipment exceeds that being produced by the dynamo.

The dynamo is of the two brush type and works in conjunction with the voltage regulator and cut-out. The dynamo is cooled by a multi-bladed fan mounted behind the dynamo pulley, and blows air through cooling holes in the dynamo end brackets. The output from the dynamo is controlled by the voltage regulator which ensures a high output if the battery is in a low state of charge or the demands from the electrical equipment high, and a low output if the battery is fully charged and there is little demand from the electrical equipment.

2 Battery - removal and refitting

1 Disconnect the positive and negative leads from the battery terminals.
2 Disconnect the battery clamp at the rear of the battery and withdraw the unit to the rear out of the front clamp.
3 Keep the battery level during removal so that the electrolyte does not spill.
4 Refitting is a reversal of removal. Apply petroleum jelly to the terminals to prevent corrosion.

3 Battery - maintenance and inspection

1 Normal weekly battery maintenance consists of checking the electrolyte level of each cell to ensure that the separators are covered by ¼ inch (6.35 mm) of electrolyte. If the level has fallen, top up the battery using distilled water only. Do not overfill. If the battery is overfilled or any electrolyte spilled, immediately wipe away the excess as electrolyte attacks and corrodes any metal it comes into contact with very rapidly.
2 As well as keeping the terminals clean and covered with petroleum jelly, the top of the battery, and especially the top of the cells, should be kept clean and dry. This helps prevent corrosion and ensures that the battery does not become partially discharged by leakage through dampness and dirt.
3 Once every six months remove the battery and inspect the battery securing bolts, the battery clamp plate, tray, and battery leads for corrosion (white fluffy deposits on the metal which are brittle to touch). If any corrosion is found, clean off the deposits with ammonia and paint over the clean metal with an anti-rust/anti-acid paint.
4 At the same time inspect the battery case for cracks. If a crack is found, clean and plug it with one of the proprietary compounds marketed by firms such as Holts for this purpose. If leakage through the crack has been excessive then it will be necessary to refill the appropriate cell with fresh electrolyte as detailed later. Cracks are frequently caused to the top of the battery cases by pouring in distilled water in the middle of winter **after** instead of **before** a run. This gives the water no chance to mix with the electrolyte and so the former freezes and splits the battery case.
5 If topping up the battery becomes excessive and the case has been inspected for cracks that could cause leakage, but none are found, the battery is being overcharged and the voltage regulator will have to be checked and reset.
6 With the battery on the bench at the six monthly interval check, measure its specific gravity with a hydrometer to determine its state of charge and the condition of the electrolyte. There should be very little variation between the different cells and if a variation in excess of 0.025 is present it will be due to either:

a) Loss of electrolyte from the battery at some time caused by spillage or a leak resulting in a drop in the specific gravity of the electrolyte, when the deficiency was replaced with distilled water instead of fresh electrolyte.
b) An internal short circuit caused by buckling of the plates or a similar malady pointing to the likelihood of total battery failure in the near future.

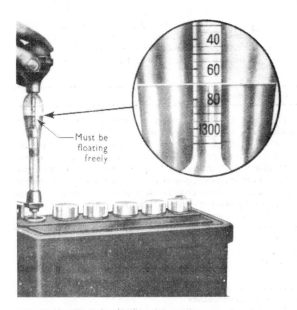

Fig. 10.1. Checking battery specific gravity with a hydrometer

7 The specific gravity for the electrolyte for fully charged conditions at the electrolyte temperature indicated, is listed in Table 1. The specific gravity of a fully discharged battery at different temperatures of the electrolyte is given in Table 2.

Table 1

Specific gravity - battery fully charged

1.268 at 100°F or 38°C	electrolyte temperature		
1.272 at 90°F or 32°C	''	''	
1.276 at 80°F or 27°C	''	''	
1.280 at 70°F or 21°C	''	''	
1.284 at 60°F or 16°C	''	''	
1.288 at 50°F or 10°C	''	''	
1.292 at 40°F or 4°C	''	''	
1.296 at 30°F or -1.5°C	''	''	

Table 2

Specific gravity - battery fully discharged

1.098 at 100°F or 38°C	electrolyte temperature		
1.102 at 90°F or 32°C	''	''	
1.106 at 80°F or 27°C	''	''	
1.110 at 70°F or 21°C	''	''	
1.114 at 60°F or 16°C	''	''	
1.118 at 50°F or 10°C	''	''	
1.122 at 40°F or 4°C	''	''	
1.126 at 30°F or -1.5°C	''	''	

4 Electrolyte - replenishment

1 If the battery is in a fully charged state and one of the cells maintains a specific gravity reading which is 0.025 or more lower than the others, and a check of each cell has been made with a voltage meter to check for short circuits (a four to seven second test should give a steady reading of between 1.2 to 1.8 volts), then it is likely that electrolyte has been lost from the cell with the low reading at some time.

2 Top the cell up with a solution of 1 part sulphuric acid to 2.5 parts of water. If the cell is already fully topped up, draw some electrolyte out of it with a pipette. When mixing the sulphuric acid and water **never add water to sulphuric acid** - always pour the acid slowly onto the water in a glass container. **If water is added to sulphuric acid it will explode.** Continue to top up the cell with the freshly made electrolyte and then recharge the battery and check the hydrometer readings.

5 Battery - charging

1 In winter time when heavy demand is placed upon the battery, such as when starting from cold, and much electrical equipment is continually in use, it is a good idea to occasionally have the battery fully charged from an external source at a rate of 3.5 to 4 amps. Continue to charge the battery at this rate until no further rise in specific gravity is noted over a four hour period. Alternatively, a trickle charger charging at the rate of 1.5 amps can be safely used overnight. Specially rapid boost charges which are claimed to restore the power of the battery in 1 to 2 hours are dangerous as they can cause serious damage to the battery plates through overheating. While charging the battery note that the temperature of the electrolyte should never exceed 100°F.

6 Dynamo - maintenance

1 Routine maintenance consists of checking the tension of the fan belt, and lubricating the dynamo rear bearing once every 5000 miles (8000 km).

2 The fan belt should be tight enough to ensure no slip between the belt and the dynamo pulley. If a shrieking noise comes from the engine when the unit is accelerated rapidly, it is likely that it is the fan belt slipping. On the other hand, the belt must not be too taut or the bearings will wear rapidly and cause dynamo failure or bearing seizure. Ideally ½ inch (12.7 mm) of total free movement should be available at the fan belt midway between the fan and the dynamo pulley. To adjust the fan belt tension slightly slacken the three dynamo retaining bolts and swing the dynamo on the upper two bolts outwards to increase the tension and inwards to lower it. It is best to leave the bolts fairly tight so that considerable effort has to be used to move the dynamo; otherwise it is difficult to get the correct setting. If the dynamo is being moved outwards to increase the tension and the bolts have only been slackened a little, a long spanner acting as a lever placed behind the dynamo with the lower end resting against the block works very well in moving the dynamo outwards. Retighten the dynamo bolts and check that the dynamo pulley is correctly aligned with the fan belt.

3 Lubrication on the dynamo consists of inserting three drops of SAE 30 engine oil in the small oil hole in the centre of the commutator end bracket. This lubricates the rear bearing. The front bearing is pre-packed with grease and requires no attention.

Fig. 10.2. Fan belt adjustment diagram (total deflection ½ in. (12.7 mm)

7 Dynamo - testing in position

1 If, with the engine running, no charge comes from the dynamo, or the charge is very low, first check that the fan belt is in place and is not slipping. Then check that the leads from the control box to the dynamo are firmly attached and that one has not come loose from its terminal.

2 The lead from the 'D' terminal on the dynamo should be connected to the 'D' terminal on the control box, and similarly, the 'F' terminals on the dynamo and control box should also be connected together. Check that this is so and that the leads have not been incorrectly fitted.

3 Make sure none of the electrical equipment (such as the lights or radio) is on and then pull the leads off the dynamo terminals marked 'D' and 'F', join the terminals together with a short length of wire.

4 Attach to the centre of this length of wire the positive clip of a 0 - 20 volts voltmeter and run the other clip to earth on the dynamo yoke. Start the engine and allow it to idle at approximately 750 rpm. At this speed the dynamo should give a reading of about 15 volts on the voltmeter. There is no point in raising the engine speed above a fast idle as the reading will then be inaccurate.

5 If no reading is recorded then check the brushes and brush connections. If a very low reading of approximately 1 volt is observed then the field winding may be suspect.

6 If a reading of between 4 to 6 volts is recorded it is likely that the armature winding is at fault.

7 The dynamo end plate must be removed before the commutator or brushes can be serviced (see Section 9).

8 If the voltmeter shows a good reading then, with the temporary link still in position, connect both leads from the control box to 'D' and 'F' on the dynamo ('D' to 'D' and 'F' to 'F'). Release the lead from the 'D' terminal at the control box end and clip one lead from the voltmeter to the end of the cable, and the other lead to a good earth. With the engine running at the same speed as previously, an identical voltage to that recorded at the dynamo should be noted on the voltmeter. If no voltage is recorded then there is a break in the wire. If the voltage is the same as recorded at the dynamo then check the 'F' lead in similar fashion. If both readings are the same as at the dynamo then it will be necessary to test the control box.

8 Dynamo - removal and refitting

1 Slacken the two dynamo retaining bolts and the nut on the sliding adjustment link, and move the dynamo in towards the engine so that the fan belt can be removed.

2 Disconnect the two leads from the dynamo terminals.

3 Remove the nut from the sliding link bolt and remove the two upper bolts. The dynamo is then free to be lifted away from the engine.

4 Replacement is a reversal of the above procedure. Do not finally tighten the retaining bolts and the nut on the sliding link until the fan belt has been tensioned correctly.

9 Dynamo - dismantling and inspection

1 Mount the dynamo in a vice and unscrew and remove the two tie bolts from the commutator end bracket.

2 Mark the commutator end bracket and the dynamo casing so the end bracket can be replaced in its original position. Pull the end bracket off the armature shaft. Some versions of the dynamo may have a raised pip on the end bracket which locates in a recess on the edge of the casing. If so, marking the end bracket and casing is not necessary. A pip may also be found on the drive end bracket at the opposite end of the casing.

3 Lift the two brush springs and draw the brushes out of the brush holders (arrowed in photo).

4 Measure the brushes and if worn down to 5/16 inch (8.0 mm) or less, unscrew the screws holding the brush leads to the end bracket. Take off the brushes complete with leads. Old and new brushes are compared in the photograph.

5 If no locating pip can be found, mark the drive end bracket and the dynamo casing so the drive end bracket can be replaced in its original position. Then pull the drive end bracket complete with armature out of the casing (photo).

6 Check the condition of the ball bearing in the drive end plate by firmly holding the plate and noting if there is visible side movement of the armature shaft in relation to the end plate. If play is present the armature assembly must be separated from the end plate. If the bearing is sound there is no need to carry out the work described in the following two paragraphs.

7 Hold the armature in one hand (mount it carefully in a vice if preferred) and undo the nut holding the combined plastic pulley wheel and fan in place. Pull off the pulley wheel fan assembly taking care not to break it (photo).

8 Next remove the Woodruff key (arrowed) from its slot in the armature shaft and also the bearing locating ring (photo).

9 Place the drive end bracket across the open jaws of a vice with the armature downwards and gently tap the armature shaft from the bearing in the end plate with the aid of a suitable drift (photo).

10 Carefully inspect the armature and check it for open or short circuited windings. It is a good indication of an open circuited armature when the commutator segments are burnt. If the armature has short circuited the commutator segments will be very badly burnt, and the overheated armature windings badly discoloured. If open or short circuits are suspected then test by substituting the suspect armature for a new one.

11 Check the resistance of the field coils. To do this, connect an ohmmeter between the field terminal and the yoke and note the reading on the ohmmeter which should be about 6 ohms. If the ohmmeter reading is infinity this indicates an open circuit in the field winding. If the ohmmeter reading is below 5 ohms this indicates that one of the field coils is faulty and must be replaced.

12 Field coil replacement involves the use of a wheel operated screwdriver, a soldering iron, caulking and riveting and this operation is considered to be beyond the scope of most owners. Therefore, if the field coils are at fault, either purchase a rebuilt dynamo, or take the casing to a Ford dealer or electrical engineering works for new field coils to be fitted.

13 Next check the condition of the commutator (arrowed). If it is dirty and blackened as shown, clean it with a petrol dampened rag. If the commutator is in good condition, the surface will be smooth and quite free from pits or burnt areas, and the insulated segments clearly defined.

14 If, after the commutator has been cleaned, pits and burnt spots are still present, wrap a strip of glass paper round the commutator taking great care to move the commutator ¼ of a turn every ten rubs till it is thoroughly clean (photo).

15 In extreme cases of wear the commutator can be mounted in a lathe and with the lathe turning at high speed, a very fine cut may be taken off the commutator. Then polish the commutator with glass paper. If the commutator has worn so that the insulators between the segments are level with the top of the segments, then undercut the insulators to a depth of 1/32 inch (0.8 mm). The best tool to use for this purpose is half a hacksaw blade ground to a thickness of the insulator, and with the handle end of the blade covered in insulating tape to make it comfortable to hold. This is the sort of finish the surface of the commutator should have when finished.

16 Check the bush bearing (arrowed) in the commutator end bracket for wear by noting if the armature spindle rocks when placed in it. If worn it must be renewed (photo).

17 The bush bearing can be removed by a suitable extractor or by screwing a 5/8 inch tap four or five times into the bush. The tap complete with bush is then pulled out of the end bracket.

18 Before fitting the new bush bearing as it is of the porous bronze type, it is essential that it is allowed to stand in SAE 30 engine oil for at least 24 hours before fitment. In an emergency the bush can be immersed in hot oil (100°C) for 2 hours.

19 Carefully fit the new bush into the end plate, pressing it in until the end of the bearing is flush with the inner side of the end plate. If available, press the bush in with a smooth shouldered mandrel the same diameter as the armature shaft.

10 Dynamo - repair and reassembly

1 To renew the ball bearing fitted to the drive end bracket, drill out the rivets which hold the bearing retainer plate to the end bracket and lift off the plate.

2 Press out the bearing from the end bracket and remove the corrugated and felt washers from the bearing housing.

3 Thoroughly clean the bearing housing, and the new bearing and pack with high melting point grease.

4 Place the felt washer and corrugated washer in that order in the end bracket bearing housing (photo).

5 Then fit the new bearing as shown (photo).

6 Gently tap the bearing into place with the aid of a suitable drift (photo).

7 Replace the bearing plate and fit three new rivets (photo).

8 Open up the rivets with the aid of a suitable cold chisel.

9 Finally peen over the open end of the rivets with the aid of a ball hammer (photo).

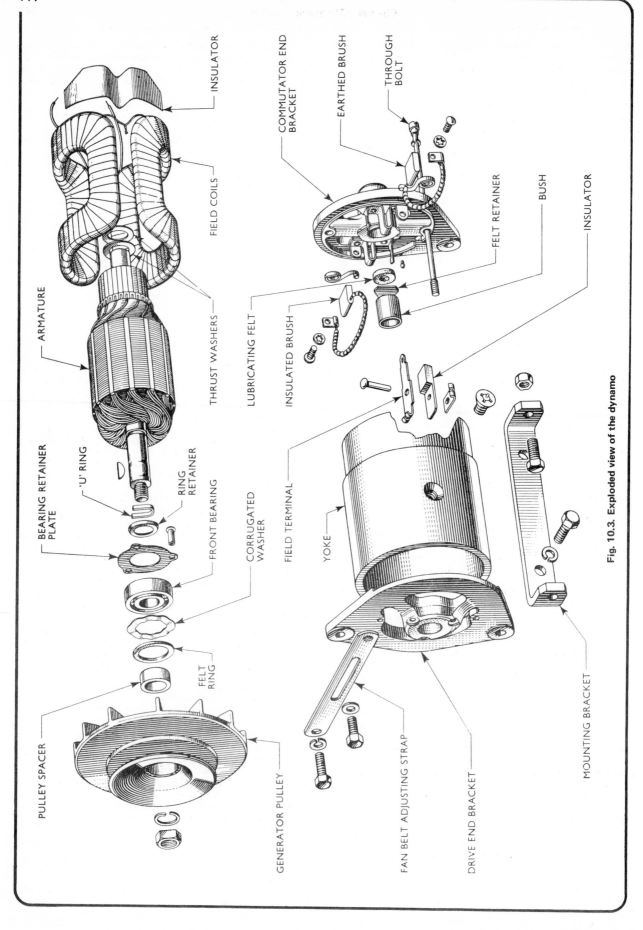

INSULATOR

FIELD COILS

COMMUTATOR END BRACKET

EARTHED BRUSH

THROUGH BOLT

FELT RETAINER

BUSH

INSULATOR

ARMATURE

THRUST WASHERS

LUBRICATING FELT

INSULATED BRUSH

BEARING RETAINER PLATE

'U' RING

RING RETAINER

FRONT BEARING

CORRUGATED WASHER

FIELD TERMINAL

YOKE

FELT RING

PULLEY SPACER

GENERATOR PULLEY

FAN BELT ADJUSTING STRAP

DRIVE END BRACKET

MOUNTING BRACKET

Fig. 10.3. Exploded view of the dynamo

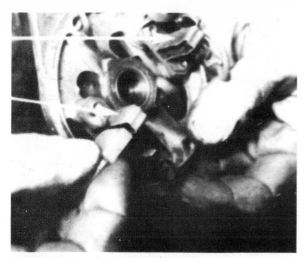

9.3 Removing dynamo brushes from holders

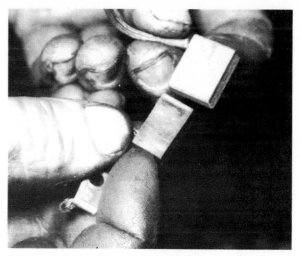

9.4 Dynamo old and new brush comparison

9.5 Withdrawing dynamo drive end bracket and armature

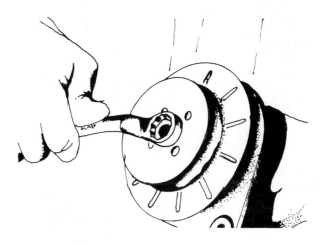

9.7 Removing dynamo pulley nut

9.8 Removing Woodruff key from armature shaft slot

9.9 Drifting armature shaft from end plate

9.14 Cleaning dynamo commutator

9.16 Checking armature spindle for wear

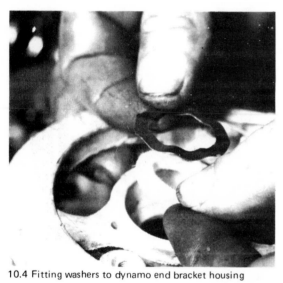
10.4 Fitting washers to dynamo end bracket housing

10.5 Fitting new dynamo end bearing

10.6 Drifting new dynamo end bracket bearing into position

10.7 Locating dynamo end bracket bearing plate

10 Refit the drive end bracket to the armature shaft. Do not try and force the bracket on but with the aid of a suitable socket abutting the bearing, tap the bearing on gently, so pulling the end bracket down with it (photo).

11 Slide the spacer up the shaft and refit the Woodruff key (photo).

12 Replace the fan and pulley wheel and then fit the spring washer and nut and tighten the latter. The drive bracket end of the dynamo is now fully assembled (photo).

13 If the brushes are little worn and are to be used again then ensure that they are placed in the same holders from which they were removed. When refitting brushes, either new or old, check that they move freely in their holders. If either brush sticks, clean with a petrol moistened rag and, if still stiff, lightly polish the sides of the brush with a very fine file until the brush moves quite freely in its holders.

14 Tighten the two retaining screws and washers which hold in position the brush leads (photo).

15 It will be easier if the end plate complete with brushes is slipped over the commutator while the brushes are held in their raised position by allowing the springs to press against the brush sides (photo).

16 Refit the armature to the casing and then the commutator end plate and screw up the two through bolts (photo).

17 Finally, hook the ends of the two springs off the flanks of the brushes and onto their heads so the brushes are forced down into contact with the armature (photo).

---

11 Control box - general description

The control box comprises the voltage regulator and the cut-out. The voltage regulator controls the output from the dynamo depending on the state of the battery and the demands of the electrical equipment, and ensures that the battery is not overcharged. The cut-out is really an automatic switch and connects the dynamo to the battery when the dynamo is turning fast enough to produce a charge. Similarly it disconnects the battery from the dynamo when the engine is idling or stationary so that the battery does not discharge through the dynamo.

---

12 Voltage regulator - adjustment

1 The regulator requires very little attention during its service life, and should there be any reason to suspect its correct functioning, tests of all circuits should be made to ensure that they are not the reason for the trouble.

2 These checks include the tension of the fan belt, to make sure that it is not slipping and so providing only a very low charge rate. The battery should be carefully checked for possible low charge rate due to a faulty cell, or corroded battery connections.

3 The leads from the generator may have been crossed during replacement, and if this is the case, then the regulator points will have stuck together as soon as the generator starts to charge. Check for loose or broken leads from the generator to the regulator.

4 If after a thorough check it is considered advisable to test the regulator, this should be carried out as follows.

5 Disconnect the leads from the regulator terminals 'D' and 'F' and join the leads together.

6 Attach the negative lead of a moving coil voltmeter (calibrated to 30 volts) to the junction of the leads 'D' and 'F' and the voltmeter positive lead to a good earth.

7 Start the engine and gradually increase the idling speed to approximately 1000 rev/min, when the voltmeter reading should rise rapidly without fluctuation to above 24 volts. Failure to perform as specified may be due to broken or disconnected dynamo leads, a faulty dynamo or one that has become demagnetised due to the leads having been crossed. In the latter event, the regulator points will be found welded together.

8 On completion of the test, reconnect the leads to the 'D' and

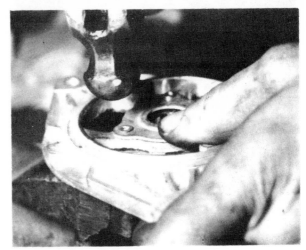
10.9 Peening bearing plate rivets

10.10 Refitting dynamo drive end bracket

10.11 Fitting dynamo armature shaft spacer

10.12 Refitting dynamo fan and pulley

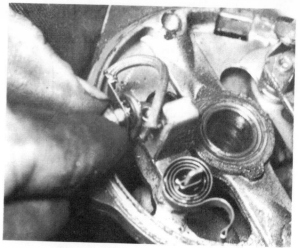

10.14 Inserting dynamo brush lead screws

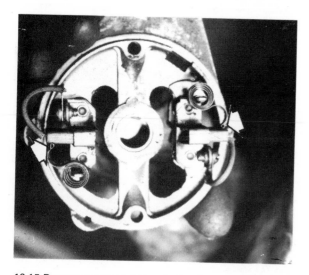

10.15 Dynamo brushes held in raised position

10.16 Tightening a dynamo tie bolt

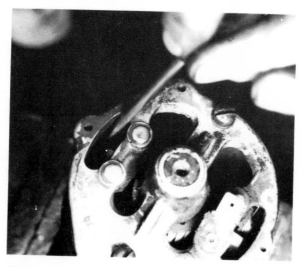

10.17 Releasing dynamo brush springs using a hooked rod

Fig. 10.4. Voltage regulator (early Cortina) located above parcels shelf

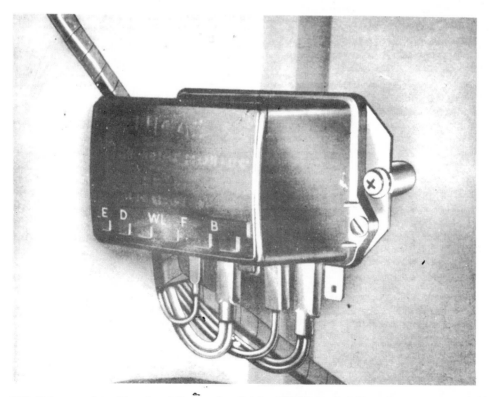

Fig. 10.5. Voltage regulator (Corsair and Cortina after October 1964) located within engine compartment (LH side)

'F' terminals of the regulator.

9   The following operations must be carried out within a period of 30 seconds to avoid inaccuracy due to rapid temperature rises in the shunt coil windings.

10 Disconnect the lead from the regulator 'B' terminal.

11 Connect the negative lead of a 0 - 25 volt moving coil voltmeter to the regulator 'D' or 'WL' terminal and the positive lead to the regulator baseplate.

12 Start the engine and gradually increase its idling speed until the voltmeter needle flicks and then steadies. This will occur at between 14.2 and 14.8 volts at an ambient temperature of 20°C (68°F). If the climatic conditions vary from the standard, apply the following correction:

For every 10°C (18°F) above 20°C (68°F) subtract 0.20 volts.

For every 10°C (18°F) below 20°C (68°F) add 0.20 volts.

13 Where the voltmeter reading is outside the limits specified, carry out the following further check before adjusting the unit. Increase the engine speed and if the voltmeter reading continues to rise (even swinging the needle right over) then this may indicate that the regulator points are not opening or there is a poor or no earth contact between the regulator and the bodyshell.

14 Switch off the ignition and remove the regulator cover (photo). To do this, push out the centre pins from the plastic retainers.

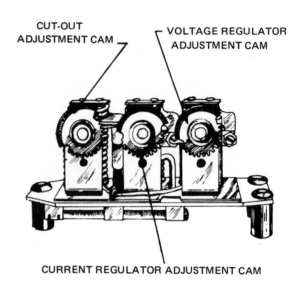

CUT-OUT ADJUSTMENT CAM

VOLTAGE REGULATOR ADJUSTMENT CAM

CURRENT REGULATOR ADJUSTMENT CAM

Fig. 10.6. Voltage regulator adjustment cams

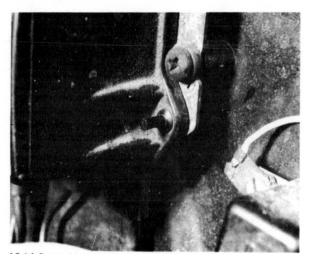

12.14 Control box cover securing plug and pin

15 Start the engine and repeat the procedure described in the preceding paragraph 12.

16 Using a Lucas type tool, adjust the cam (1) within the regulator until the voltage lies within that specified. Remake the original connections and refit the cover.

17 To adjust the cut-in/cut-out voltage, connect the negative lead of the voltmeter to the 'D' or 'WL' regulator terminals and the positive lead to the regulator baseplate.

18 Connect a test load of 100 watts (three standard headlamp bulbs) across the battery terminals to ensure that the drop in the voltmeter test reading will be immediately observed.

19 Start the engine and increase the idling speed until maximum voltage is indicated which should be between 12.6 and 13.4 volts. Immediately after reaching this voltage level, the voltmeter needle should drop, indicating that the cut-out contacts have closed.

20 Where the voltage cut-in or cut-out level must be adjusted, apply the tool to the appropriate cam (2) and turn it fractionally

in either direction.

21 Remake the original connections and refit the cover.

22 To check the cut-out drop-off voltage, disconnect the lead from the regulator terminal 'B'. Connect the negative lead of the voltmeter to terminal 'B' and the positive lead to the regulator baseplate.

23 Run the engine with the throttle about half open and then gradually reduce the speed, noting the indicated voltage at the moment when the needle suddenly flicks back to zero. This indicates that the cut-out contacts are open and should occur between 9.3 and 11.2 volts.

24 Where the drop-off voltage is outside the limits specified, stop the engine, remove the regulator cover and carefully bend the cut-out fixed contact bracket to vary the gap (reduce the gap to increase the drop-off voltage, widen the gap to decrease the drop-off voltage).

25 Recheck the drop-off voltage with the engine running, remake the original connections and refit the cover.

26 To check the current regulator, short-circuit the voltage regulator contacts by using a crocodile clip to bridge the gap between the adjustable contact and the armature limb.

27 Disconnect the lead from terminal 'B' and then connect an ammeter (moving coil 40-0-40 amps).

28 Connect a test load of 100 watts (three standard headlamp bulbs) across the battery terminals to ensure that the drop in the voltmeter test reading will be immediately observed.

29 Start the engine and run it at near maximum speed (4500 rev/min) and observe the ammeter which should indicate 23.5 amps. An unsteady reading will be due to a slipping fan belt, an internal fault in the dynamo, or dirty regulator contacts. If the voltage is steady but outside the limits specified, adjust the cam (3) in either direction (only fractionally) using the adjustment tool.

30 Remake the original connections and fit the cover.

13 Cut-out and regulator contacts - maintenance

1   Every 12,000 miles (19,000 km) check the cut-out and regulator contacts. If they are dirty or rough or burnt place a piece of fine glass paper (**do not use emery paper or carborundum**

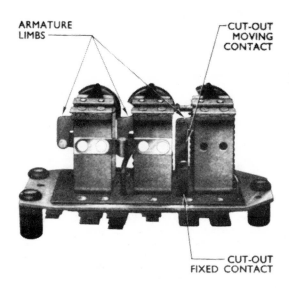

Fig. 10.7. Cut-out contacts

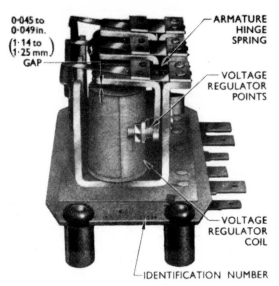

Fig. 10.8. Voltage regulator air gap adjustment

paper) between the cut-out contacts, close them manually and draw the glass paper through several times.

2 Clean the regulator contacts in exactly the same way, but use emery or carborundum paper and not glass paper. Carefully clean both sets of contacts from all traces of dust with a rag moistened in methylated spirit.

3 Air gap settings are set during production and do not normally require adjustment; however, where the points have been removed or dismantled they must be set in the following manner.

4 To adjust the current/voltage regulator air gap, remove the regulator from the vehicle and turn the adjustment cam fully anticlockwise. Slacken the contact locknut and screw the contact point a few turns outward.

5 Insert an 0.045 inch (1.14 mm) feeler gauge between the armature and the copper shim and press the armature fully down. Holding the armature in this position, screw in the contact point until it just touches the fixed point and then tighten the locknut. Release the armature and check the air gap which should be between 0.045 and 0.049 inch (1.14 and 1.25 mm).

6 The cut-out armature to core air gap should be between 0.035 and 0.045 inch (0.89 to 1.14 mm) measured with a feeler gauge.

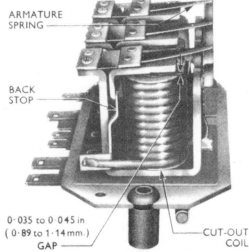

Fig. 10.9. Cut-out air gap adjustment

7 Having carried out either of the previous adjustments, the electrical settings must be checked and adjusted as described in the preceding Section.

14 Starter motor - general description

1 The starter motor is held in position by two bolts which also clamp the bellhousing flange.

2 The motor is of the four field coil, four pole piece type, and utilises four spring-loaded commutator brushes. Two of these brushes are earthed, and the other two are insulated and attached to the field coil ends.

15 Starter motor - testing on engine

1 If the starter motor fails to operate then check the condition of the battery by turning on the headlamps. If they glow brightly for several seconds and then gradually dim, the battery is in an uncharged condition.

2 If the headlamps glow brightly and it is obvious that the battery is in good condition then check the tightness of the battery wiring connections (and in particular the earth lead from the battery terminal to its connection on the body frame). If the negative terminal on the battery becomes hot when an attempt is made to work the starter, this is a sure sign of a poor connection on the battery terminal. To rectify remove the terminal, clean the inside of the cap and the terminal post thoroughly and reconnect. Check the tightness of the connections at the relay switch and at the starter motor. Check the wiring with a voltmeter for breaks or shorts.

3 If the wiring is in order then check that the starter motor is operating. To do this, press the rubber covered button in the centre of the solenoid under the bonnet. If it is working the starter motor will be heard to 'click' as it tries to rotate. Alternatively check it with a voltmeter.

4 If the battery is fully charged, the wiring in order, and the switch working and the starter motor fails to operate, then it will have to be removed from the car for examination. Before this is done, however, ensure that the starter pinion has not jammed in mesh with the flywheel. Check by turning the square end of the armature shaft with a spanner. This will free the pinion if it is stuck in engagement with the flywheel teeth. On some models the square on the end of the shaft will be covered by a metal clip.

16 Starter motor - removal and refitting

1 Disconnect the battery earth lead from the positive terminal.
2 Disconnect the starter motor cable from the terminal on the starter motor end plate.
3 Remove the upper starter motor securing bolt.
4 Working under the car, loosen, and then remove, the lower starter motor securing bolt taking care to support the motor so as to prevent damage to the drive components.
5 Lift the starter motor out of engagement with the flywheel ring and lower it out of the car.
6 Replacement is a straightforward reversal of the removal procedure.

17 Starter motor - dismantling and reassembly

1 With the starter motor on the bench, loosen the screw on the cover band and slip the cover band off. With a piece of wire bent into the shape of a hook, lift back each of the brush springs in turn and check the movement of the brushes in their holders by pulling on the flexible connectors. If the brushes are so worn that their faces do not rest against the commutator, or if the ends of the brush leads are exposed on their working face, they must be renewed.
2 If any of the brushes tend to stick in their holders then wash them with a fuel moistened cloth and, if necessary, lightly polish the sides of the brush with a very fine file, until the brushes move quite freely in their holders.
3 If the surface of the commutator is dirty or blackened, clean it with a fuel dampened rag. Secure the starter motor in a vice and check it by connecting a heavy gauge cable between the starter motor terminal and a 12 volt battery.
4 Connect the cable from the other battery terminal to earth in the starter motor body. If the motor turns at high speed it is in good order.
5 If the starter motor still fails to function, or if it is wished to renew the brushes, it is necessary to further dismantle the motor.
6 Lift the brush springs with the wire hook and lift all four brushes out of their holders one at a time.
7 Remove the terminal nuts and washers from the terminal post on the commutator end bracket.
8 Unscrew the two tie bolts which hold the end plates together and pull off the commutator end bracket. Also remove the driving end bracket which will come away complete with the armature.
9 At this stage, if the brushes are to be renewed, their flexible connectors must be unsoldered and the connectors of new brushes soldered in their place. Check that the new brushes move freely in their holders as detailed above. If cleaning the commutator with fuel fails to remove all the burnt areas and spots, then wrap a piece of glass paper round the commutator and rotate the armature. If the commutator is very badly worn, remove the drive gear as detailed in the following section. Then mount the armature in a lathe and with the lathe turning at high speed, take a very fine cut out of the commutator and finish the surface by polishing with glass paper. **Do not undercut the mica insulators between the commutator segments.**
10 With the starter motor dismantled, test the four field coils for an open circuit. Connect a 12 volt battery with a 12 volt bulb in one of the leads between the field terminal post and the tapping point of the field coils to which the brushes are connected. An open circuit is proved by the bulb not lighting.
11 If the bulb lights, it does not necessarily mean that the field coils are in order, as there is a possibility that one of the coils will be earthing to the starter yoke or pole shoes. To check this, remove the lead from the brush connector and place it against a clean portion of the starter yoke. If the bulb lights the field coils are earthing. Replacement of the field coils calls for the use of a wheel operated screwdriver, a soldering iron, caulking and riveting operations and is beyond the scope of the majority of owners. The starter yoke should be taken to a reputable electrical engineering works for new field coils to be fitted. Alternatively,

purchase an exchange starter motor.
12 If the armature is damaged this will be evident after visual inspection. Look for signs of burning, discolouration, and for conductors that have lifted away from the commutator. Reassembly is a straight reversal of the dismantling procedure.

18 Starter motor drive - servicing

1 The starter motor drive is of the outboard type. When the starter motor is operated the pinion moves into contact with the flywheel gear ring by moving in towards the starter motor.
2 If the engine kicks back, or the pinion fails to engage with the flywheel gear ring when the starter motor is actuated, no undue strain is placed on the armature shaft as the pinion sleeve disengages from the pinion and turns independently.
3 When the starter motor is removed the drive should be well washed in paraffin to remove any dirt or corrosion which may be the cause of a sticking pinion. This operation should be carried out regularly at three monthly intervals on vehicles fitted with automatic transmission as in damp operating conditions, the air ducts at the base of the clutch bellhousing tend to draw in moisture which causes surface rusting of the starter drive sliding surfaces. Apply a little thin oil to the spiral of the starter drive before refitting the starter motor.
4 To dismantle the drive, compress the main starter drive spring using a proprietary compressor and extract the circlip from the shaft recess.
5 Always renew the pinion drive as an assembly, installing it on the armature shaft so that the teeth are towards the armature windings.

19 Direction indicator flasher circuit - fault tracing and rectification

1 The flasher unit is located in a cylindrical metal container behind the instrument panel.
2 If the flasher circuit fails to operate, or works very slowly or very rapidly, check out the flasher indicator circuit as detailed below, before assuming there is a fault in the unit itself.
3 Examine the direction indicator bulbs front and rear for broken filaments.
4 If the external flashers are working but the internal flasher warning light has ceased to function, check the filament of the warning bulb and replace as necessary.
5 With the aid of the wiring diagram, check all the flasher circuit connections if a flasher bulb is sound but does not work.
6 With the ignition turned on, check that current is reaching the flasher unit by connecting a voltmeter between the 'plus' or 'B' terminal and earth. If this test is positive connect the 'plus' or 'B' terminal and the 'L' terminal and operate the flasher switch. If the flasher bulb lights up the flasher unit itself is defective and must be replaced as it is not possible to dismantle and repair it.

20 Windscreen wiper mechanism - maintenance

1 Renew the windscreen wiper blades at intervals of 12,000 miles (19,000 km) or more frequently if necessary (photo).
2 The washer round the wheelbase spindle can be lubricated with several drops of glycerine. The windscreen wiper links can be lightly oiled at the same time (located behind the instrument panel).

21 Windscreen wiper mechanism - fault diagnosis and rectification

1 The windscreen wiper motor and linkage may be of Autolite, AC-Delco or Lucas manufacture. Although differing in detail design, they all operate using a similar mechanical linkage which is located at the rear of the instrument panel.
2 Should the windscreen wipers fail, or work very slowly, then check the terminals for loose connections, and make sure the insulation of the external wiring is not cracked or broken. If this

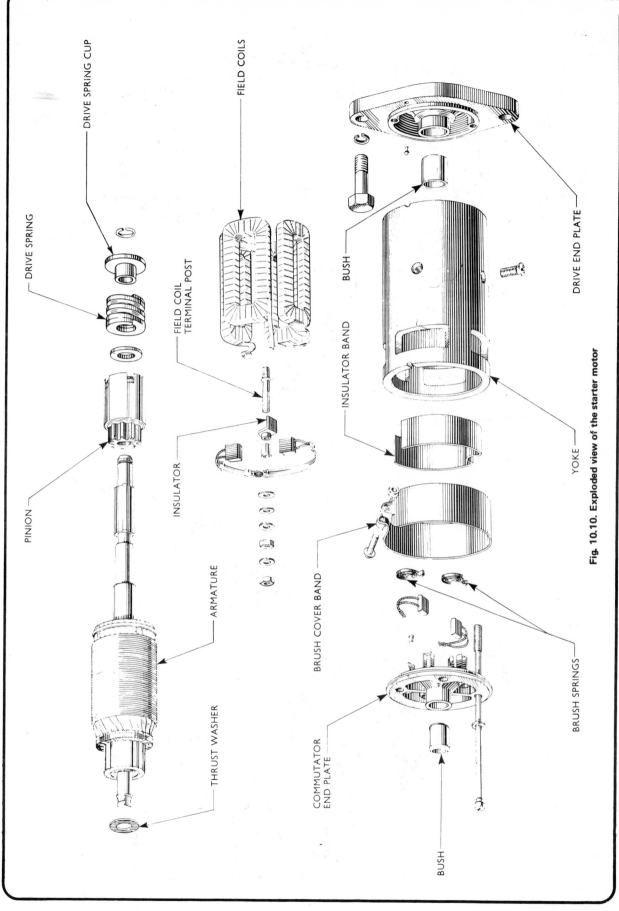

DRIVE SPRING CUP

DRIVE SPRING

FIELD COILS

PINION

FIELD COIL TERMINAL POST

INSULATOR

BUSH

INSULATOR BAND

ARMATURE

YOKE

DRIVE END PLATE

THRUST WASHER

BRUSH COVER BAND

COMMUTATOR END PLATE

BRUSH SPRINGS

BUSH

Fig. 10.10. Exploded view of the starter motor

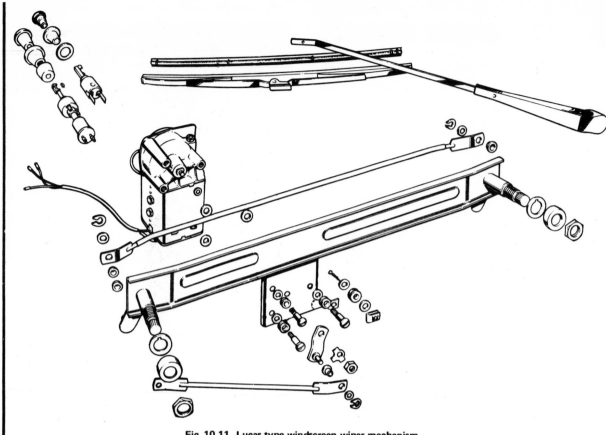

Fig. 10.11. Lucas type windscreen wiper mechanism

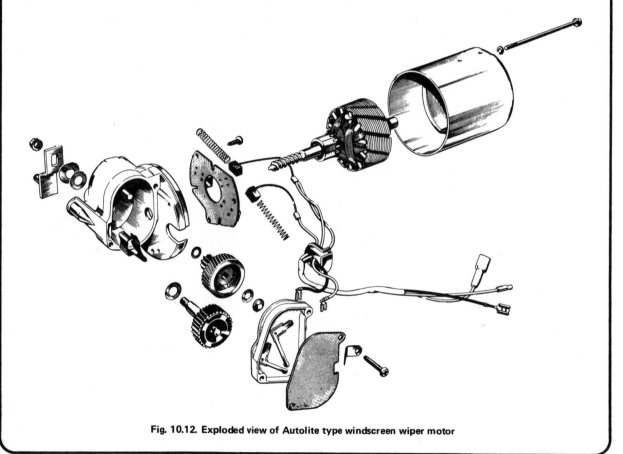

Fig. 10.12. Exploded view of Autolite type windscreen wiper motor

20.1 Removing a windscreen wiper blade

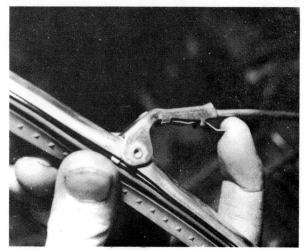

21.8 Removing a windscreen wiper arm

is in order then check the current the motor is taking by connecting up a 1 - 20 volt voltmeter in the circuit and turning on the wiper switch. Consumption should be between 2.3 to 3.1 amps.
3 If no current is passing through, check the wiper switch.
4 If the wiper motor takes a very high current, check the wiper blades for freedom of movement. If this is satisfactory, check the gearbox cover and gear assembly for damage and measure the armature endfloat which should be between 0.009 to 0.012 inch (0.20 to 0.30 mm).
5 If the motor takes a very low current ensure that the battery is fully charged. Check the brush gear after removing the commutator end bracket and ensure that the brushes are bearing on the commutator. If not, check the brushes for freedom of movement and if necessary, renew the tension spring. If the brushes are very worn they should be replaced with new ones. The brush levers should be quite free on their pivots. If stiff, loosen them by moving them backwards and forwards by hand and by applying a little thin machine oil.
6 It is not recommended that further dismantling of the wiper motor is carried out but rather that a new or reconditioned wiper motor is fitted.
7 Where the arc of travel of the wiper arms increases and so causes the blades to contact the screen frame, then this will be due to elongation of the holes in the linkage and the worn components must be renewed.
8 Removal of all types of linkage is carried out by disconnecting the link from the wiper motor crank and then removing the wiper arms from the splined spindles (photo). Unscrew the spindle housing locknuts and withdraw the complete support member, linkage and spindle assembly from beneath the instrument panel.
9 The wiper motor is separately mounted and before removing it, disconnect the leads at the snap connectors, first identifying them for correct reconnection.

22 Windscreen washer - description and maintenance

1 The windscreen washer may be one of several designs having either a rigid or flexible fluid container.
2 Apart from maintaining the level in the fluid container as described in 'Routine Maintenance', occasionally check to see that the plastic pipes are secure and not compressed by other components.
3 Adjustment of the washer nozzles may be carried out by inserting a pin into the ball jet and moving it as required.
4 Failure of the washer unit will either be due to a faulty non-return valve or wear in the plunger. Neither component can be repaired and should be renewed.

23 Horn - fault tracing and rectification

1 If the horn works badly or fails to work altogether, check all the wiring leading to the horn for cracks or breaks and also check that the snap connectors on the horn are clean and free from corrosion.
2 Check that the horn is secure on its mounting and that nothing is lying on the horn body.
3 If the fault is not an external one then the horn will have to be replaced as it is not possible to effect repairs.

24 Headlamp sealed beam unit (Cortina) - renewal

1 Remove the crosshead screw from the lower edge of the headlamp bezel (photo). Pull the bezel forward and lift it slightly to disengage it from its upper clips.
2 Unscrew and remove the three screws which secure the lamp retaining bezel and remove the bezel (photo). Do not move the slotted headlamp alignment screws.
3 Withdraw the sealed beam unit sufficiently to permit disconnection of the wiring plug at its rear (photo).
4 Installation of the new sealed beam unit is a reversal of removal and provided the adjustment screws have not been disturbed, no alignment of beam will be necessary.

25 Headlamp sealed beam unit (Corsair) - renewal

The operation is similar to that described in the preceding Section except that the headlamp bezel includes a seal and is retained by two screws at the top and two bolts at the bottom.

26 Headlamp - alignment

It is recommended that the headlamps are aligned on modern optical beam setting equipment.

27 Front direction indicator and side lamp bulbs - renewal

1 On Cortina models the lens is removed after unscrewing the two retaining screws (four on later models).
2 The bulb is now accessible and it is of double filament, bayonet type.
3 On Corsair models, separate lenses are used for side and flasher lamps, also separate bulbs.

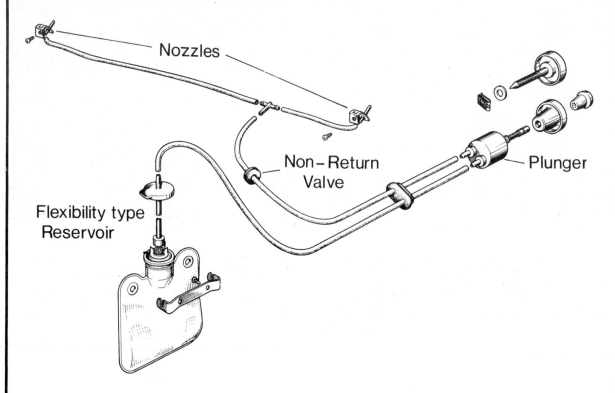

Fig. 10.13. Components of windscreen washer

24.1 Headlamp bezel securing screw

24.2 Headlamp unit securing screw

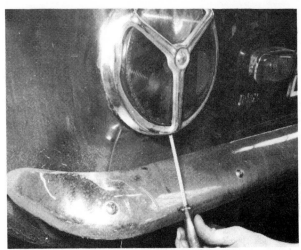

28.1 Removing a rear lamp cluster rim screw

24.3 Withdrawing a sealed beam headlamp unit

Fig. 10.14. Removing sealed beam headlamp (early Cortina)

Fig. 10.16a. Renewing front side and indicator bulbs on early and later type Cortinas

28 Rear direction indicator, stop and tail bulbs - renewal

1   On Cortina models, unscrew and remove the crosshead screw located on the bottom edge of the lens bezel (photo). Pull the bezel forward; lift slightly, to disengage its tongue and then withdraw it.

2   Unscrew the now exposed large centre screw and then the two lens screws as appropriate. Renew the bayonet type bulbs for either the direction indicator or the double filament stop and tail.

3   On Corsair models, the bulbs may be renewed from within the luggage compartment simply by pulling their spring type holders out of their locations.

29 Combined lighting, direction indicator, horn switch (Cortina up to October 1964 and Corsair models) - removal and refitting

1   Pull off the steering column half-shroud from the side opposite to the switch assembly. This is retained by four spring sockets.

2   Identify and then disconnect the switch assembly leads at the snap connectors behind the instrument panel.

3   Unscrew the four dome-headed screws which retain the switch housing to the steering column and withdraw the switch.

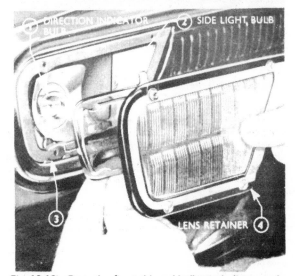

Fig. 10.16b. Renewing front side and indicator bulbs on early and later type Cortinas

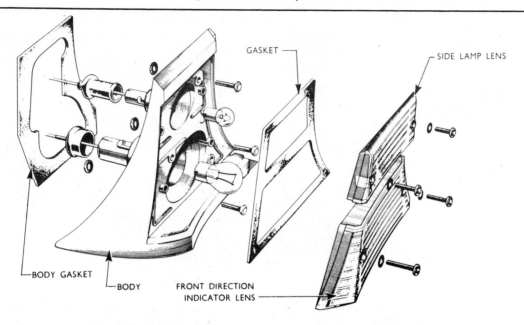

GASKET

SIDE LAMP LENS

BODY GASKET

BODY

FRONT DIRECTION
INDICATOR LENS

Fig. 10.17. Exploded view of front side and direction indicator lamp (Corsair)

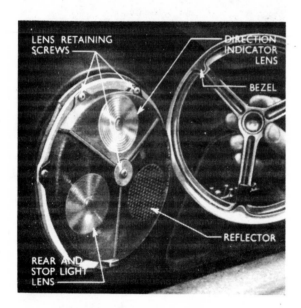

LENS RETAINING
SCREWS

DIRECTION
INDICATOR
LENS

BEZEL

REFLECTOR

REAR AND
STOP LIGHT
LENS

**Fig. 10.18. Tail, stop and direction indicator lamp cluster
(Cortina)**

4   To refit the switch, locate it on its four mounting lugs on the
steering column and screw in the four retaining bolts but do not
fully tighten them at this stage.
5   Position the switch by moving it up or down the steering
column within the limits of the mounting lug slots so that there
is a clearance of 0.060 inch (0.153 mm) between the top of the
cancelling pawl and the cancelling cam.
6   Tighten the retaining bolts fully and then check that the
direction indicator switch cancels correctly by jacking up the
front of the vehicle under the crossmember and turning the
steering wheel from lock to lock.
7   Push the switch cover into position over the heads of the
four retaining bolts.
8   Reconnect the switch leads and check the operation of all
units.

**30   Combined lighting, direction indicator, dipswitch and horn
button (Cortina after October 1964) - removal and refitting**

1   Disconnect the battery.
2   Unscrew the four crosshead screws from the base of the
steering column shroud. Remove both halves of the shroud from
vehicles with manual gearboxes (photo) but on vehicles fitted with
automatic transmission do not pull the upper half away but
support it on the parcel shelf as it will have the speed selector
quadrant lamp lead attached.
3   Disconnect the switch leads at the snap connectors behind
the instrument panel.
4   Remove the two crosshead screws which secure the switch to
the steering column and remove the switch (photo).

**31   Steering column direction indicator cancelling arm (Cortina
October 1964 onward) - removal and refitting**

1   Remove the steering column shroud and the steering wheel (as
described in Chapter 11).
2   Pull the cam off the column splines (photo).
3   When refitting, the cam should be pressed onto the steering
column splines until there is the specified clearance as shown in
the diagram (Fig 10.23) according to transmission type.
4   Refit the steering wheel as described in Chapter 11 and
replace the shroud.

**32   Instrument panel (Cortina up to October 1964) - removal and
refitting**

1   Reach behind the instrument panel and disconnect the
speedometer cable from the speedometer head by unscrewing the
knurled ring.
2   Prise away the wiring loom clips from the lower edge of the
facia panel.
3   Remove the bezel retaining screws and withdraw the bezel.
4   Remove the two panel securing screws now exposed and ease
the instrument panel from the facia.
5   Disconnection of wiring and individual instruments may be
carried out as necessary by reference to the appropriate loom
layout diagram.
6   Refitting is a reversal of removal.

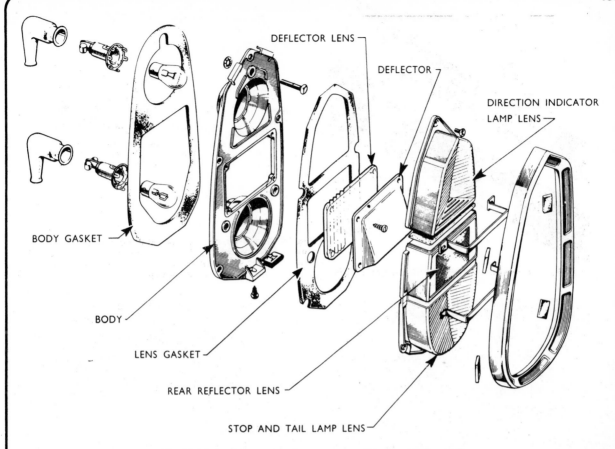

DEFLECTOR LENS

DEFLECTOR

DIRECTION INDICATOR
LAMP LENS

BODY GASKET

BODY

LENS GASKET

REAR REFLECTOR LENS

STOP AND TAIL LAMP LENS

Fig. 10.19. Tail, stop and direction indicator lamp cluster (Corsair)

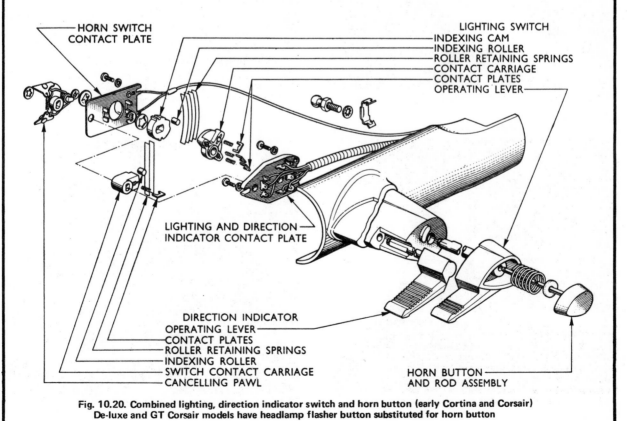

HORN SWITCH
CONTACT PLATE

LIGHTING SWITCH
INDEXING CAM
INDEXING ROLLER
ROLLER RETAINING SPRINGS
CONTACT CARRIAGE
CONTACT PLATES
OPERATING LEVER

LIGHTING AND DIRECTION
INDICATOR CONTACT PLATE

DIRECTION INDICATOR
OPERATING LEVER
CONTACT PLATES
ROLLER RETAINING SPRINGS
INDEXING ROLLER
SWITCH CONTACT CARRIAGE
CANCELLING PAWL

HORN BUTTON
AND ROD ASSEMBLY

Fig. 10.20. Combined lighting, direction indicator switch and horn button (early Cortina and Corsair)
De-luxe and GT Corsair models have headlamp flasher button substituted for horn button

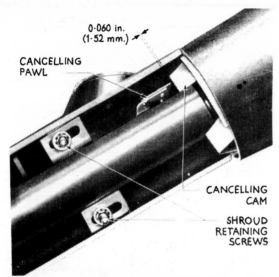

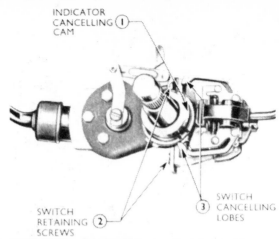

Fig. 10.21. Steering column switch setting diagram (early Cortina and Corsair)

Fig. 10.22. Flasher, direction indicator, dip switch and horn button (Cortina October 1964 onwards). Automatic transmission version shown. Note position of cam lobes with steering in straight ahead position

30.2 Removing steering column shroud

30.4 Combined lighting, flasher switch (indicator)

31.2 Location of flasher switch (indicator) cancelling cam

32.1 Speedometer cable connection (instrument panel removed in the interest of clarity)

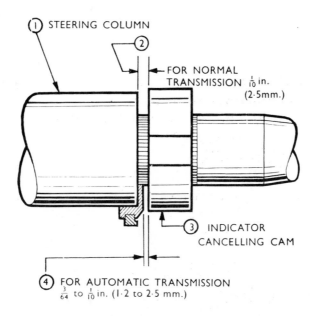

Fig. 10.23. Indicator cancelling cam setting diagram (Cortina October 1964 onwards)

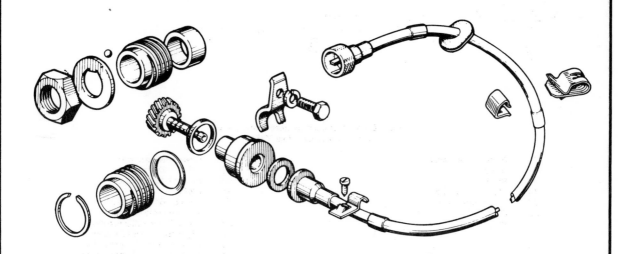

Fig. 10.24. Speedometer drive and cable

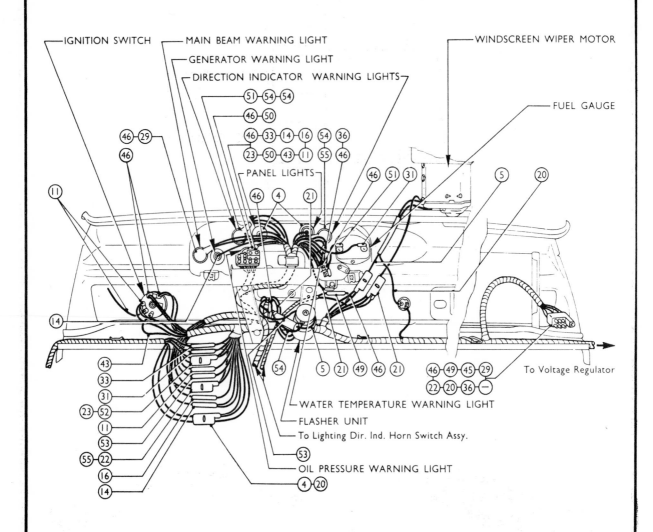

**Fig. 10.25. Rear view of instrument panel
(Cortina up to October 1964)**

4	Red—White tracer	36	Green—Blue tracer
5	Green	43	White—Red tracer
11	Brown	45	Brown—Green tracer
14	Blue—White tracer	46	White
16	Blue—Red tracer	49	Purple—Black tracer
20	Red	50	White—Brown tracer
21	Black	51	Light Green—Blue tracer
22	Green—White tracer	52	Light Green—Red tracer
23	Green—Red tracer	53	Light Green—Brown tracer
29	Brown—Yellow tracer	54	Light Green—Purple tracer
31	Green—Black tracer	55	Light Green—White tracer
33	Green—Yellow tracer		

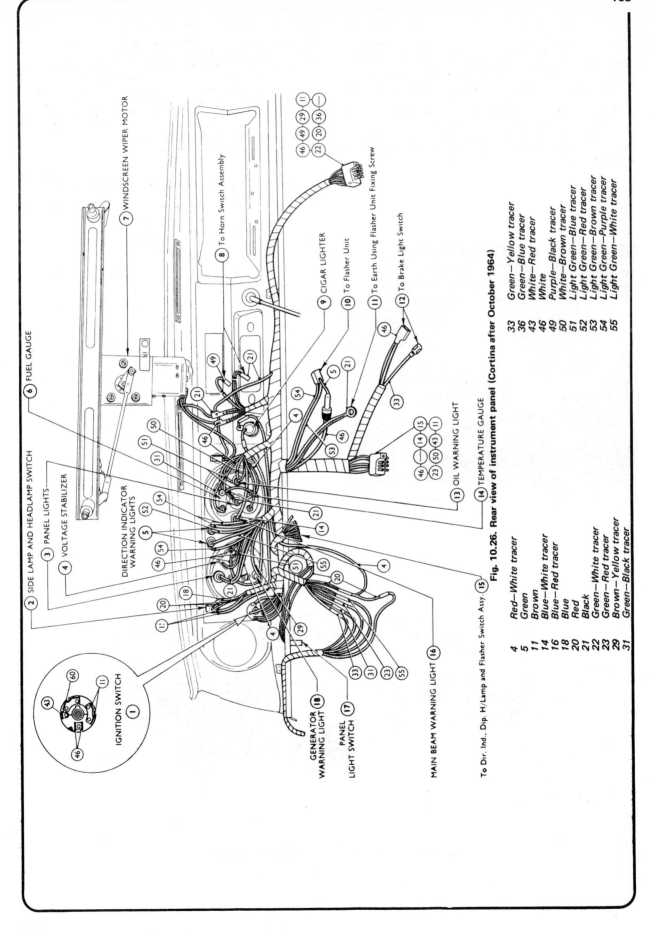

Fig. 10.26. Rear view of instrument panel (Cortina after October 1964)

To Dir. Ind., Dip. H/Lamp and Flasher Switch Assy.

4	Red—White tracer
5	Green
11	Brown
14	Blue—White tracer
16	Blue—Red tracer
18	Blue
20	Red
21	Black
22	Green—White tracer
23	Green—Red tracer
29	Brown—Yellow tracer
31	Green—Black tracer
33	Green—Yellow tracer
36	Green—Blue tracer
43	White—Red tracer
46	White
49	Purple—Black tracer
50	White—Brown tracer
51	Light Green—Blue tracer
52	Light Green—Red tracer
53	Light Green—Brown tracer
54	Light Green—Purple tracer
55	Light Green—White tracer

33   Instrument panel and individual instruments (Cortina October 1964 onward) - removal and refitting

1   Disconnect the battery and disconnect the speedometer cable as described in the preceding Section.
2   Remove the steering column shroud and the bezels from the instrument panel switches and washer plunger.
3   Pull the panel to the rear and disconnect the wiring as necessary after reference to the appropriate loom layout diagram (photo).

33.3 Withdrawing the instrument panel

4   On GT versions a supplementary instrument panel is fitted and this is secured by two crosshead screws.
5   All instruments are secured to the instrument panels by a bayonet type fitting and they can be removed individually by gripping the instrument at the rear of the panel, turning it clockwise and pushing it out through the front of the panel.
6   Instruments fitted to later model Cortinas operate on 5 volts whereas those fitted to early models operate on 10 volts and the units must not be interchanged.
7   Refitting is a reversal of removal.

34   Instrument panel and individual instruments (Corsair) - removal and refitting

1   The instrument panel is of self-contained, printed circuit type. All electrical connections to the panel are made through the medium of a 13 pin plug connector which can only be connected in one position.
2   Panel bulbs may be renewed by reaching under the panel and turning each bulb holder one quarter-turn anticlockwise.
3   To remove the panel, unscrew and remove the three crosshead screws which secure the instrument panel shroud and raise the shroud off its ball studs.
4   Unscrew and remove the three panel securing screws.
5   Lift the panel slightly forward and upwards and disconnect the multi-pin plug and the speedometer cable from the speedometer head.
6   Removal of the instrument regulator (voltage/temperature controller) which is installed to ensure accurate gauge readings even when the battery is in a low state of charge, is achieved simply by pulling it from its location.
7   The fuel and temperature gauges and the speedometer head may be removed after the screws have been removed which retain

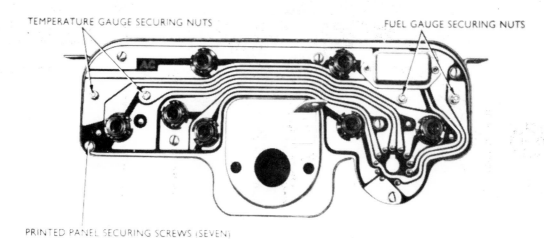

TEMPERATURE GAUGE SECURING NUTS   FUEL GAUGE SECURING NUTS

PRINTED PANEL SECURING SCREWS (SEVEN)

Fig. 10.27. Corsair printed circuit type instrument panel

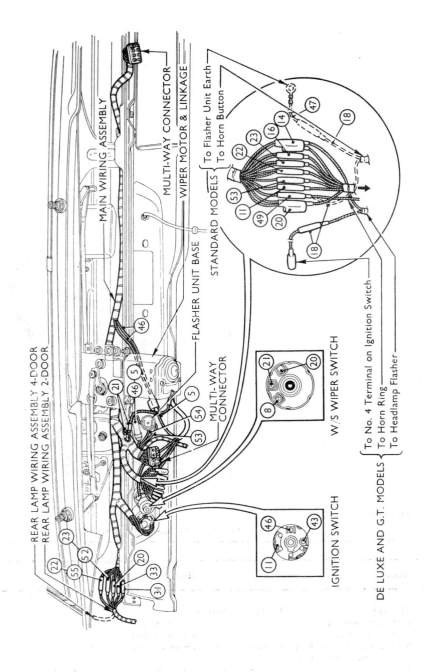

REAR LAMP WIRING ASSEMBLY 4-DOOR
REAR LAMP WIRING ASSEMBLY 2-DOOR

MAIN WIRING ASSEMBLY

MULTI-WAY CONNECTOR

WIPER MOTOR & LINKAGE

FLASHER UNIT BASE

MULTI-WAY CONNECTOR

STANDARD MODELS { To Flasher Unit Earth
To Horn Button

DE LUXE AND G.T. MODELS { To No. 4 Terminal on Ignition Switch
To Horn Ring
To Headlamp Flasher

IGNITION SWITCH

W/S WIPER SWITCH

Fig. 10.28. Corsair wiring layout at rear of fascia panel

5	Green	33	Green—Yellow tracer
8	Yellow	36	Green—Blue tracer
10	White—Black tracer	37	Purple—White tracer
11	Brown	43	White—Red tracer
14	Blue—White tracer	45	Brown—Green tracer
16	Blue—Red tracer	46	White
18	Blue	47	Blue—Black tracer
20	Red	49	Purple—Black tracer
21	Black	50	White—Brown tracer
22	Green—White tracer	52	Light Green—Red tracer
23	Green—Red tracer	53	Light Green—Brown tracer
29	Brown—Yellow tracer	54	Light Green—Purple tracer
31	Green—Black tracer	55	Light Green—White tracer

the panel to the housing and the individual instrument securing nuts and screws.

8   On GT versions an electrically operated tachometer is mounted on the steering column.

9   Refitting is a reversal of removal but treat the printed circuit carefully when handling.

35 Auxiliary lamps - fitting

1   There are many types of auxiliary lamps which may be fitted and most of them are fitted with brackets that will suit a variety of mounting positions.

2   These may be on the front bumper supports or behind the overrider attachment nuts.

3   If Ford produced accessories are purchased then this will facilitate installation as they are produced to fit the vehicle.

4   Remember that if the lamps are to be used during normal driving then their centres must be at least 24 inches (406.4 mm) from the ground. If they are mounted at a lower level then they can only be used in conditions of fog or falling snow. The maximum height to which the lamp centres may be fitted is 3½ feet (1.07 m) and the maximum distance from the extreme outside of the vehicle to the lamp centre is 16 inches (406.4 mm).

5   Both lamps should be wired through one switch and the current taken from the 'B' terminal of the control box. Ensure that each lamp is well earthed.

36 Radio - installation

1   Fitting a radio is a job for an expert if really satisfactory performance is to be obtained but the following will give some guidance to owners who are contemplating installation.

2   Select the location for the receiver and speaker very carefully before cutting or drilling the vehicle interior. Check that they will not be in the way of the knees or obstruct gear changing.

3   Ensure that the set is **positive earthed**. Many receivers can be simply altered from one polarity to another but make sure this can be done before fitting it.

4   Always incorporate a fuse in the supply lead, which should be connected to the ignition switch ('ACC' or No '4' terminal).

5   Install the aerial securely. There is no substitute for an outside telescopic type aerial, internal types limit the signal strength particularly on roads with banking at either side.

6   Check that the ignition leads are all suppressed by suppressors fitted in the coil lead and at the spark plugs.

7   When the radio is installed and the engine running any interference is most likely to come from the dynamo or (when operated) the windscreen wiper motor. Both these units can be fitted with suppressors if necessary.

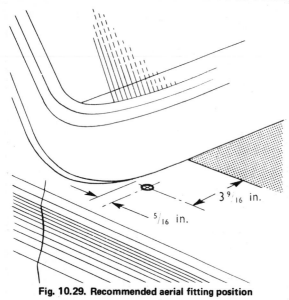

Fig. 10.29. Recommended aerial fitting position

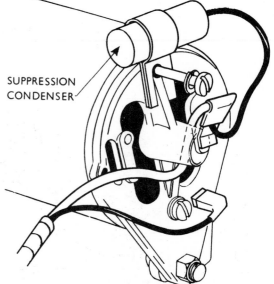

Fig. 10.30. Suppressor fitted to dynamo

37 Fault diagnosis - electrical system

Symptom	Reason/s	Remedy
	STARTER MOTOR FAILS TO TURN ENGINE	
No electricity at starter motor	Battery discharged	Charge battery.
	Battery defective internally	Fit new battery.
	Battery terminal leads loose or earth lead not securely attached to body	Check and tighten leads.
	Loose or broken connections in starter motor circuit	Check all connections and tighten any that are loose.
	Starter motor switch faulty	Test and replace faulty components with new.
Electricity at starter motor: faulty motor	Starter motor pinion jammed in mesh with flywheel gear ring	Remove motor, free drive and clean.
	Starter brushes badly worn, sticking, or brush wires loose	Examine brushes, replace as necessary, tighten down brush wires.
	Commutator dirty, worn or burnt	Clean commutator, recut if badly burnt.
	Starter motor armature faulty	Overhaul starter motor, fit new armature.

| | Field coils earthed | Exchange starter motor. |

STARTER MOTOR TURNS ENGINE VERY SLOWLY

Electrical defects	Battery in discharged condition	Charge battery.
	Starter brushes badly worn, sticking, or brush wires loose	Examine brushes, replaces as necessary, tighten down brush wires.
	Loose wires in starter motor circuit	Check wiring and tighten as necessary.

STARTER MOTOR OPERATES WITHOUT TURNING ENGINE

| Dirt or oil on drive gear | Starter motor pinion sticking on the screwed sleeve | Remove starter motor, clean starter motor drive. |
| Mechanical damage | Pinion or flywheel gear teeth broken or worn | Fit new gear ring to flywheel and new pinion to starter motor drive. |

STARTER MOTOR NOISY OR EXCESSIVELY ROUGH ENGAGEMENT

Lack of attention or mechanical damage	Pinion or flywheel gear teeth broken or worn	Fit new gear teeth to flywheel, or new pinion to starter motor drive.
	Starter drive main spring broken	Dismantle and fit new main spring.
	Starter motor retaining bolts loose	Tighten starter motor securing bolts. Fit new spring washer if necessary.

BATTERY WILL NOT HOLD CHARGE FOR MORE THAN A FEW DAYS

Wear or damage	Batery defective internally	Remove and fit new battery.
	Electrolyte level too low or electrolyte too weak due to leakage	Top up electrolyte level to just above plates.
	Plate separators no longer fully effective	Remove and fit new battery.
Insufficient current flow to keep battery charged	Battery plates severely sulphated	Remove and fit new battery.
	Fan belt slipping	Check belt for wear, replace if necessary, and tighten.
	Battery terminal connections loose or corroded	Check terminals for tightness and remove all corrosion.
	Dynamo not charging	Remove and overhaul.
	Short in lighting circuit causing continual battery drain	Trace and rectify.
	Regulator unit not working correctly	Check setting, clean and renew if defective.

IGNITION LIGHT FAILS TO GO OUT, BATTERY RUNS FLAT IN A FEW DAYS

Dynamo not charging	Fan belt loose and slipping or broken	Check, replace and tighten as necessary.
	Brushes worn, sticking, broken or dirty	Examine, clean or renew brushes as necessary.
	Brush springs weak or broken	Examine and test. Renew as necessary.
	Commutator dirty, greasy, worn or burnt	Clean commutator and undercut segment separators.
	Dynamo field coils burnt, open or shorted	Remove and fit rebuilt unit.
	Commutator worn	Remove and fit rebuilt unit.
	Pole pieces very loose	Remove and fit rebuilt unit.
Regulator or cut-out fails to work correctly	Regulator incorrectly set	Adjust regulator correctly.
	Cut-out incorrectly set	Adjust cut-out correctly.
	Open circuit in wiring of cut-out and regulator unit	Remove, examine, and renew as necessary.

Failure of individual electrical equipment to function correctly is dealt with alphabetically, item by item, under the headings listed below:

HORN

Horn operates all the time	Horn push either earthed or stuck down	Disconnect battery earth. Check and rectify source of trouble.
	Horn cable to horn push earthed	Disconnect battery earth. Check and rectify source of trouble.
Horn fails to operate	Cable or cable connection loose, broken or disconnected	Check all connections for tightness and cables for breaks.
	Horn has an internal fault	Remove and overhaul horn.
Horn emits intermittent or unsatisfactory noise	Cable connections loose	Check and tighten all connections.
	Horn incorrectly adjusted	Adjust horn until best note obtained.

LIGHTS

Lights do not come on	If engine not running, battery discharged	Push-start car, charge battery.
	Light bulb filament burnt out or bulbs broken	Test bulbs in live bulb holders.
	Wire connections loose, disconnected or broken	Check all connections for tightness and wire cable for breaks.

	Light switch shorting or otherwise faulty	By-pass light switch to ascertain if fault is in switch and fit new switch as appropriate.
Lights come on but fade out	If engine not running, battery discharged	Push-start car, and charge battery.
	Light bulb filament burnt out or bulbs or sealed beam units broken	Test bulbs in live bulb holder, renew sealed beam units.
	Wire connections loose, disconnected or broken	Check all connections for tightness and wire cable for breaks.
	Light switch shorting or otherwise faulty	By-pass light switch to ascertain if fault is in switch and fit new switch as appropriate.
Lights gives very poor illumination	Lamp glasses dirty	Clean glasses.
	Lamps badly out of adjustment	Adjust lamps correctly.
Lights work erratically - flashing on and off, especially over bumps	Battery terminals or earth connection loose	Tighten battery terminals and earth connection.
	Lights not earthing properly	Examine and rectify.
	Contacts in light switch faulty	By-pass light switch to ascertain if fault is in switch and fit new switch as appropriate.

WIPERS

Wiper motor fails to work	Wire connections loose, disconnected, or broken	Check wiper wiring. Tighten loose connections.
	Brushes badly worn	Renew wiper motor.
	Armature worn or faulty	Renew wiper motor.
	Field coils faulty	Renew wiper motor.
Wiper motor works very slowly and takes excessive current	Commutator dirty, greasy or burnt	Renew wiper motor.
	Armature bearings dirty or unaligned	Renew wiper motor.
	Armature badly worn or faulty	Renew wiper motor.
Wiper motor works slowly and takes little current	Brushes badly worn	Renew.
	Commutator dirty, greasy or burnt	Clean.
	Armature badly worn or faulty	Renew wiper motor.
Wiper motor works but wiper blades remain static	Wiper motor gearbox parts badly worn	Renew wiper motor.

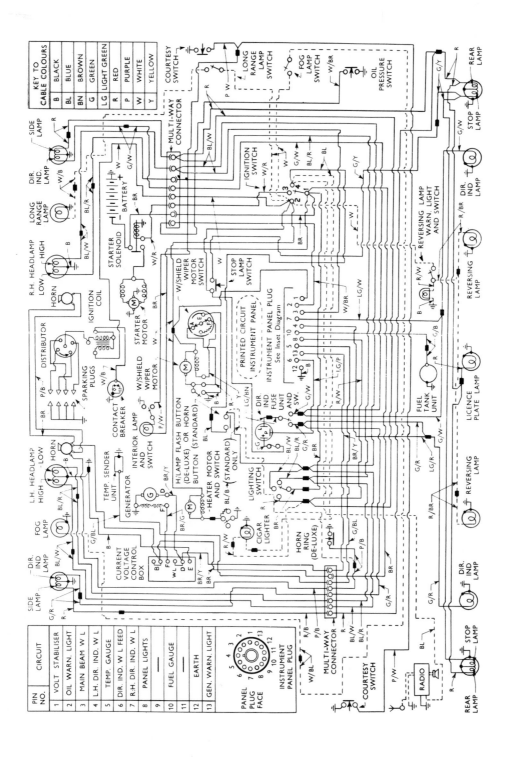

Wiring Diagram; Corsair Standard and DeLuxe

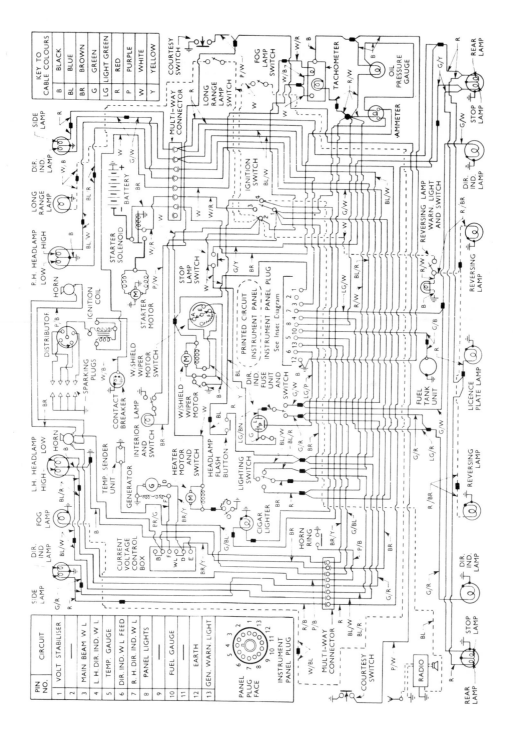

Wiring Diagram; Corsair GT

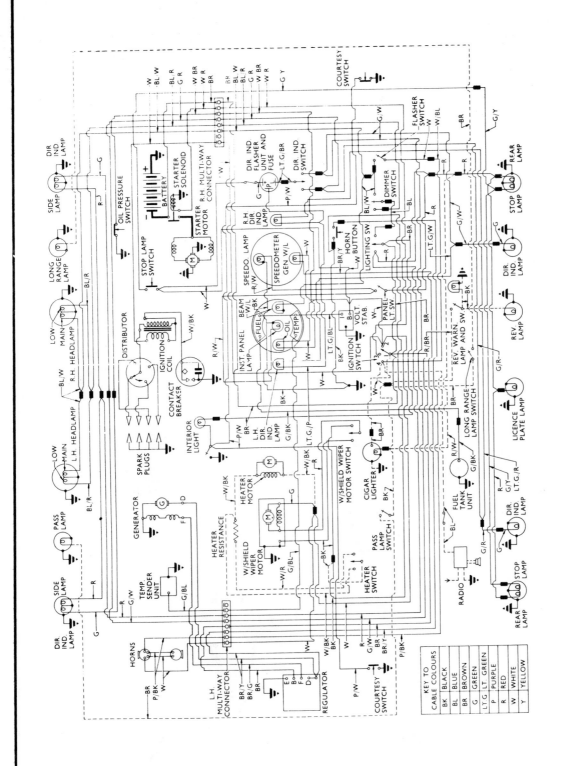

Wiring Diagram; Standard and DeLuxe cars only (1964 onwards)

KEY TO CABLE COLOURS	
BK	BLACK
BL	BLUE
BR	BROWN
G	GREEN
LT.G	LT. GREEN
P	PURPLE
R	RED
W	WHITE
Y	YELLOW

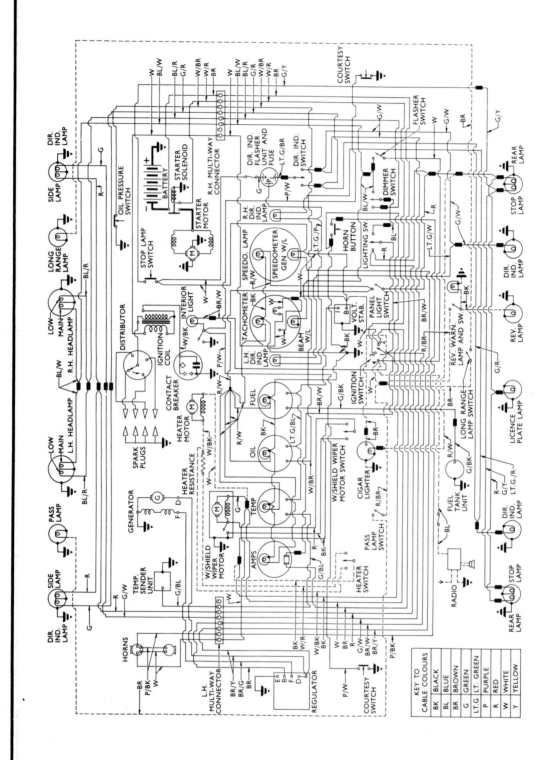

Wiring Diagram; GT October 1964 onwards

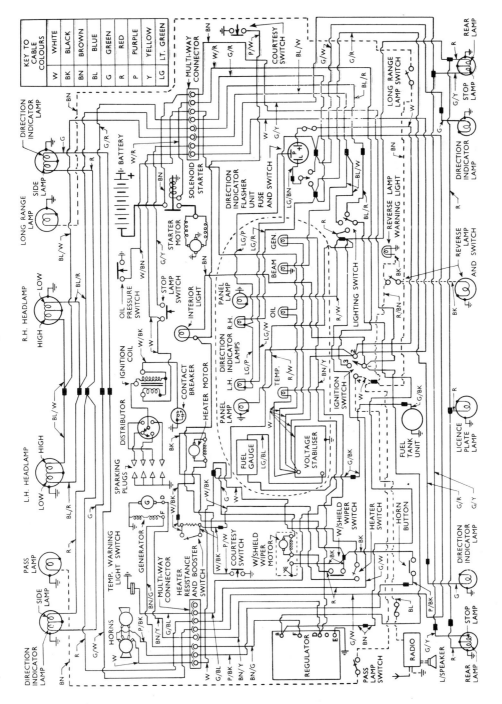

Wiring Diagram; Cars up to October 1964

KEY TO CABLE COLOURS	
W	WHITE
BK	BLACK
BN	BROWN
BL	BLUE
G	GREEN
R	RED
P	PURPLE
Y	YELLOW
LG	LT. GREEN

Chapter 11 Suspension and steering

Contents

Specifications

Front suspension

Type ... ...   McPherson strut with coil spring and stabiliser bar

Coil springs

	Cortina	Cortina GT	Corsair	Corsair GT
Free length	12.25 in	10.01 in	12.86 in	11.39 in
	(31.1 cm)	(25.55 cm)	(32.64 cm)	(28.92 cm)
Number of coils	7.19	6.85	7.07	6.70
Diameter of coils	5.0 in	5.0 in	5.0 in	5.0 in
	(1.27 cm)	(1.27 cm)	(1.27 cm)	(1.27 cm)

Shock absorbers

Type ... ...   Double acting, hydraulic (incorporated in suspension struts)
Fluid capacity ... ...   330 cc

Rear suspension

Type ... ...   Semi-elliptic leaf
Spring length (between eye centres) ... ...   47 in (119.4 cm)

	Cortina	Cortina GT	Corsair
Number of leaves	4	5	6
Width of leaves	2 in (5.1 cm)	2 in (5.1 cm)	2 in (5.1 cm)

Shock absorbers ... ...   Double acting, telescopic hydraulic (lever arm type on Estate cars)

Steering geometry

	Cortina	Corsair
Castor	1° 12' to 2° 42'	1° 15' to 2° 45'
Camber	0° 40' to 2° 10'	0° 10' to 2° 10'
Steering axis ('king pin') inclination	4° 26' to 5° 56'	4° 26' to 5° 56'
Toe-in	1/16 to 1/8 in (1.6 to 3.2 mm)	1/16 to 1/8 in (1.6 to 3.2 mm)
Front track	50.0 in (127.0 cm)	50.0 in (127.0 cm)
Rear track	49.5 in (125.7 cm)	49.5 in (125.7 cm)
Turning circle (between kerbs)	34.67 ft (10.38 m)	36.6 ft (11.13 m)
Wheelbase	8.1 ft (2.49 m)	8.5 ft (2.565 m)

Steering gear

Type ... ...   Recirculatory ball
Capacity (oil) ... ...   ¾ pint (0.42 litre)

	Cortina	Cortina GT	Corsair	Corsair GT
Ratio (steering box)	15.1 : 1	13.4 : 1	15.1 : 1	13.4 : 1
Ratio (overall)	22.6 : 1	15.6 : 1	16.9 : 1	15.6 : 1

Steering wheel diameter ... ...   15.94 in (40.5 cm)

Wheels and tyres

Wheel type and size ... ...   Pressed steel 13 x 4J
Tyre size:
     Cortina ... ...   520 x 13
     Corsair and all GT models ... ...   5.60 x 13

Tyre pressures:

	Cortina	Cortina GT	Corsair	Corsair GT
Front	24 lb in^2 (1.7 kg cm^2)	22 lb in^2 (1.547 kg cm^2)	22 lb in^2 (1.547 kg cm^2)	24 lb in^2 (1.7 kg cm^2)
Rear	24 lb in^2 (1.7 kg cm^2)	24 lb in^2 (1.7 kg cm^2)	22 lb in^2 (1.547 kg cm^2)	26 lb in^2 (1.547 kg cm^2)

Where high speeds are sustained add 6 lb in^2 (0.42 kg cm^2) to the above recommended pressures

Torque wrench settings	lb ft	kg m
Stabiliser bar mounting bolts	18	2.49
Stabiliser bar end nuts	30	4.15
Front suspension leg thrust bearing nut	55	7.60
Front suspension leg upper support nuts	18	2.49
Front track control arm ball joint	35	4.84
Front track control arm inner pivot	27	3.73
Rear shock absorber upper mounting	25 to 30	3.46 to 4.15
Rear shock absorber lower mounting	40 to 45	5.53 to 6.22
Rear road spring 'U' bolts	20 to 25	2.76 to 3.46
Rear spring front shackle	30	4.15
Rear spring rear shackle	15	2.07
Steering ball joints	18 to 22	2.48 to 3.03
Brake backplate bolts	18 to 22	2.49 to 3.03
Drop arm nut	60 to 70	8.30 to 9.68
Steering box top cover bolts	12 to 15	1.66 to 2.07
Steering wheel nut	20 to 25	2.76 to 3.46
Steering column flange bolts	12 to 15	1.66 to 2.07
Rear suspension radius arm to body (GT models)	50	6.91
Rear suspension radius arm to rear axle casing (GT models) ..	25	3.46

1 General description

The suspension and steering is similar on all models covered by this manual but there are certain detail differences in steering ratios, coil spring lengths and other items. Reference should be made to the Specifications at the beginning of this Chapter.

The front suspension consists of two vertical shock absorber units each of which is surrounded by a coil spring.

At the upper end each unit is secured to a reinforcing mounting under each wing inner panel pressing.

To each unit a track control arm is connected, the inner ends of each being mounted on rubber bushes in the front cross-member, while the outer ends are connected to the steering arms through ball joints.

A stabiliser bar is connected to the outer ends of each track rod and is secured to the main structure by rubber-insulated brackets.

Directly associated with this suspension are two adjustable track rods which are connected to the steering arms and the drop arm to idler arm rod. The steering lock is determined by means of adjustable stops mounted on the front suspension crossmember, which contact lugs forged on the drop arm to idler arm connecting rod.

On earlier models there are six grease points, two on the track rod to steering arm ball joints, two on the track rod to drop arm to idler arm rod, and two on the suspension unit to track control arm joint.

On later models, of the nine joints in the linkage, seven are of

the sealed type and are packed with lubricant during manufacture and the remaining two are rubber-bonded joints, similarly requiring no lubrication.

After dismantling and reassembly of any part of the front suspension or steering, the alignment of the front wheels must be checked as described later in this Chapter.

The steering gear is of worm and nut, recirculatory ball type.

Provision is made for adjustment; but only adjustment to the rocker shaft should be carried out with the steering gear in the vehicle.

A two spoked steering wheel is splined to the steering column shaft.

The rear suspension comprises leaf springs and double-acting hydraulic shock absorbers. These are of telescopic type on cars but of lever type on Estate cars.

GT versions are equipped with rubber bushed radius arms as an additional refinement to the rear suspension arrangement.

2 Maintenance and inspection

1 In addition to the maintenance operations described in Routine Maintenance, the following work should also be carried out at a maximum of six monthly intervals.
2 Inspect the condition of all rubber gaiters and ball joint covers for splits or deterioration and renew as necessary.
3 Check the security of the outer track rod clamps.

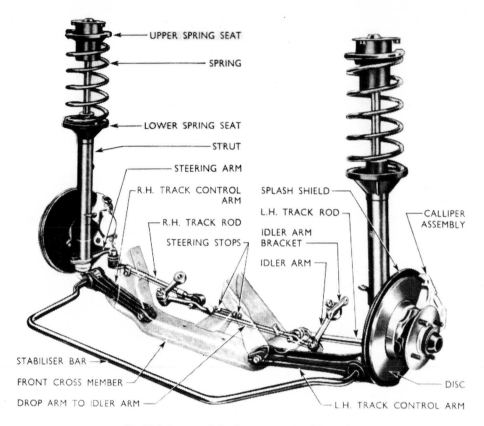

Fig. 11.1. Layout of the front suspension (Corsair)

4   Examine the condition of the track control arm bushes, also the rubber bushes at the stabiliser bar mounting brackets.

5   Check the rear road springs for cracked leaves, worn shackle bushes and loose shackle bolts. Tighten these and the 'U' bolt nuts to the specified torque.

6   The top end of the suspension unit should have no discernible movement and to check it grip the strut at the lower spring seat and try pushing it from side to side. There should be no detectable movement either between the outer cylinder and the inner piston rod or at the top of the piston rod near the upper mounting.

7   Any sign of oil on the outside of the rear shock absorber bodies will indicate that the seals have started to leak and the units must be renewed as assemblies. Where the shock absorber has failed internally, this is more difficult to detect although rear axle patter or tramp, particularly on uneven road surfaces, may provide a clue. When a shock absorber is suspected to have failed, remove it from the vehicle and holding it in a vertical position operate it for the full length of its stroke eight or ten times. Any lack of resistance in either direction will indicate the need for immediate renewal.

3 Stabiliser bar - removal and refitting

1   Before removing the stabiliser bar, the front coil springs on each of the front suspension units must be restrained. This can be done by having an assistant sit on the front wing to compress the coil spring and then fitting three clips and a safety strap to the spring. These clips are available from Ford dealers (Part No P5030) or from motor accessory factors. An alternative spring compressor of the adjustable rod type will also prove satisfactory. **Do not** be tempted to make home-made spring clamps.

2   Support the front of the vehicle on axle stands placed under the jacking points.

3   Remove the engine splash shield.

4   Remove the two clamps which attach the stabiliser bar to the bodyframe.

5   Remove the split pins and remove the nuts which secure the ends of the stabiliser bar to the track control arm. Withdraw the stabiliser bar together with bushes and sleeves.

6   Refitting is a reversal of removal but note that the end nuts must be tightened evenly to a torque of between 25 and 30 lb ft (3.46 and 4.148 kg m). Tighten the attachment clamp bolts to a torque of between 15 and 18 lb ft (2.074 and 2.489 kg m) and use new tab washers.

4 Track control arm and ball joint - removal and refitting

1   Restrain the front coil spring by fitting clips or threaded compressors as described in the preceding Section.

2   Withdraw the split pin and unscrew the ball joint stud nut at the base of the suspension unit.

3   Separate the track control arm from the ball joint stud by using an extractor or forked ('Smallbone' type) wedges.

4   Unscrew and remove the track control arm pivot bolt and withdraw the track control arm from the front crossmember.

5   Withdraw the split pin and unscrew the castellated nut from the end of the stabiliser bar and then detach the track control arm from the bar.

6   The track control arm ball joint is located at the bottom of the suspension leg and can be dismantled after disconnecting the track rod end ball joint from the steering arm on the suspension leg.

7   Remove the rubber gaiter and its retaining ring and then unscrew and remove the two bolts which secure the steering arm assembly to the suspension leg.

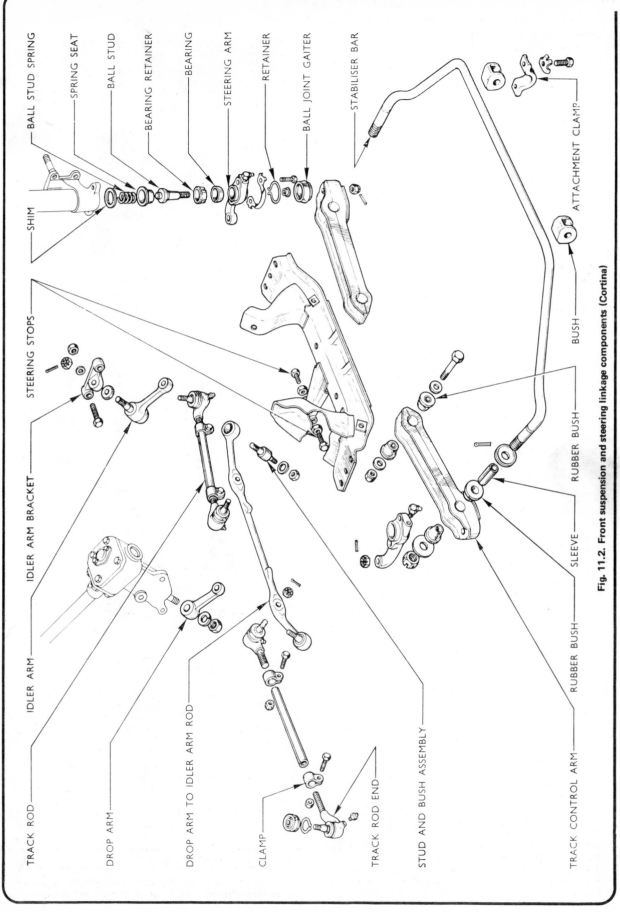

Fig. 11.2. Front suspension and steering linkage components (Cortina)

TRACK ROD

IDLER ARM

IDLER ARM BRACKET

STEERING STOPS

BALL STUD SPRING

SPRING SEAT

BALL STUD

BEARING RETAINER

BEARING

STEERING ARM

RETAINER

BALL JOINT GAITER

STABILISER BAR

SHIM

DROP ARM

DROP ARM TO IDLER ARM ROD

CLAMP

TRACK ROD END

STUD AND BUSH ASSEMBLY

TRACK CONTROL ARM

RUBBER BUSH

SLEEVE

RUBBER BUSH

BUSH

ATTACHMENT CLAMP.

8 Examine the surfaces of the ball and bearing. If these are corroded, rusty or scored, renew the joint complete.

9 When fitting a new track control arm ball joint the endfloat must be checked. To do this, fit the ball stud spring seat and the ball stud but not the spring. Refit the steering arm and bearing assembly and tighten the two securing bolts.

Cortina models

10 Ideally a dial gauge should be used to check the ball joint endfloat but a threaded rod inserted into the hole in the steering arm and a flat bar secured to the rod with two nuts so that the bar just makes light contact with the end of the track control arm ball joint stud will provide a good alternative. Push the ball joint stud inwards and take the dial gauge reading, or using feeler gauges, measure the gap between the end of the ball joint stud and the flat bar, whichever method is being used. Now pull the ball joint stud outwards and check the amount of movement (endfloat). This should be between 0.009 and 0.025 inch (0.23 and 0.035 mm).

11 If the endfloat is incorrect, adjust the shims (maximum of three shims).

Corsair models

12 With Corsair models the track control arm ball joint is of somewhat different design and the endfloat should be checked after the inner bearing has been correctly installed (with its lug located in the groove provided) also the outer bearing and the spring seat.

13 Using a press and tubular distance piece, press the bearing fully home but ensure that the outer bearing lug engages with the slot in the lower bearing.

14 Using feeler gauges, measure the gap between the spring seat and the lower edge of the steering arm upper rim. Where the clearance does not exceed 0.061 inch (1.549 mm) a shim does not have to be fitted. Where the clearance is between 0.061 and 0.072 inch (1.549 and 1.829 mm) fit one shim and if the clearance is greater fit two shims. All shims should be fitted below the spring seat.

All models

15 Refitting the track control ball joint and arm is a reversal of removal but ensure that nuts and bolts are tightened to their specified torque.

16 Pack the ball joint assembly and gaiter with molybdenum disulphide lithium grease.

17 Ensure that the rubber gaiter is not twisted during reassembly or reconnection.

18 If new rubber bushes are being fitted to the track control arm, use soapy water or brake fluid to facilitate their installation.

5 Front suspension leg (drum brake models) - removal

1 Before removing a suspension leg, fit spring clips or compressors to the coil spring as described in Section 3.

2 Jack up the front of the vehicle and support it securely on axle stands or blocks.

3 Remove the road wheel, the hub dust cap, split pin, hub nut, thrust washer and withdraw the brake drum taking care that the outer bearing does not drop to the ground during the process.

4 Unscrew and remove the bolts from the backplate and support it so that the brake hydraulic pipe is not strained. There is no need to dismantle the brake shoes or fluid lines.

5 Remove the split pin and castellated nut from the ball joint stud at the base of the suspension leg and using a suitable extractor, disconnect the ball joint stud from the track control arm.

6 Disconnect the track rod end ball joint from the suspension leg steering arm again using a suitable extractor.

7 Open the bonnet and remove the rubber dust cap from the suspension leg upper bearing.

8 Unscrew the three bolts which secure the suspension unit to the bodyshell support ring. Lift the suspension leg from under the front wing.

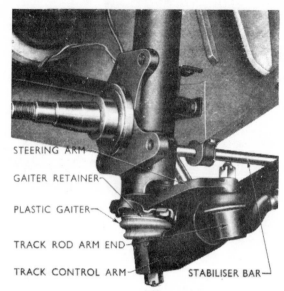

Fig. 11.3. Track control arm balljoint at base of front suspension leg

STEERING ARM

GAITER RETAINER

PLASTIC GAITER

TRACK ROD ARM END

TRACK CONTROL ARM   STABILISER BAR

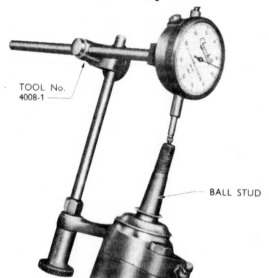

TOOL No. 4008-1

BALL STUD

Fig. 11.4. Checking track control arm balljoint end-float (Cortina)

6 Front suspension leg (disc brake models) - removal

1 Removal of this type of suspension leg is similar to the procedure described in the preceding Section.

2 The caliper unit can be moved to one side and supported without disconnecting the hydraulic fluid line. To do this, unscrew and remove the two caliper securing bolts and then release the fluid pipe locknut at the securing bracket (photo). Carefully move the caliper complete with flexible and rigid pipelines from its location over the disc.

3 The suspension leg may be withdrawn complete with hub/disc assembly for later removal, or alternatively, the components may be withdrawn from the stub axle before the suspension leg is lifted from the vehicle.

7 Front suspension leg - servicing

1 It is recommended that the suspension leg is exchanged for a new or reconditioned unit, in which case the coil spring still in

6.2 Disc brake type front suspension leg showing flexible brake hose bracket

its compressed state can be removed and refitted to the new leg.

2 Where it is decided however to dismantle and recondition the original unit, unscrew the self-locking nut at the top of the leg which retains the upper thrust bearing. Hold the upper spring seat firmly during this operation to prevent the piston rod turning (photo).

3 Pull off the upper mounting, spring seat and coil spring (still in clips or compressors).

4 Unscrew the filler plug from the outer casing and expel the fluid from the suspension leg by operating the piston.

5 Relieve the staking at the gland nut and in the absence of a suitable tool, use a blunt cold chisel to unscrew the nut.

6 Remove the rubber sealing ring, grip the piston rod and pull the piston/cylinder assembly from the leg.

7 Complete sealed cartridge units are available for installation into the original legs but where individual repair kit components are available then continue to dismantle as follows:

8 Withdraw the compression and foot valve assembly from the bottom of the cylinder. Do not touch the small screw in the compression valve nut.

9 Withdraw the piston rod from the cylinder.

10 Remove the upper guide, wave washer, gland seat and gland.

11 Bend back the tab washers and remove the piston valve nut from the piston rod.

12 Withdraw the valve assembly and spring from the piston rod.

13 Remove the rebound stop tube from the top of the cylinder if essential. Dismantling of the track control arm ball joint is described in Section 4.

14 Check all components for wear and renew as necessary. The piston/piston rod are supplied as one unit.

15 Ensure that all fluid ports and drillings are clear.

16 Reassembly of internal components is a reversal of removal but the following points must be observed: Where a sealed cartridge unit is being installed then the outer casing must not be refilled with oil but the filler plug should be refitted.

17 Check that the rebound stop is flush with the top of the cylinder.

18 Fit a new lockwasher to the piston rod with its tongue located in the piston rod slot. Refit the valve nut and fully tighten. Bend over the lockwasher tab.

19 Make sure that the gland seat has its dished side towards the upper guide and the gland has its grooved face uppermost.

20 Use a new upper guide sealing ring and tighten the gland cap to a torque of between 23 and 31 lb ft (3.180 to 4.286 kg m). Stake the outer casing into the gland cap slot.

21 Refill the unit with approved fluid through the filler plug

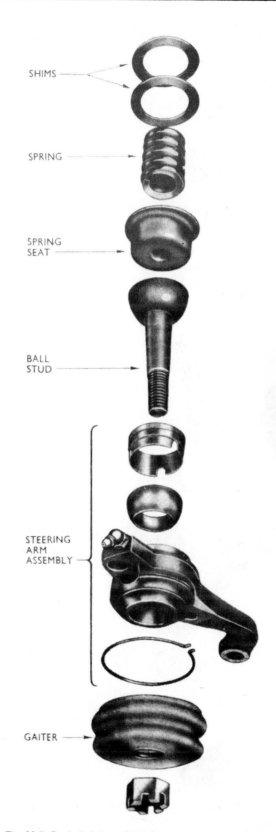

SHIMS

SPRING

SPRING SEAT

BALL STUD

STEERING ARM ASSEMBLY

GAITER

Fig. 11.5. Exploded view of Cortina type track control arm balljoint

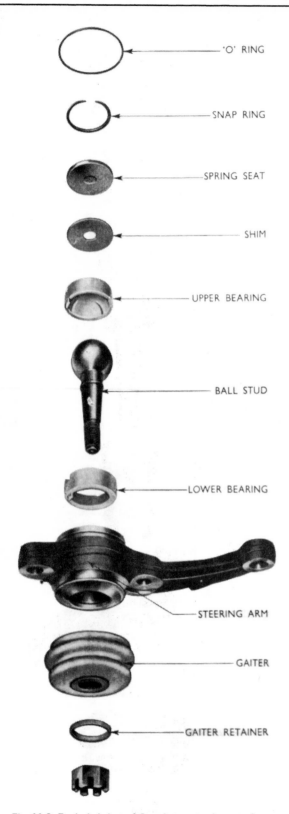

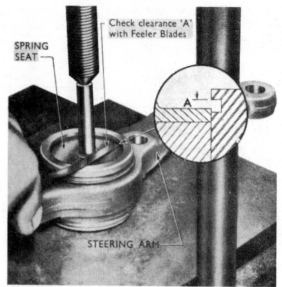

Fig. 11.7. Checking track control arm balljoint end-float (Corsair)

7.2 Suspension leg upper mounting

hole, replace the plug and then operate the piston at least six times to the limit of its travel. With the piston at its lowest position and the suspension leg held vertically top up to the level of the filler plug.

22 Pack the bearing cages with lithium based grease.

23 Tighten the thrust bearing locknut to a torque of between 45 and 55 lb ft (6.22 and 7.60 kg m).

24 Reassembly of the track control arm ball joint is described in Section 4.

8 Front suspension leg (drum brake models) - refitting

1   Offer up the suspension leg to its upper mounting ring.

2   Locate the track control arm ball joint, the track rod end ball joint and the stabiliser bar to their points of attachment on the suspension leg.

3   Tighten the upper mounting nuts to a torque of between 15 and 18 lb ft (2.07 and 2.49 kg m) and then fit the dust cap.

4   Tighten the track control arm ball joint stud nut to a torque of between 30 and 35 lb ft (4.15 and 4.84 kg m).

5   Tighten the stabiliser end nut to a torque of between 25 and 30 lb ft (3.46 to 4.148 kg m).

6   Tighten the track rod end ball joint stud nut to a torque of

Fig. 11.6. Exploded view of Corsair type track control arm balljoint

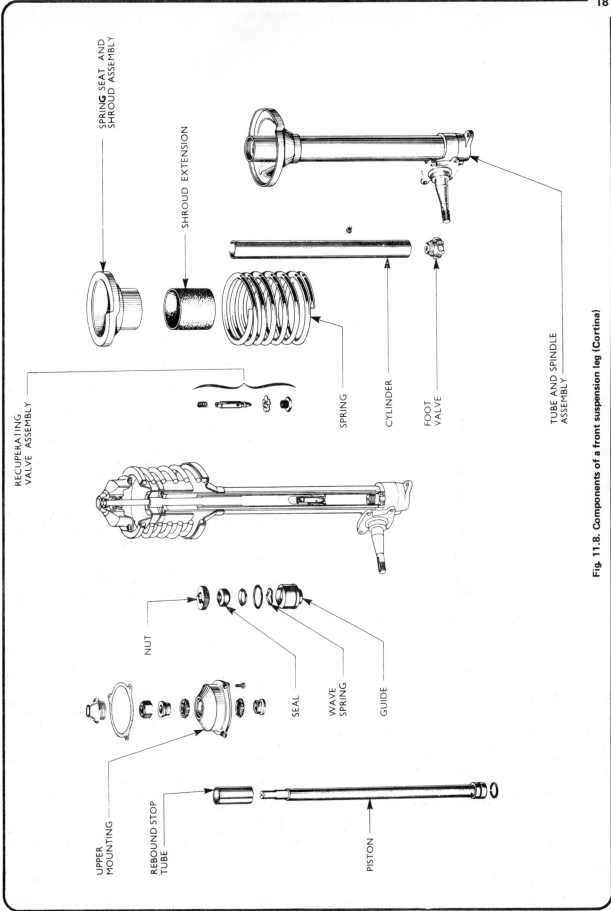

Fig. 11.8. Components of a front suspension leg (Cortina)

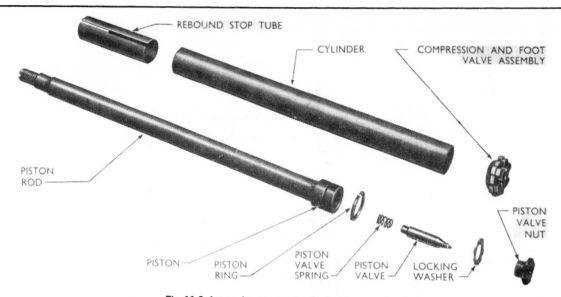

Fig. 11.9. Internal components of a front suspension leg

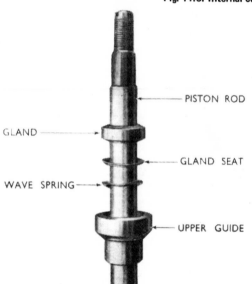

Fig. 11.10. Suspension leg upper piston rod detail

between 18 and 22 lb ft (2.48 and 3.03 kg m). Always use new split pins when fitting castellated nuts.

7   Fit the brake backplate and tighten the securing bolts to a torque of between 18 and 22 lb ft (2.49 and 3.03 kg m).

8   Reassemble and adjust the front hub/drum assembly as described in Chapter 9, Section 4.

9   Refit the road wheel, lower the vehicle and remove the coil spring clips or compressors.

10 With the weight of the vehicle on the suspension, remove the suspension leg filler plug and top up if necessary. Topping up of fluid in the suspension leg is not a routine maintenance operation and will only be required at major overhaul of a unit.

9   Front suspension leg (disc brake models) - refitting

The procedure is similar to that described in the preceding Section but the disc/hub assembly should be adjusted as detailed in Chapter 9, Section 13.

10 Front hub bearings - servicing and renewal

1   Every 5000 miles (8000 km) the front hub endfloat should be

checked and the bearings adjusted as described in Chapter 9, Section 9 or 13, according to brake design.

2   Every 15,000 miles (24,000 km) the hubs should be removed, the old grease wiped out with a piece of non-fluffy rag and new wheel bearing grease packed in the space between the inner and outer bearings. Pack the grease around the sides of the hub interior bearing adequate space for the stub axle. Do not fill the dust cap with grease. Adjust as previously described.

3   If the bearings are worn, remove the inner oil seal and drift out the bearing tracks. Tap in the new bearing tracks using a tube as a drift and ensuring that the new bearings are kept as matched sets and not mixed with bearing components for the opposite hub. Always fit a new oil seal.

11 Track rods and track rod ends - removal and refitting

1   Two track rods are used; these are attached at their inner ends through ball joints to the steering box drop arm to idler arm rod. At their outer ends the track rods are attached to the suspension leg steering arms, again through ball joints.

2   Each track rod is adjustable and is fitted with a socket end at each of its extremities. The socket ends have opposing (left and right hand) tapped threads.

3   Two clamps with pinch bolts are fitted to each track rod to retain the rod in its set position.

4   To remove a track rod, unscrew the castellated nuts from the ball joint studs at either end and disconnect the ball joints from steering arm and drop arm to idler arm rod. Disconnecting a ball joint is best achieved by using a ball joint extractor or a pair of forked ('Smallbone' type) wedges. It is possible to release a ball joint stud by striking opposite sides of the eye in which the taper stud locates simultaneously with two club hammers. However, unless great care is taken, damage to adjacent components can result.

5   Unscrew each track rod end from its track rod (left or right hand as marked).

6   To refit a track rod end, first locate the clamp on the track rod so that the pinch bolt head will be nearer the drop arm to idler arm rod when fitted.

7   Check that the ball joint gaiter is secured by its clip.

8   Screw on the left or right hand track rod end to the appropriately threaded end of the track rod until it covers the same number of threads (bright in appearance) which the original one did.

9   Position the clamps at a point about 1/8 inch (3.18 mm) from each end of the track rod.

10 Engage both track rod end ball joints in their respective eyes

Fig. 11.11. Track control arm and track rod components (one side) - Corsair

and tighten the stud nuts to a torque of between 18 and 22 lb ft (2.48 and 3.03 kg m). Fit new split pins and repeat with the opposite track rod.
11 Align the front wheels as described in Section 17.

12 Idler arm, bracket and rod - removal, servicing, refitting

1 Disconnect the track rod ball joints from the drop arm to idler arm rod as described in the preceding Section.
2 Disconnect the ball joints at both ends of the drop arm to idler arm rod from the steering drop arm and idler arm using a suitable extractor or forked wedges.
3 The idler arm bracket can be removed from the bodyframe after withdrawal of the two securing bolts.
4 The idler arm may be removed from its bracket using an extractor or forked wedges.
5 The idler arm cannot be repaired but in the event of wear occurring in the ball joint it must be renewed as an assembly.
6 The stud and bush assemblies can be pressed out from each end of the idler arm rod and new ones installed ensuring that the outer sleeves are flush with the boss on each end of the rod.
7 Refitting is a reversal of removal; tighten the ball joint stud nuts to a torque of between 18 and 22 lb ft (2.48 and 3.03 kg m) and the idler arm to bracket stud nut to a torque of between 25 and 30 lb ft (3.46 and 4.15 kg m).

13 Steering gear and linkage - inspection

1 Wear in the steering gear and linkage is indicated when there is considerable movement in the steering wheel without corresponding movement at the road wheels. Wear is also indicated when the car tends to wander off the line one is trying to steer. There are three main steering 'groups' to examine in such circumstances. These are the wheel bearings, the linkage joints and bushes and the steering box itself.
2 First jack up the front of the car and support it on stands under the side frame members so that both front wheels are clear of the ground.
3 Grip the top and bottom of the wheel and try to rock it. It will not take any great effort to be able to feel any play in the wheel bearing. If this play is very noticeable it would be as well to adjust it straight away as it could confuse further examinations. It is also possible that during this check play may be discovered also in the lower suspension track control arm ball joint (at the foot of the suspension strut). If this happens, the ball joint will need renewal as described in Section 4.
4 Next grip each side of the wheel and try rocking it laterally. Steady pressure will, of course, turn the steering but an alter-

nated back and forth pressure will reveal any loose joint. If some play is felt it would be easier to get assistance from someone so that while one person rocks the wheel from side to side, the other can look at the joints and bushes on the track rods and connections. Excluding the steering box itself, there are seven places where wear may be detected. The two outer ball joints on the two track rods are the most likely followed by the two inner ones where they join the central drop arm to idler arm rod. Any play in these components will necessitate immediate renewal. Next are the two stud and bush assemblies, one at each end of the drop arm to idler arm rod. Also check the ball joint which connects the idler arm to the bracket on the body side frame.
5 Finally, the steering box itself is checked. Make sure that the bolts holding the steering box to the side frame member are tight, then get another person to help examine the mechanism. One should look at, or get hold of, the drop arm at the bottom of the steering box while the other turns the steering wheel a little way from side to side. The amount of lost motion between the steering wheel and the drop arm indicates the degree of wear somewhere in the steering box mechanism. This check should be carried out with the wheels first of all in the straight ahead position and then at nearly full lock on each side. If the play only occurs noticeably in the straight ahead position then the wear is most probably in the worm and/or nut. If it occurs at all positions of the steering then the wear is probably in the rocker shaft bush. An oil leak at this point is another indication of such wear. In either case the steering box will need removal for closer examination and repair.

14 Steering gear - adjustment

1 Rocker shaft adjustment is the only adjustment which should be carried out with the steering gear in the vehicle. Need for adjustment will probably be first indicated by knocking from the steering when traversing rough surfaces.
2 To verify the need for adjustment, disconnect the steering linkage from the drop arm.
3 Centralise the steering wheel (drop arm pointing straight ahead and parallel to steering column).
4 Using a spring balance attached to the steering wheel rim apply a pull of between 1¼ and 1½ lbs (0.57 and 0.69 kg) which should turn the wheel. If the force required to turn the wheel is too low, remove the steering box cover, the shim pack, gaskets, two coil springs and the thrust button.
5 Remove a paper shim (0.002 to 0.003 in/0.051 to 0.076 mm) or a steel shim (0.005 in/0.127 mm or 0.010 in/0.254 mm).

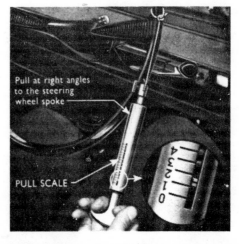

Fig. 11.12. Checking rocker shaft adjustment using a spring balance

6 Refit the reduced shim pack, gaskets, springs, thrust button and cover, tightening the bolts to a torque of between 12 and 15 lb ft (1.66 and 2.07 kg m).

7 Recheck the turning force with the spring balance and further adjust the shim pack if necessary.

8 Where during the original test, the pull indicated on the spring balance was high, **add** shims and repeat the operations described for low reading.

9 When adjustment is correct refit the linkage to the drop arm and tighten to a torque of between 18 and 22 lb ft (2.49 to 3.04 kg m).

10 Top up the steering box with fluid of the specified grade.

15 Steering gear - removal and installation

1 Disconnect the battery and centralise the steering so that the road wheels are in the straight ahead position.

2 Prise the motif from the centre of the steering wheel.

3 On cars fitted with a tachometer, remove the securing screws and also support it away from the steering column.

4 On Corsair DeLuxe and GT cars, detach the horn contact terminal from the direction indicator cam and also remove the horn ring (two screws) and motif.

5 Bend back the locking tab, unscrew the steering wheel retaining nut and remove the tab washer and steering wheel. If the wheel is stuck on its splines, attempt to jar it from behind the spokes using the palms of the hands. Where this fails, use a three-legged puller but adequately protect the steering wheel hub against damage.

6 Remove the steering column cover plate (two screws).

7 Pull off one side of the steering column shroud (left hand for rhd, right hand for lhd) and remove the now exposed bolts which secure the opposite half shroud. Support the shroud away from the column without straining or disconnecting the electrical leads.

8 Remove the parcel tray (two screws at each end) also the angular support bracket from the left hand side of the heater.

9 Unscrew the cover plate and remove it and the sealing gasket from the bulkhead.

10 Remove the two bolts from the steering column mounting clamp also the single bolt from the pedal bracket.

11 Where steering column gearchange mechanism is fitted, withdraw the pin from the connection of the gearchange tube to the gearchange housing within the engine compartment. Within the driving compartment withdraw the gearchange lever/tube

assembly from its location.

12 At the bottom of the steering column, remove the bolts which secure the gearchange housing to the steering box and tie the linkage to one side.

13 Jack up the front of the vehicle and support the bodyframe securely on stands or blocks, also support the wheels under the track control arms. Remove the engine splash shield.

14 Disconnect the steering linkage from the drop arm.

15 Unscrew and remove the bolts which secure the steering box to the body side frame.

16 The steering gear may now be withdrawn downwards and out from below and to the front of the vehicle.

17 Installation of the steering gear is a reversal of removal but observe the following points.

18 Initially fit the steering box bolts loosely until the steering column upper clamp and lower bracket bolts have been fitted. Finally, tighten all bolts securely. When installation is complete, top up the steering box to the level of the filler plug.

16 Steering gear - dismantling, servicing, reassembly

1 Drain the oil from the steering box through the filler plug hole.

2 Mark the relative position of the drop arm to the rocker shaft and then remove the drop arm using a suitable puller.

3 Remove the cover plate and its gasket from the top face of the steering box and withdraw the two coil springs and thrust button.

4 Remove the large top cover (four bolts) together with gaskets and shim pack.

5 Remove the roller from the peg on the steering nut and pull out the rocker shaft.

6 Remove the four bolts which secure the steering column flange to the steering box. Pull the column and flange assembly off the inner shaft and remove the gaskets and shim pack, noting their sequence of fitting.

7 Withdraw the spacer and then unscrew the steering shaft to release the nut complete with its thirteen balls.

8 Remove the steering shaft, upper bearing cup and twelve balls.

9 Remove the twelve balls from the lower cup and then remove the lower bearing cup.

10 Discard the rocker shaft oil seal and the felt bush from the upper end of the steering column.

11 Inspect all components for wear and scoring and renew as appropriate. If the rocker shaft bush requires renewal it should

Fig. 11.13. Steering column shroud retaining bolts (Corsair)

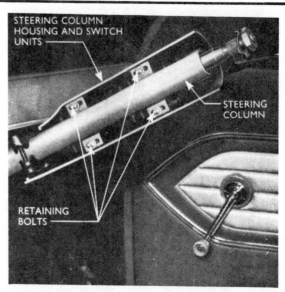

Fig. 11.14. Steering column shroud retaining bolts (Cortina)

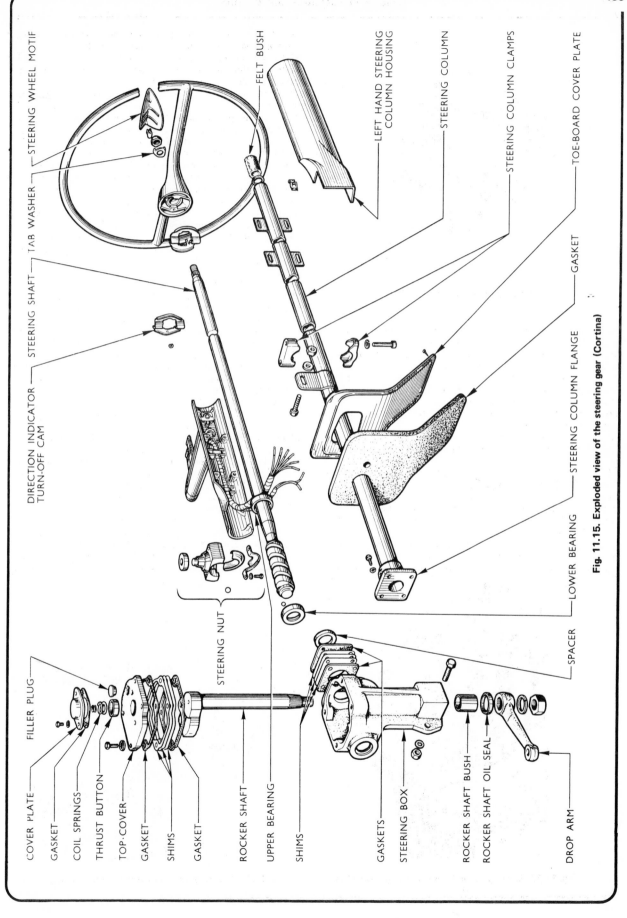

Fig. 11.15. Exploded view of the steering gear (Cortina)

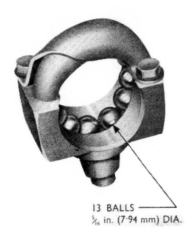

13 BALLS
⁵⁄₁₆ in. (7·94 mm) DIA.

Fig. 11.16. The steering nut and balls

be pressed from its housing location after first having tapped a 5/8 inch BSP thread in it. Leave the tap in position in the full length of the bush and press it out of the bottom of the housing when it will bring the bush with it.

12 The new bush will have to be pressed into position (with the open end of the oil groove towards the steering shaft) until its inner edge abuts the machined edge in the steering box housing. Broaching will then be required (Tool P3022) and the housing washed clean of all swarf.

13 Fit a new rocker shaft oil seal and a new upper column felt seal which has previously been soaked in molten heavy grease or tallow.

14 Refit the lower bearing (track uppermost) and retain the twelve 7/32 inch (5.56 mm) diameter balls in it with grease. It should be noted that the steering box balls are of different sizes: upper and lower steering shaft bearing balls (24) are 1/32 inch (5.56 mm) in diameter. The steering nut balls (13) are 5/16 inch (7.94 mm) in diameter.

15 Fit the thirteen larger diameter balls into the steering nut, retaining them in position with grease and then locate the nut

assembly in the steering box (either way round but with the spigot end uppermost). Screw the steering shaft into the nut.

16 Grease the upper bearing and locate it over the steering shaft. Position the remaining twelve 7/32 inch (5.56 mm) diameter balls in the bearing track.

17 Fit the shaft and bearings in their correct locations so that the lower bearing track is in contact with the lower balls and the upper bearing pushed in so that the balls are in contact with the track at the upper end of the shaft worm.

18 Locate the spacer so that it abuts the upper bearing.

19 At this stage adjust the steering shaft bearing pre-load. To do this, locate a new paper gasket (0.010 in/0.254 mm thick) against the column flange mating face of the steering box and then refit the shim pack originally removed during dismantling. Fit a second new paper gasket. Slide the outer column into position over the inner shaft and insert and tighten the flange bolts evenly in diagonal sequence at the same time rotating the steering shaft. If stiff operation or binding is noted, remove the column and increase the shim pack. Shims are available in thicknesses of 0.004 inch (0.102 mm), 0.010 inch (0.254 mm) and paper gaskets in thicknesses of 0.010 inch (0.254 mm) and 0.0025 inch)0.064 mm).

20 With the flange bolts tightened to between 12 and 15 lb ft (1.66 to 2.07 kg m) if the shaft rotates freely, check the endfloat of the inner shaft using a dial gauge or a block and feeler gauges until by adjustment of the shim pack, the endfloat is 0.001 inch (0.025 mm). When this is achieved, remove one 0.004 inch (0.102 mm) shim to provide the necessary bearing pre-load.

21 Refit the flange bolts coating their threads with gasket cement and tighten to a torque of between 12 and 15 lb ft (1.66 to 2.07 kg m).

22 Insert the rocker shaft (well lubricated) into the steering box so that its fork connects with the steering nut spigot.

23 Fit the roller to the spigot.

24 Locate a new paper gasket (0.010 in/0.254 mm thick) on the steering box. Refit the original shim pack plus another new paper gasket (0.010 in/0.254 mm thick) and tighten down the top cover ensuring that the roller engages correctly in the top cover groove.

25 Using a dial gauge or fixed block and feeler gauges, check the rocker shaft endfloat. Adjust by removal or addition of paper shims (0.002 in/0.051 mm) or metal shims (0.005 in/0.127 mm) until the endfloat is between 0.002 and 0.003 inch (0.051 and 0.076 mm) with the steering in the straight ahead position. When this has been achieved, remove one 0.005 inch (0.127 mm thick) shim from below the cover to provide the correct pre-load and

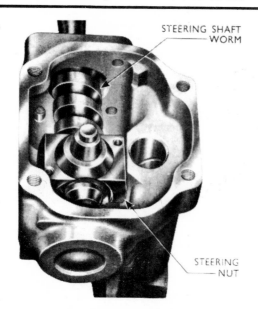

STEERING SHAFT WORM

STEERING NUT

Fig. 11.17. Steering nut and shaft correctly assembled

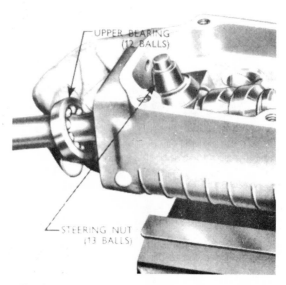

UPPER BEARING (12 BALLS)

STEERING NUT (13 BALLS)

Fig. 11.18. Locating the steering shaft upper bearing

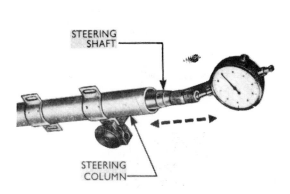

Fig. 11.19. Fitting the steering column and shims

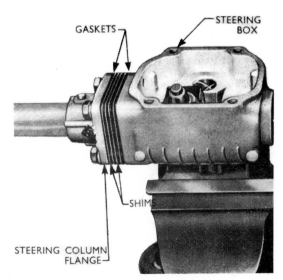

Fig. 11.20. Checking steering shaft end-float

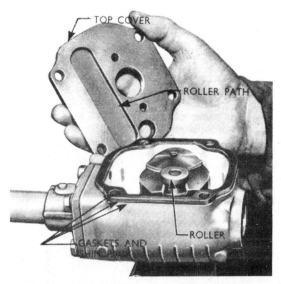

Fig. 11.21. Fitting the steering box top cover

Fig. 11.22. Fitting thrust button and springs into steering box top cover aperture

then tighten the cover bolts (coated with gasket cement) to a torque of between 12 and 15 lb ft (1.66 to 2.07 kg m).

26 Insert the thrust button and two coil springs into the top cover aperture and locate a new gasket and the small cover plate and tighten the two securing bolts to the same torque as the larger cover bolts.

27 Fit the drop arm to the rocker shaft splines ensuring that the alignment marks made before removal are correctly positioned. Fit a new spring washer and then tighten the securing nut to a torque of between 60 and 70 lb ft (8.29 and 9.67 kg m).

17 Steering geometry and front wheel alignment

1 Accurate front wheel alignment is essential for good steering and slow tyre wear. Before considering the steering geometry check the following factors:

The tyres are correctly inflated
The road wheels are not buckled

The front wheel bearings are correctly adjusted
The stabiliser clamp bolts are tight
The steering ball joints are not worn

2 Wheel alignment embraces four angles:

Camber, which is the angle at which the front wheels are inclined from the vertical when they are viewed from the front of the vehicle. The camber is regarded as positive when the wheels are tilted outwards at the top.

Castor is the angle between the steering axis and a vertical line when viewed from each side of the vehicle. Castor is regarded as positive when the steering axis is inclined rearward at the top.

Steering axis ('kingpin') inclination is the angle (when viewed from the front of the vehicle) between the vertical and an imaginary line drawn between the centres of the upper and lower suspension leg pivots.

3 All the foregoing angles are set in manufacture and cannot be adjusted. An incorrect castor angle may be due to a loosely

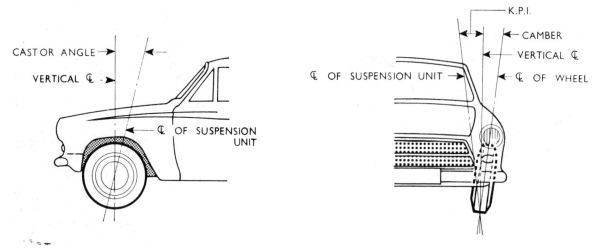

Fig. 11.23. Steering angle diagram

mounted stabiliser bar. An incorrect camber angle or an incorrect steering axis inclination may be due to a bent or distorted stub axle, a worn lower suspension leg ball joint or a worn track control arm bush.

4 Toe-in is the amount by which the distance between the front inside edges of the road wheels (measured at hub height) is less than the distance measured between the inside edges at the rear of the wheel, also taken at hub height.

5 Front wheel alignment (track adjustment) is best carried out with modern setting equipment at a service station but a satisfactory alternative adjustment method is described in the following paragraphs.

6 Place the vehicle on level ground with the road wheels in the straight ahead position.

7 Loosen both clamps on each of the two track rods and rotate the track rods if necessary so that their 'between track rod ends' measurements are equal.

8 Obtain or make a tracking gauge. One may be easily made up from a length of tubing or bar, cranked to clear the sump and bellhousing and having an adjustable nut and setscrew at one end.

9 With the gauge, measure the distance between the two inner wheel rims at the front of the road wheel, at hub height.

10 Push or pull the vehicle so that the road wheel turns through 180º (half a turn) and measure the distance between the inner wheel rims at hub height at the rear of the front road wheels. This measurement should be greater than that taken previously at the front of the wheel by between 1/16 and 1/8 inch (1.6 and 3.2 mm).

11 If the toe-in is found to be incorrect, rotate each track rod ¼ of a turn and recheck the alignment. If a mark is made on the top of each track rod and the rod is turned so that the mark moves to the rear then the toe-in will be decreased and vice versa.

12 When the toe-in has been correctly set, tighten the clamp bolts so that the clamp jaws are in alignment with a slot in the track rod. The clamp bolt should be located at the bottom of the clamp with its nut towards the rear of the vehicle. Before tightening the clamp bolt make sure that the track rod ends are set correctly with their ball joints at the centres of their arcs of travel.

13 Never attempt to check or adjust the toe-in with the front road wheels jacked up. If the front of the vehicle has recently been jacked up, the vehicle must be moved and the steering wheel turned in both directions in order to settle the suspension components into their normal operating attitude before carrying out any wheel alignment checks or adjustments.

18 Steering lock - adjustment

1 The steering lock is limited by the provision of bolts and locknuts fitted to a centrally positioned bracket. Failure to set the steering stop locks correctly may cause the rocker shaft to damage the steering box and the tyres to rub against the body side frame members.

2 With the car standing on the ground, turn the steering to full left lock and then adjust the steering wheel slightly until the gap between the inside wall of the left hand tyre and the bodyframe is 1.85 inch (47.0 mm). Now screw out the left hand lock stop bolt until it just contacts the lug on the drop arm to idler arm rod. Tighten the locknut ensuring that the setting of the bolt does not alter.

3 Repeat the operation on the opposite lock stop bolt with the steering turned to full right lock.

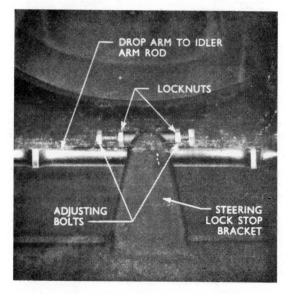

Fig. 11.24. Location of steering lock stop bolts

19 Rear shock absorbers (telescopic type) - removal and refitting

1   Chock the front wheels, jack up the rear of the car and support the axle on firmly based stands. Remove the rear wheel.
2   Undo and remove the shock absorber upper and lower mounting nuts and bolts. Lift away the shock absorbers (photo).
3   Should it be necessary to fit new rubber bushes, use a suitable diameter drift and drive out the spacer sleeve and then the rubber bushes. Refitting new bushes is the reversal of the removal sequence.
4   Examine the shock absorber for signs of damage to the body, distorted piston rod or hydraulic leakage. If evident, a new unit should be fitted.
5   To test for damper efficiency, hold the unit in the vertical position and gradually extend and contract the unit between its maximum and minimum limits ten times. It should be apparent that there is equal resistance in both directions of movement. If this is not apparent a new unit should be fitted. Always renew shock absorbers in pairs.
6   Refitting the shock absorber is the reverse sequence to removal.

19.1 Rear shock absorber upper mounting

20 Rear shock absorbers (lever type) - removal and refitting

1   This type of shock absorber is only fitted to Cortina Estate cars and is removed in the following way.
2   Chock the front wheels to prevent the car moving then jack up the rear of the car and for convenience sake remove the road wheels.
3   Undo the two self-locking nuts and spring washers which retain the shock absorber to the body side frame and then undo the nut and spring washer holding the link arm to the axle casing.
4   The shock absorber can now be removed from the car and the link arm removed from the shock absorber by undoing the single retaining nut and spring washer.
5   Replacement of the unit is a direct reversal of the above instructions.

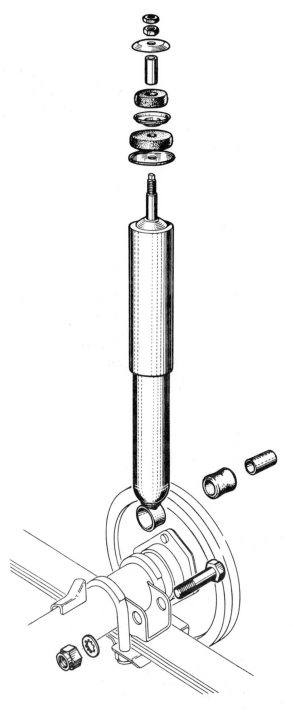

Fig. 11.25. A rear telescopic type shock absorber

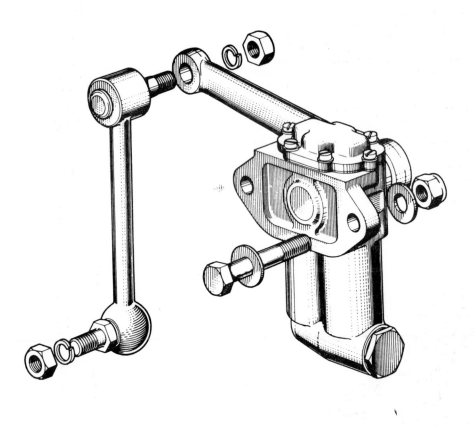

Fig. 11.26. A lever type shock absorber (Estate car)

21 Rear road springs - removal and refitting

1 Chock the front wheels to prevent the car moving, then jack up the rear of the car and support it on suitable stands. To make the springs more accessible remove the road wheels.

2 Then place a further jack underneath the differential to give support to the rear axle when the springs are removed. Do not raise the jack under the differential so that the springs are flattened, but raise it just enough to take the full weight of the axle with the spring fully extended.

3 Undo the rear shackle nuts and remove the combined shackle bolt and plate assemblies. Then remove the four rubber bushes.

4 Undo the nut from the front mounting bracket and take out the bolt running through the mounting.

5 Undo the nuts on the ends of the four 'U' bolts and remove the 'U' bolts together with the attachment plates under the nuts. The spring can now be removed from the car.

7 Replacement is a direct reversal of the above procedure. The nuts on the spring 'U' bolts, spring front mounting and spring rear mounting shackles must be torqued down to the figures given in the Specifications at the beginning of this Chapter but **after the car has been lowered onto its wheels.**

8 On GT versions, radius arms are fitted in conjunction with the rear road springs. These are simply removed by removing the securing bolts at either end which retain the arm to the axle casing lugs and the front mounting bracket.

22 Wheels and tyres

1 In the interests of safety and reduced driving fatigue the following operations should be carried out.

2 Every 5000 miles (8000 km) check the depth of tread at the centre of each tyre. When the tread has worn to 1.0 mm the tyre must be renewed.

3 When buying new tyres, make sure that a new valve is fitted and the wheel balanced at the same time.

4 Radial tyres must not be fitted to the front if crossply tyres are fitted at the rear. Radial and crossply tyres must never be mixed on the same axle.

5 If the wheels have been balanced off the vehicle then it is a good idea to move their position every two or three thousand miles to equalise tread wear. Include the spare in the pattern of rotation and if radial tyres are fitted, change them on the same side only between front and rear so that their direction of travel remains constant. Remember to adjust the pressures after moving the wheels round. Where the wheels have been balanced on the vehicle then the wheels should not be moved periodically.

6 When the tyres are about half worn it is recommended that the wheels are rebalanced as by this stage the characteristics of the tyres will have changed due to the loss of rubber.

8 If a kerb has been hit, check the wheel for run-out by jacking it up and spinning it with a fixed pointer held almost in contact with its rim. The run-out of a road wheel should not exceed 1/8 inch (3.18 mm).

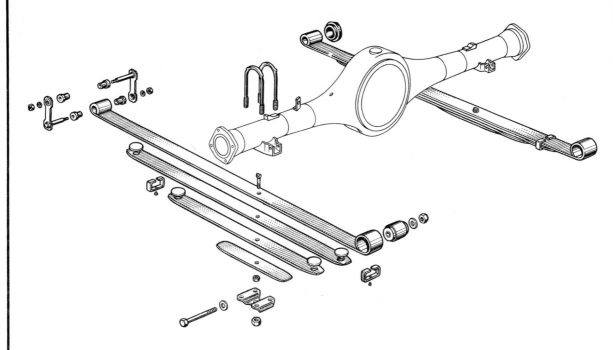

Fig. 11.27. Rear suspension details (not GT)

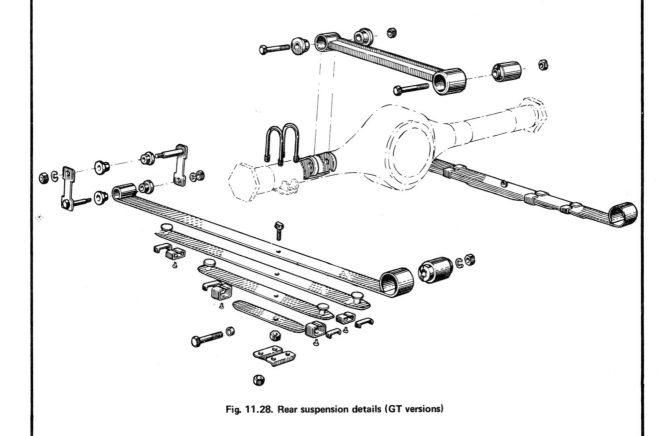

Fig. 11.28. Rear suspension details (GT versions)

23 Fault diagnosis - suspension and steering

Symptom	Reason/s	Remedy
Steering feels vague, car wanders and floats at speed	Tyre pressures uneven	Check pressures and adjust as necessary.
	Shock absorbers worn or require topping up	Top up shock absorbers, test, and replace if worn.
	Spring clips broken	Renew spring clips.
	Steering gear ball joints badly worn	Fit new ball joints.
	Suspension geometry incorrect	Check and rectify.
	Steering mechanism free play excessive	Adjust or overhaul steering mechanism.
	Front suspension and rear axle pick-up points out of alignment	Normally caused by poor repair work after a serious accident. Extensive rebuilding necessary.
Stiff and heavy steering	Tyre pressures too low	Check pressures and inflate tyres.
	No oil in steering gear	Top up steering gear.
	No grease in steering and suspension ball joints (early models)	Clean nipples and grease thoroughly.
	Front wheel toe-in incorrect	Check and reset toe-in.
	Suspension geometry incorrect	Check and rectify.
	Steering gear incorrectly adjusted too tightly	Check and re-adjust steering gear.
	Steering column badly misaligned	Determine cause and rectify (usually due to bad repair after severe accident damage and difficult to correct).
Wheel wobble and vibration	Wheel nuts loose	Check and tighten as necessary.
	Front wheels and tyres out of balance	Balance wheels and tyres and add weights as necessary.
	Steering ball joints badly worn	Renew steering gear ball joints.
	Hub bearings badly worn	Remove and fit new hub bearings.
	Steering gear free play excessive	Adjust and overhaul steering gear.
	Front springs loose, weak or broken	Inspect and overhaul as necessary.

Chapter 12 Bodywork and underframe

Contents

Specifications

	Cortina	Corsair
Length	14 ft ½ in (4.28 m)	14 ft 8½ in (4.486 m)
Width	5 ft 2½ in (1.59 m)	5 ft 3½ in (1.610 m)
Height (unladen)	56.65 in (144.0 cm)	57.50 in (152.0 cm)
Ground clearance (from differential)	6.4 in (16.25 cm)	6.7 in (17.02 cm)
Weight:		
Standard 2 door (1200 cc)	1716 lb (778 kg)	—
Standard 4 door (1200 cc)	1758 lb (797 kg)	
Standard 2 door (1500 cc)	—	1943 lb (881 kg)
Standard 4 door (1500 cc)	—	1980 lb (898 kg)
Deluxe 2 door (1200 cc)	1775 lb (805 kg)	—
Deluxe 4 door (1200 cc)	1803 lb (818 kg)	
Deluxe 2 door (1500 cc)	1780 lb (807 kg)	1956 lb (887 kg)
Deluxe 4 door (1500 cc)	1813 lb (822 kg)	1994 lb (905 kg)
GT 2 door	1795 lb (814 kg)	1988 lb (902 kg)
GT 4 door	1828 lb (827 kg)	2026 lb (919 kg)

1 General description

The bodyshell of all models is of steel, welded construction of the unitary principle without a separate chassis or bodyframe.

Apart from the obvious difference in body styling between the Cortina and Corsair, the operations described in this Chapter apply to all models (unless specifically stated otherwise) even though the components used may differ in detail design.

Bench type front seats are fitted in conjunction with automatic transmission and steering column gearchange. On later model vehicles, through-flow type ventilation is installed and quarterlight ventilators deleted.

GT versions are basically the same as standard or Deluxe models except for additional instrumentation.

2 Maintenance - bodywork and underframe

1 The condition of your car's bodywork is of considerable importance as it is on this that the secondhand value of the car will mainly depend. It is very much more difficult to repair neglected bodywork than to renew mechanical assemblies. The hidden portions of the body, such as the wheel arches and the underframe and the engine compartment are equally important,

though obviously not requiring such frequent attention as the immediately visible paintwork.

2   Once a year it is a sound scheme to visit your local main agent and have the underside of the body steam cleaned. This will take about 1½ hours. All traces of dirt and oil will be removed and the underside can then be inspected carefully for rust, damaged hydraulic pipes, frayed electrical wiring and similar maladies.

3   At the same time the engine compartment should be cleaned in the same manner. If steam cleaning facilities are not available then brush Gunk or a similar cleanser over the whole engine and engine compartment with a stiff paintbrush, working it well in where there is an accumulation of oil and dirt. Do not paint the ignition system but protect it with oily rags when the Gunk is washed off. As the Gunk is washed away it will take with it all traces of oil and dirt, leaving the engine looking clean and bright.

4   The wheel arches should be given particular attention as undersealing can easily come away here and stones and dirt thrown up from the road wheels can soon cause the paint to chip and flake, and so allow rust to set in (photo). If rust is found, clean down the bare metal with wet and dry paper, paint on an anti-corrosive coating such as Kurust, or if preferred, red lead, and renew the paintwork and undercoating.

2.4 Example of under wing corrosion at suspension unit upper mounting

5   The bodywork should be washed once a week or when dirty. Thoroughly wet the car to soften the dirt and then wash the car down with a soft sponge and plenty of clean water. If the surplus dirt is not washed off very gently, in time it will wear the paint down as surely as wet and dry paper. It is best to use a hose if this is available. Give the car a final wash down and then dry with a soft chamois leather to prevent the formation of spots.

6   Spots of tar and grease thrown up from the road can be removed by a rag dampened with fuel.

7   Once every six months, or every three months if wished, give the bodywork and chromium trim a thoroughly good wax polish. If a chromium cleaner is used to remove rust on any of the car's plated parts, remember that the cleaner also removes part of the chromium, so use sparingly.

3   Maintenance - upholstery and carpets

1   Remove the carpets or mats and thoroughly vacuum clean the interior of the car every three months or more frequently if necessary.

2   Beat out the carpets and vacuum clean them if they are very dirty. If the upholstery is soiled apply an upholstery cleaner with a damp sponge and wipe off with a clean dry cloth.

4   Maintenance - PVC external roof covering

Under no circumstances try to clean any external PVC roof covering with detergents, caustic soaps or spirit cleaners. Plain soap and water is all that is required with a soft brush to clean dirt that may be ingrained. Wash the covering as frequently as the rest of the car.

5   Minor body repairs

1   At some time during the ownership of your car it is likely that it will be bumped or scraped in a mild way, causing some slight damage to the body.

2   Major damage must be repaired by your local Ford agent, but there is no reason why you cannot successfully beat out, repair and respray minor damage yourself. The essential items which the owner should gather together to ensure a really professional job are:
a) a plastic filler such as Holts Cataloy
b) paint whose colour matches exactly that of the bodywork, either in a can for application by a spray gun, or in an aerosol can
c) fine cutting paste
d) medium and fine grade wet and dry paper.

3   Never use a metal hammer to knock out small dents as the blows tend to scratch and distort the metal. Knock out the dent with a mallet or rawhide hammer and press on the underside of the dented surface a metal dolly or smooth wooden block roughly contoured to the normal shape of the damaged area.

4   After the worst of the damaged area has been knocked out, rub down the dent and surrounding area with medium wet and dry paper and thoroughly clean away all traces of dirt.

5   The plastic filler comprises a paste and hardener which must be thoroughly mixed together. Mix only a small quantity at a time as the paste sets hard within five to fifteen minutes depending on the amount of hardener used.

6   Smooth on the filler with a knife or stiff plastic to the shape of the damaged portion and allow to thoroughly dry, a process which takes about six hours. After the filler has dried it is likely that it will have contracted slightly, so spread on a second layer of filler if necessary.

7   Smooth down the filler with fine wet and dry paper wrapped round a small flat block of wood and continue until the whole area is perfectly smooth and it is impossible to feel where the filler joins the rest of the paintwork.

8   Spray on from an aerosol can, or with a spray gun, an anti-rust undercoat, smooth down with wet and dry paper, and then spray on two coats of the final finish using a circular motion.

9   When thoroughly dry, polish the whole area with a fine cutting paste to smooth the resprayed area into the remainder of the wing or panel and to remove the small particles of spray paint which will have settled round the area.

10   This will leave the area looking perfect with not a trace of the previous unsightly dent.

6   Major body repairs

1   Because the body is built on the monocoque principle and is integral with the underframe, major damage must be repaired by competent mechanics with the necessary welding and hydraulic straightening equipment.

2 If the damage has been serious it is vital that the body is checked for correct alignment, as otherwise the handling of the car will suffer and many other faults such as excessive tyre wear and wear in the transmission and steering may occur.

3 There is a special body jig which most large body repair shops have and to ensure that all is correct, it is important that this jig be used for all major repair work.

7 Maintenance - hinges and locks

Once every 3000 miles (5000 km) or 4 months, the door, bonnet and boot or tailgate hinges and locks should be oiled with a few drops of oil from an oil can. The door striker plates can be given a thin smear of grease to reduce wear and ensure free movement.

8 Windscreen glass - removal and refitting

1 If you are unfortunate enough to have a windscreen shatter, or should you wish to renew your present windscreen, fitting a replacement is one of the few jobs which the average owner is advised to leave to a professional. For the owner who wishes to attempt the job himself the following instructions are given.

2 Cover the bonnet with a blanket or cloth to prevent accidental damage and remove the windscreen wiper blades and arms.

3 If the windscreen is intact, put on a pair of plimsoles and sit in one of the front seats. With a piece of soft cloth between the soles of your shoes and the windscreen glass, place both feet in one top corner of the windscreen and push firmly.

4 When the weatherstrip has freed itself from the body flange in that area repeat the process at frequent intervals along the top edge of the windscreen until, from outside the car the glass and weatherstrip can be removed together.

5 If you are having to replace your windscreen due to a shattered screen, remove all traces of sealing compound and broken glass from the weatherstrip and body flange.

6 Gently prise out the clip which covers the joint of the chromium finisher strip and pull the finisher strip out of the weatherstrip. Then remove the weatherstrip from the glass or if it is still on the car, as in the case of a shattered screen, remove it from the body flange.

7 To fit a new windscreen start by fitting the weatherstrip around the new windscreen glass.

8 Apply a suitable sealer to the weatherstrip to body groove. In this groove then fit a fine but strong piece of cord right the way round the groove allowing an overlap of about six inches at the joint.

9 From outside the car, place the windscreen in its correct position, making sure that the loose end of the cord is inside the car.

10 With an assistant pressing firmly on the outside of the windscreen, get into the car and slowly pull out the cord thus drawing the weatherstrip over the body flange.

11 Apply a further layer of sealer to the underside of rubber to glass groove from outside the car.

12 Replace the chromium finisher strip into its groove in the weatherstrip and replace the clip which covers its joint.

13 Carefully clean off any surplus sealer from the windscreen glass before it has a chance to harden and then replace the windscreen wiper arms and blades.

14 The glass in the rear window can be removed or refitted in a similar manner.

9 Door rattles - tracing and rectification

1 The most common cause of door rattles is a misaligned loose or worn striker plate but other causes may be:

  a) Loose door handles or window winder handles

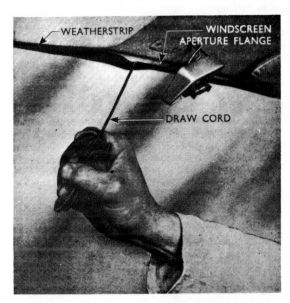

Fig. 12.1. Using a cord to refit windscreen and rubber surround

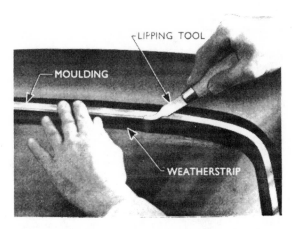

Fig. 12.2. Refitting windscreen surround strip moulding

  b) Loose or misaligned door lock components
  c) Loose or worn remote control mechanism

2 It is quite possible for door rattles to be the result of a combination of the above faults so a careful examination must be made to determine the causes of the fault.

3 If the nose of the striker plate is worn and as a result the door rattles, renew and then adjust the plate.

4 Should the inner door handle or window winder rattle, this is easily cured by putting a rubber washer between the escutcheon and the handle.

5 If the door lock is found to be worn and rattles as a consequence, then fit a new lock.

10 Door striker plate - removal, refitting and adjustment

1 If it is wished to renew a worn striker plate, mark its position on the door pillar with a pencil so that a new plate can

be fitted in the same position.

2 To remove the plate simply undo the three Phillips screws which hold the plate and anti-slip shim in position. Replacement is equally straightforward.

3 To adjust the striker plate, slightly loosen the three retaining screws and, with the outside door push button depressed, close the door and release the button.

4 Move the door in and out until it is flush with the surrounding bodywork then depress the button and open the door, being careful not to disturb the striker plate.

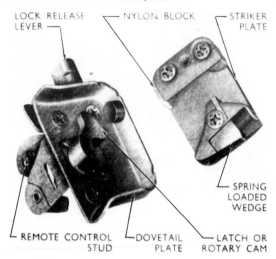

LOCK RELEASE LEVER — NYLON BLOCK — STRIKER PLATE

SPRING LOADED WEDGE

REMOTE CONTROL STUD — DOVETAIL PLATE — LATCH OR ROTARY CAM

Fig. 12.3. Door lock and striker plate (front door)

5 Check that the striker plate is vertical and tighten down the three screws. Adjustment is now complete.

11 Door trim, locks and remote control - removal and refitting

1 Wind up the window and remove the door remote control handle and the window regulator handle by undoing their centre screws and lifting off the washer, handles and escutcheon plates in that order (photos).

2 Remove the combined arm rest and door pull by undoing its two retaining screws (photo).

3 Insert a thin strip of metal with all the sharp edges removed between the recessed trim panel and the door. This will release one or two of the trim panel clips without damaging the trim. A short metal ruler is ideal for this job. The trim panel can then be eased off by hand and the polythene waterproof sheet removed.

4 Take off the spring clip which secures the door remote control operating arm to the lock mechanism and disconnect the operating arm.

5 To remove the outside door handle from inside the door panel remove the screw and washer holding the rear of the handle to the door, then, through the door access hole, undo and remove the screw and washer securing the front of the handle. The handle and sealing gasket can now be withdrawn.

6 From the rear end of the door remove the single screw and washer which secure the bottom of the door window glass rear lower run in position. Pull the run downwards to free the metal backing channel from the window frame.

7 On the driver's door of Cortina models and on both front doors of Corsair models, detach the lock from the private lock (see next Section) operating shaft.

8 Unscrew and remove the three screws which hold the dovetail plate to the door frame edge (photo), move the lower glass run to one side and withdraw the lock mechanism through the door aperture.

9 The remote control assembly can be removed by unscrewing the three retaining screws from its mounting plate (photo).

10 Refitting is a reversal of removal.

11.1a Removing a window regulator handle

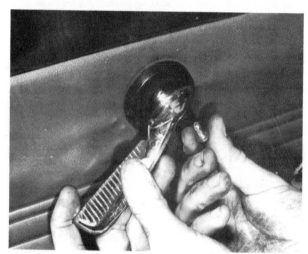

11.1b Removing a door lock interior handle

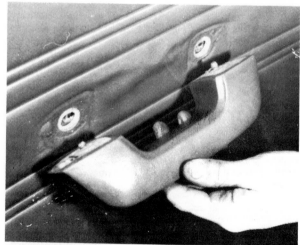

11.2 Removing an arm rest from the door interior panel

11.8 A door lock dovetail

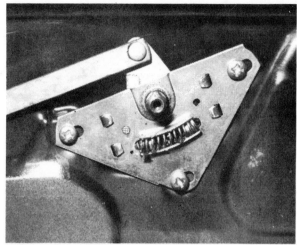

11.9 Door lock remote control securing plate

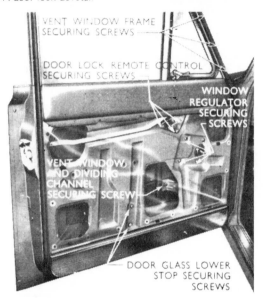

Fig. 12.4. Front door detail (Cortina)

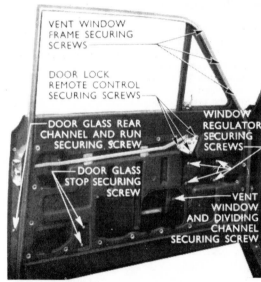

Fig. 12.5. Front door detail (Corsair)

12 Door private lock (Cortina) - removal and refitting

1   On Cortina models, the private cylinder type lock is fitted to the driver's door only and mounted within the door external release plunger.
2   To remove the lock, remove the external door handle as described in the preceding Section and then withdraw the two screws from the lock cylinder cover plate.
3   Remove the coil tension spring and extract the lock cylinder and plunger.
4   Slacken the adjuster stud locknut and unscrew and remove the plunger stud. Insert the ignition key and withdraw the lock cylinder.
5   Refitting is a reversal of removal.

13 Door private lock (Corsair) - removal and refitting

1   On Corsair models, the private cylinder type lock is fitted to each front door and located just below the door release plunger.
2   Remove the door lock as described in Section 11 and using a pair of pliers, compress the spring clip which retains the private lock and which is accessible from within the door cavity. Withdraw the lock cylinder from the outside of the door.

3   The barrel is retained within the cylinder by a tapered pin and this will be revealed after removal of the surrounding clip. Drive out the pin to dismantle.
4   Refitting is a reversal of removal.

14 Door release plunger - adjustment

1   Access to the plunger stud and locknut may be gained after removal of the door interior trim and lock mechanism as described in Section 11.
2   Slacken the locknut and screw the stud in or out until the correct operation is obtained. Retighten the locknut and apply a little grease to the end of the stud.

15 Rear door locks - removal and refitting

1   The rear door locks are of similar design to those fitted to the front doors except that on all Corsair models and on later Cortina models, they incorporate a childproof safety catch.
2   Close the window and remove the door interior trim and handles as described in Section 11.
3   Remove the spring clip and detach the lock remote control

rod.

4 Unscrew and remove the three screws which secure the dovetail plate and withdraw the lock assembly through the door aperture.

5 Refitting is a reversal of removal.

16 Window regulators - removal and refitting

1 Lower the window and remove the door remote control handle, the window regulator handle and the door trim panel as described in Section 11.

2 Support the window glass by means of a block of wood or similar object and undo the four screws holding the window regulator assembly to the door.

3 Disconnect the window regulator operating arm from the window glass lower run and then withdraw the regulator assembly through the door access hole.

4 Replacement is a reversal of the removal sequence.

17 Front door ventilators - removal, refitting, adjustment

1 Remove the door interior trim and handles as described in Section 11.

2 Temporarily refit the regulator handle and wind the window right down and then remove the glass lower stop.

3 Disengage the window regulator from the glass lower channel and lower the glass right to the bottom of the door cavity.

4 Pull down the glass flexible channel from the top corner adjacent to the ventilator frame.

5 Remove the three screws which secure the ventilator outer frame to the door.

6 Remove the ventilator dividing channel lower securing screw.

7 Prise out the inner and outer weatherstrips and then pull the ventilator frame rearwards at the same time disengaging the dividing channel from the main window glass. Lift out the ventilator assembly.

8 If the ventilator has been too easy or too stiff to operate, adjust its action by means of the pinch bolt on its lower pivot.

9 Installation is a reversal of removal.

18 Front door window glass - removal and refitting

1 Remove the ventilator assembly as described in the preceding Section. Where a fixed type quarterlight is fitted in conjunction with through-flow ventilation, the door glass should be removed as described in the following Section.

2 Lift the main door glass from the door cavity, prising open the door frame if necessary to permit it and its lower channel to pass through.

19 Rear door glass - removal and refitting

1 Wind the window fully down and remove the door interior trim and handles as described in Section 11.

2 Prise out the glass weatherstrip from their clips.

3 Prise out a short length of the upper door glass channel and let it hang down.

4 Remove the window dividing channel by drilling out one pop rivet at the top and removing one screw at the lower end. Pull out the dividing channel, prising the door frame open if necessary to permit it and its bracket to pass through. Remove the quarterlight and frame.

5 Remove the two securing screws from the door glass lower stop.

6 Disengage the window regulator from the glass lower channel, turn the glass through 90° and remove it from the door cavity.

7 Refitting is a reversal of removal but, of course, a new pop rivet will be required at the top end of the dividing channel.

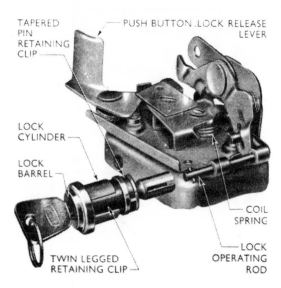

Fig. 12.6. Front door private lock (Corsair)

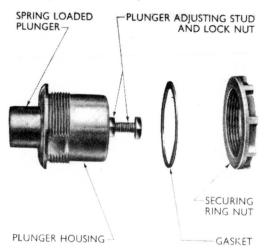

Fig. 12.7. Door release plunger detail

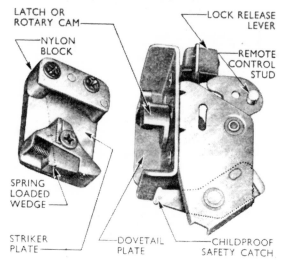

Fig. 12.8. Rear door lock and striker plate (Corsair and late Cortina)

20 Fixed rear quarter windows - removal and refitting

1   This type of window is fitted to two door standard Cortina models.
2   The glass is removed and refitted in a manner similar to that described for the windscreen in Section 8.

21 Opening rear quarter windows - removal and refitting

1   This type of window is fitted to Deluxe Cortina and standard Corsair models having two door bodywork.
2   Remove the two screws which secure the toggle type fastener to the body.
3   Open the window fully and remove the top screw from each pillar hinge.
4   Slacken, but do not remove, each of the lower hinge screws so that the slotted hinge plates can be slid out from under the screw heads and the window and frame removed.
5   The frame is assembled in two sections, secured by screws at the lower corners. Access to these screws can be obtained after removing the rubber strip. Tap the frame gently from the glass to remove it.
6   Refit the window assembly by first engaging the slotted hinge plates with the two lower screws and aligning the frame within the body aperture before fitting and tightening the remaining screws.

22 Doors - alignment, removal and refitting

1   Should the doors require adjustment within their body apertures, mark the position of the hinge plates on the edges of the door frames.
2   Slacken the hinge plate bolts and move the door fractionally in the appropriate direction. Tighten the bolts and check the door closure. The striker plate will probably require adjustment to provide positive door closure.
3   Where this movement proves insufficient or if the door is to be removed completely, then in the case of the front doors the trim panels located below the parcel shelf must be removed to provide access to the hinge plate to body pillar bolts.
4   With rear doors, remove the interior trim panel from the centre pillar.
5   Always support the door at its lower edge with jacks or blocks and a folded cloth pad to protect the paintwork before unscrewing the hinge bolts.
6   It is wise to mark the original positions of the hinge plates before adjusting or removing a door.
7   When refitting, always attempt to set the door so that the gaps at the sides and top are equal.

23 Bonnet - removal, refitting and adjustment

1   Open the bonnet lid and prop it open with the strut provided.
2   With a pencil draw a line round the hinge plates on the bonnet lid to ensure correct alignment when replacing.
3   Remove the two bolts and washers from either side of the bonnet lid and carefully lift the bonnet from the car.
4   When replacing the bonnet, loosely retain it with the bolts and then carefully line up the hinge plates with the pencil marks before finally tightening down the bolts.
5   Adjustment of the bonnet catch is carried out by compressing the coil spring on the catch bolt and slackening the locknut with a thin open-ended spanner.
6   Hold the locknut stationary with the spanner and turn the catch bolt in or out until when testing the closure of the bonnet it does not rattle, neither does it require excessive pressure to close it.
7   Tighten the locknut and grease the point of the catch bolt, also the sliding plate of the striker unit.

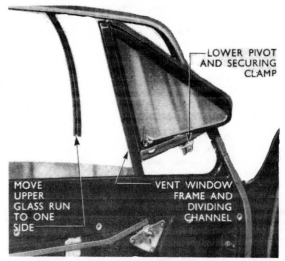

Fig. 12.9. Removing a front door ventilator (Cortina)

Fig. 12.10. Front door glass removal

Fig. 12.11. Rear door glass removal

24 Luggage boot lid - removal, refitting, adjustment

1 Place a piece of cloth over the paintwork immediately below the rear window to prevent scratching.
2 Mark the position of the hinge plates on the underside of the boot lid.
3 Remove the two bolts and washers from one hinge and rest the lid on the cloth.
4 Remove the remaining two bolts and washers from the opposite hinge and then lift the lid away.
5 Refit by resting the lid carefully on the cloth and inserting the hinge bolts finger tight only until the lid can be aligned with the original hinge plate marks made before removal.
6 The lock and striker catch may be adjusted to provide positive closure of the boot lid by loosening their securing bolts (photo).

24.6 Luggage boot lid lock assembly

7 Torsion bars are used to counterbalance the lid and reduce the effort of opening it. The effect of the torsion bars may be varied if required by connecting a length of wire about 4 feet (1.2 m) in length to one end of the torsion bar. Tie the other end of the wire to a bar or lever and using the bumper as a pivot, pull the end of the torsion bar from its bracket.
8 Reposition the torsion bar in its catch to vary the effective force of closure of the lid.

25 Tailgate door (Estate car) - adjustment, removal, refitting

1 Always adjust the alignment of the tailgate door by slackening the hinge plate bolts and moving the door about the hinge plates.
2 The lock and striker assembly can be adjusted to provide positive closure once their retaining bolts are slackened.
3 The tailgate door may be removed after marking the position of the hinge plates on it and removing the securing bolts. Do not attempt to remove the door complete with torsion bar counterbalance assembly. If necessary this can be removed separately as follows:
4 Remove the plastic rivets from the torsion bar assembly cover panel by pushing out their centre pins with a thin rod.
5 Unscrew and remove the eight bolts which secure the hinge/torsion bar assembly to the body.
6 It is not recommended that the torsion bar assembly is dismantled but if it is, then a board and the weight of an

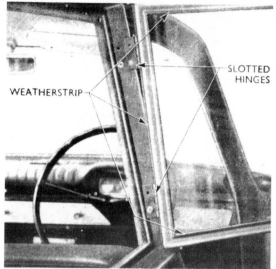

Fig. 12.12. Opening type rear quarter window

Fig. 12.13. Door hinge bolt location

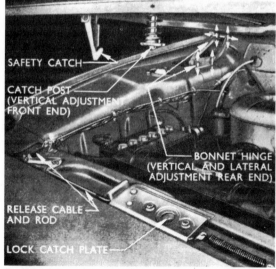

Fig. 12.14. Bonnet catch detail

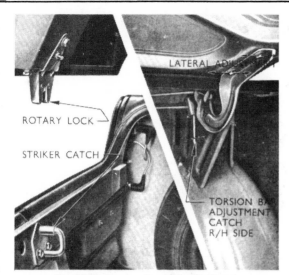

Fig. 12.15. Luggage boot lid adjustment

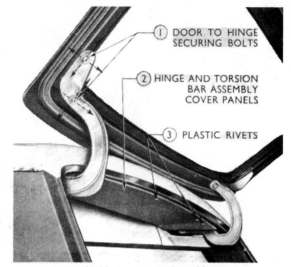

Fig. 12.16. Estate car tailgate hinges

assistant should be applied to the baseplates while the securing bolts are unscrewed carefully and evenly until the torsion bar tension is relieved.

26 Heater - general description

1 The heater fitted to most models is of conventional type and operates in conjunction with the engine cooling system. A two-speed blower fan is incorporated together with all the necessary controls to vary the heater temperature and to deflect the airflow between the windscreen outlets and the vehicle interior.

2 A heavy duty heater unit is fitted to vehicles supplied to certain overseas territories but this differs from the standard type only in detail construction.

3 Vehicles built after October 1964 incorporate a face level ventilation system which is entirely separate from the main heating and ventilating unit. The additional 'through-flow' system maintains equal pressure inside and outside the vehicle by means of the rear mounted flap valves which operate quite automatically to compensate for the increased interior pressure caused by the ram effect of the forward motion of the vehicle. The air within the vehicle interior is therefore continually changed while the vehicle is in motion.

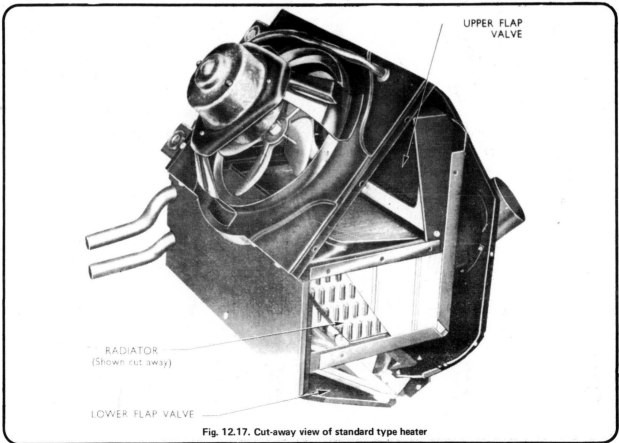

Fig. 12.17. Cut-away view of standard type heater

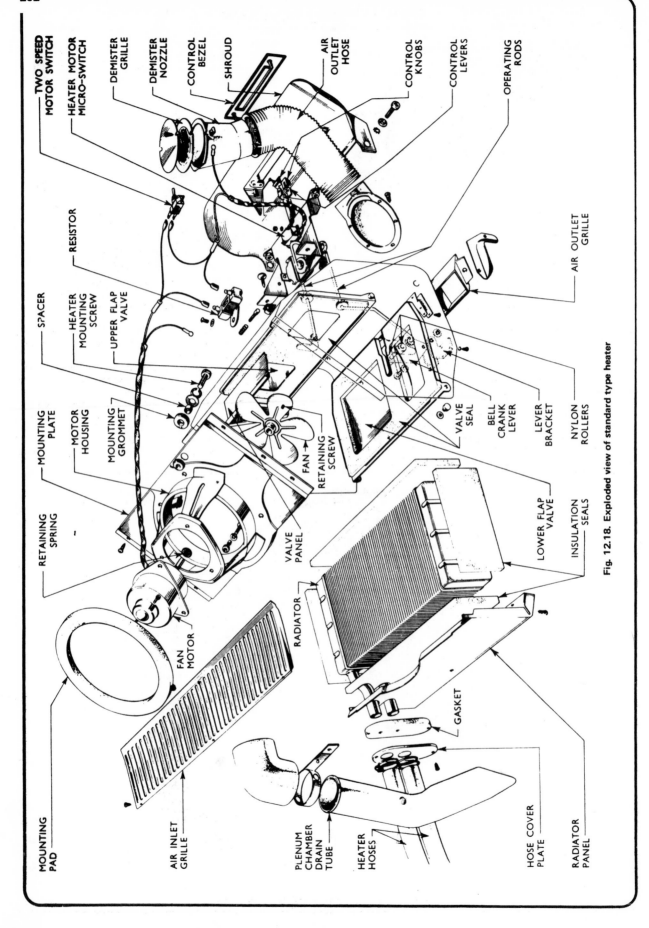

TWO SPEED MOTOR SWITCH

HEATER MOTOR MICRO-SWITCH

DEMISTER GRILLE

DEMISTER NOZZLE

CONTROL BEZEL

SHROUD

AIR OUTLET HOSE

CONTROL KNOBS

CONTROL LEVERS

OPERATING RODS

RESISTOR

SPACER

HEATER MOUNTING SCREW

UPPER FLAP VALVE

AIR OUTLET GRILLE

MOUNTING PLATE

MOTOR HOUSING

MOUNTING GROMMET

FAN

RETAINING SCREW

VALVE SEAL

BELL CRANK LEVER

LEVER BRACKET

NYLON ROLLERS

RETAINING SPRING

VALVE PANEL

FAN MOTOR

RADIATOR

LOWER FLAP VALVE

INSULATION SEALS

MOUNTING PAD

AIR INLET GRILLE

PLENUM CHAMBER DRAIN TUBE

HEATER HOSES

GASKET

HOSE COVER PLATE

RADIATOR PANEL

Fig. 12.18. Exploded view of standard type heater

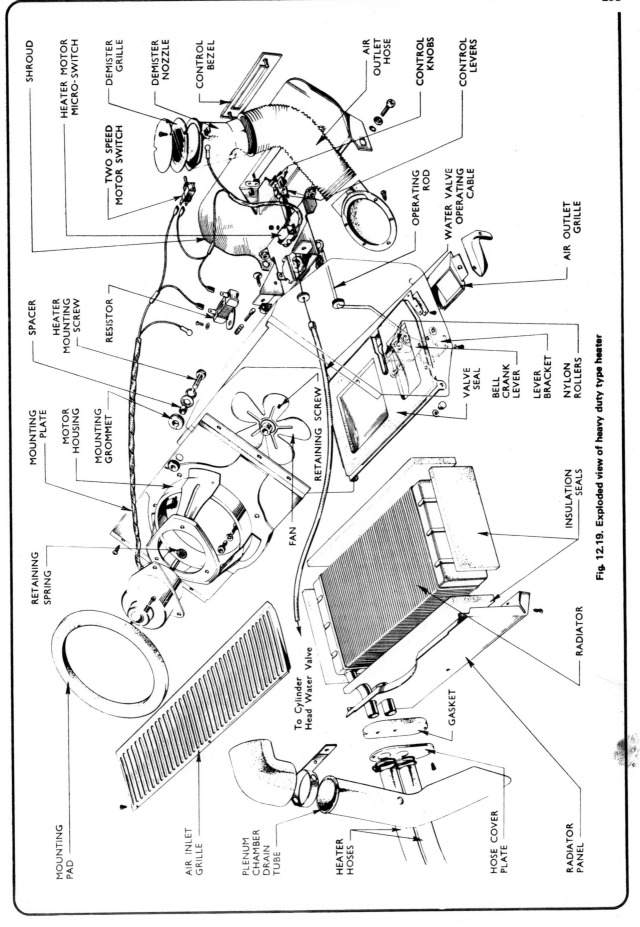

SHROUD

HEATER MOTOR MICRO-SWITCH

DEMISTER GRILLE

DEMISTER NOZZLE

CONTROL BEZEL

TWO SPEED MOTOR SWITCH

AIR OUTLET HOSE

CONTROL KNOBS

CONTROL LEVERS

OPERATING ROD

WATER VALVE OPERATING CABLE

AIR OUTLET GRILLE

SPACER

HEATER MOUNTING SCREW

RESISTOR

VALVE SEAL

BELL CRANK LEVER

LEVER BRACKET

NYLON ROLLERS

MOUNTING PLATE

MOTOR HOUSING

MOUNTING GROMMET

RETAINING SCREW

FAN

INSULATION SEALS

RETAINING SPRING

To Cylinder Head Water Valve

RADIATOR

GASKET

MOUNTING PAD

AIR INLET GRILLE

PLENUM CHAMBER DRAIN TUBE

HEATER HOSES

HOSE COVER PLATE

RADIATOR PANEL

Fig. 12.19. Exploded view of heavy duty type heater

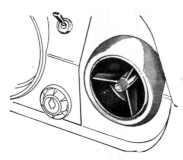

Fig. 12.20. Face level ventilation outlet

27 Heater - adjustment of controls and maintenance

1 Where hot air still enters the vehicle interior with the controls at the 'OFF' position then the lower flap valve is not closing fully.

2 On models produced prior to October 1962, move the heater control to the fully 'OFF' position and then remove the floor covering from below the heater and remove the four screws which retain the bell crank lever bracket to the heater casing.

3 Insert the finger through the outlet grille and push the bracket as far forward as it will go.

4 Retighten the securing screws and check the heater operation.

5 With vehicles produced after October 1962, loosen the grub screws from the heater control lever knobs and remove them.

6 Spring off the heater control panel bezel from its clips and then remove the heater shroud retaining screws and as the shroud is eased from the heater, disconnect the heater motor electrical leads.

7 Set the lower control lever in the 'OFF' position and then slacken the lever trunnion screw.

8 Pull the flap valve operating rod fully rearwards and then tighten the trunnion screw. Refit the heater shroud, control panel bezel and knobs. The upper flap valve can be adjusted in a similar manner.

9 Draining the cooling system will not fully drain the heater matrix and it is therefore essential that where a heater is fitted, anti-freeze mixture should always be used.

10 If the heater does not warm up, check the heater hoses for collapse and check that the tap on the cylinder head is in the fully open position.

11 Disconnect the heater hose from the return side of the heater unit and with the engine running, check for water flow. If nothing emerges from the hose then the heater matrix is blocked and must be cleared. Try reverse flushing it by disconnecting the inlet heater hose and attaching a cold water hose to the return outlet on the heater matrix. If the unit is still blocked it must be removed as described in Section 28 and exchanged for a new unit or the matrix renewed. The use of cooling system cleansers is not recommended for a blocked heater matrix as the scale or corrosion which will be dislodged will only tend to block the fine tubes elsewhere in the unit.

12 Any attempt at soldering a leaking heater matrix is not to be advised as unless the heat is localised it is likely to cause further leaks.

Fig. 12.21. Heater bellcrank lever bracket retaining screws

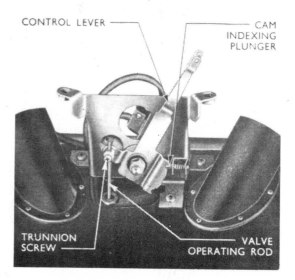

Fig. 12.22. Heater lower flap valve detail

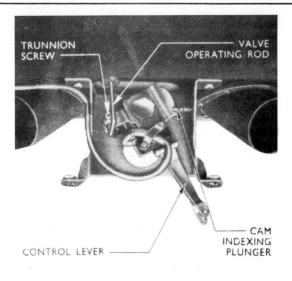

Fig. 12.23. Heater upper flap valve detail

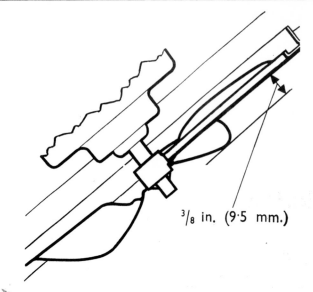

Fig. 12.24. Heater fan setting diagram

28 Heater - removal and refitting

1   Disconnect the battery and drain the cooling system.
2   Within the engine compartment, disconnect the heater hoses from the heater unit inlet and outlet pipe connections.
3   Remove the cover plate and gasket which surrounds these pipes.
4   Remove the parcel tray (two screws at each end and 'L' shaped bracket bolt).
5   Remove the two heater control knobs and pull the heater control panel bezel out of its two retaining clips.
6   Remove the heater shroud (four screws), disconnecting the motor leads as it is withdrawn.
7   Remove the screws from the demister grille plates, remove the plates and lift out the nozzles and outlet hoses.
8   Unscrew and remove the four heater mounting bolts noting the metal cored mounting grommets.
9   Refitting is a reversal of removal but check the following points:
10 Ensure that the mounting pad is evenly located on the heater unit seating.
11 Check that the lead with the black push-in connection goes to the windscreen wiper switch and the white lead to the wiring loom connector.

29 Heater - dismantling and reassembly

1   Detach the mounting pad from the motor housing and disconnect the motor earth lead from the push-in connector.
2   Unscrew and remove the thirteen screws which hold the motor housing mounting plate to the heater casing and lift off the motor, housing and mounting plate.
3   Draw the electric supply lead through the mounting plate grommet.
4   Pass a screwdriver through the fan blades and remove the three motor mounting screws and their spacers and grommets.
5   Prise the spring retainer away from the motor shaft, slacken the fan retaining screw and withdraw the fan from the shaft.
6   Withdraw the upper and lower flap valve rods after slackening their trunnion retaining screws.
7   Remove the control assembly (three screws) from the heater casing.
8   Remove the heater micro switch and the control pivot bolt, lever, plunger and spring.
9   Remove the matrix panel (four screws) and withdraw the insulation seal.
10 Invert the heater unit and let the matrix slide out of its location.
11 Remove the upper and lower flap valves and their operating linkage.
12 Reassembly is a reversal of dismantling but check the following points. Ensure that the electric supply lead to the motor is well clear of the fan blades. Apply sealer between the mounting plate flanges and the heater body.
13 Set the fan blades so that the boss is towards the motor and the greatest projection of the blades is 3/8 inch (9.5 mm) beyond the aperture in the mounting plate.

Index

Printed by
J. H. HAYNES & Co. Ltd
Sparkford Yeovil Somerset
ENGLAND